D1597171

BIBLICAL HEBREW WORKBOOK

An Inductive Study for Beginners

A. Vanlier Hunter

St. Mary's Seminary & University
Baltimore, Maryland

UNIVERSITY
PRESS OF
AMERICA

Lanham • New York • London

Library of Congress Cataloging-in-Publication Data

Hunter, A. Vanlier (Austin Vanlier), 1939–
Biblical Hebrew workbook.

Includes index.
1. Hebrew language—Grammar—1950–   . I. Title.
PJ4567.3.H86   1988   492.4'82421   88–5519
ISBN 0–8191–5715–5 (pbk. : alk. paper)

All University Press of America books are produced on acid-free
paper which exceeds the minimum standards set by the National
Historical Publications and Records Commission.

To

Donald E. Gowan

and

Jared J. Jackson

CONTENTS

PREFACE

It is customary to distinguish between "deductive" and "inductive" methods of learning a biblical language. A deductive approach systematizes the grammar of the language and then presents it in lessons which give the simplest elements first and then work toward the more complicated elements in later chapters. Accompanying the lessons are paradigms of nouns and verbs to be memorized, and exercises of the author's composition to be translated. Toward the end of such an approach, actual biblical passages are sometimes included, but normally students turn to the biblical text only after they have completed the textbook. An inductive approach starts with the text of the Bible itself and explains the grammar as actual passages are read. The elements of grammar are built up and organized in stages until the complete scope of the language emerges.

There are advantages and disadvantages to both methods, but in choosing an inductive approach for this textbook, I am responding especially to several factors that argue convincingly for such a method. First, curricular time allotted to the study of biblical languages, particularly in many seminaries, is often limited to a year's course or less. An inductive approach has a better chance of exposing students to the essentials of biblical Hebrew in that time frame, since even more complex matters, such as weak verbs, are dealt with almost from the beginning because of their high frequency. If time does not permit the completion of a deductive grammar, students will have had little or no exposure to some very frequent elements of the language, since some very common but more complex matters may be reserved for the last lessons.

Second, an inductive method stimulates motivation to learn the language. This is especially important when students are required to take language courses but may not have particular interest in Hebrew or more than average linguistic ability. Memorizing paradigms and translating "uninspired" exercises have often led students to dread such courses. But studying the language with attention to actual biblical passages makes the effort more engaging from the beginning.

Third, people who undertake the learning of biblical Hebrew do so not merely to translate but more importantly to study and understand the meaning of biblical passages. An inductive method lends itself to the task of preparing students to move on to exegesis, for some exegetical methods can be illustrated as the biblical passages are read. Consequently, the transition from a language course to an exegetical course is made more smoothly. Instructors may incorporate as much or as little exegetical content as time and their course purpose allow.

Besides these basic values in an inductive approach, this workbook incorporates several features that maximize the use of this method. First, it seems best not to base the study primarily on one book of the Bible or on isolated verses, but to choose chapter-length passages that are both well known and important and that represent a variety of types of literature derived from differing biblical traditions. In keeping with this aim, eight key biblical passages have been selected: Genesis 22, Genesis 12, Deuteronomy 5, Joshua 24, II Samuel 11-12, Genesis 1, Jeremiah 1, and Psalm 51. Their order reflects an ascending degree of difficulty. When students complete this book, they will have studied some central and theologically significant pericopes that can be the basis of fuller exegetical treatment.

Second, to be prepared for exegesis, students need to be familiar with the standard critical text of the Hebrew Bible and to be able to use a good lexicon. Therefore, except for the first reading, for which the Hebrew text and word definitions are provided, students are to use *Biblia Hebraica Stuttgartensia* and William L. Holladay's *A Concise Hebrew and Aramaic Lexicon of the Old Testament*. Brown-Driver-Briggs and Koehler-Baumgartner may also be used. In this way, students will not become dependent on the workbook's Hebrew text or glossary but will feel at home with the critical tools themselves.

Third, rather traditional grammatical terminology has been retained. Some recent grammars have moved away from this more cumbersome and sometimes inadequate nomenclature, but there is no consensus about a new terminology. More importantly, the standard lexicons and critical commentaries still use the traditional terms, so that students need to become accustomed to this grammatical vocabulary if they are to use such exegetical tools productively.

Fourth, full paradigms of nouns and verbs along with summary charts of other grammatical forms are provided so that students can see the total picture at any time. An overview helps to alleviate the sense of insecurity some students feel in the early stages of an inductive approach. Also, some instructors may want to utilize these charts to incorporate some more deductive elements into their courses.

Fifth, the Hebrew vocabulary is learned on a frequency basis. Of the 440 words that occur more than 100 times in the Hebrew Bible, 333 of them appear in the eight readings. Three vocabulary lessons are added to include the rest of the words. All the vocabulary words are listed in Appendix II, so that students can develop their own glossary. Beyond this, in these readings students encounter an additional 250 words that occur fewer than 100 times, which they look up in the lexicon. As a result of this method, students have a fairly broad exposure to Hebrew vocabulary.

In an inductive method an effort must be made to keep moving forward in the readings and not to dwell too long on any one matter. Learning results from the repeated occurrences of the vocabulary and grammar. The instructor must also avoid the temptation of saying too much too soon. Many items are intentionally introduced with rather oversimplified explanations. As subsequent examples occur, more can be said to make the initial explanations more complete. Students are often directed to review earlier explanations, so that repetition can aid the learning process.

For a more specific look at the way this workbook proceeds, see the sections on "Using the Workbook" on pp. 19-20, 74, 164, and 190. Two systems of pronunciation are introduced. The Sefardi pronunciation (pp. 3-11) is employed in the workbook, but the traditional academic pronunciation (pp. 12-18) is included for those who wish to use it.

Conceivably, the greatest value of the inductive method is that it gives students a genuine "feel" for the Hebrew text of the Bible that leads to a serious interest in exegesis. Deductive methods can complement an inductive approach, but they are better reserved for later stages of learning, especially for those who wish to develop their knowledge of Hebrew beyond a year's initial exposure in an inductive method. Appendix I offers some suggestions for further study along both inductive and deductive lines.

The basic form of this workbook was originally developed during the years I was a teaching fellow at Pittsburgh Theological Seminary in the late 1960s. I owe the insight into the inductive method employed here to David Noel Freedman, my own teacher of Hebrew, and to William F. Orr and James A. Walther, who used an inductive method in the study of New Testament Greek. Special words of appreciation need to be expressed to Donald E. Gowan and Jared J. Jackson, whose use over the years of earlier versions of this workbook resulted in numerous suggestions for improvements and in encouragement to bring it to publication. To these two former teachers and colleagues I dedicate this work with profound gratitude.

I am deeply indebted to Robert F. Leavitt, S.S., of St. Mary's Seminary & University, to James A. Brashler of the Ecumenical Institute, and to Gerald L. Brown, S.S., of the Society of St. Sulpice for the financial support I received for the sabbatical year during which the final preparation of this workbook took place. Also I express my sincere thanks to Lenore Brashler, who introduced me to the world of computers, and to Jerome T. Walsh, S.S.L., who shared with me the Hebrew fonts that I modified and adapted to the laser printer. Many other colleagues, friends, and family members were exceedingly supportive during the time I labored over this workbook. To all of them I am most grateful.

Baltimore, Maryland
February 1, 1988

A. Vanlier Hunter

ABBREVIATIONS AND SYMBOLS

Abbreviations

abs.	absolute
adj.	adjective
BDB	Brown-Driver-Briggs Lexicon
BH, BH³, BHK	*Biblia Hebraica* (Kittel)
BHS	*Biblia Hebraica Stuttgartensia*
c/com	common
consec.	consecutive
cs./const.	construct
Dt	Deuteronomy
Ex	Exodus
f/fem.	feminine
Gn	Genesis
Hif.	Hifil
Hitp.	Hitpael
Hof.	Hofal
impf.	imperfect
impv.	imperative
inf.	infinitive
Jr	Jeremiah
Js	Joshua
KB	Koehler-Baumgartner Lexicon
m/masc.	masculine
MT	Masoretic Text
Nif.	Nifal
part.	participle
p/pl.	plural
pf.	perfect
Ps	Psalms
sf.	suffix
s/sg.	singular
Sm	Samuel
v./vv.	verse,verses
w.	with

Symbols

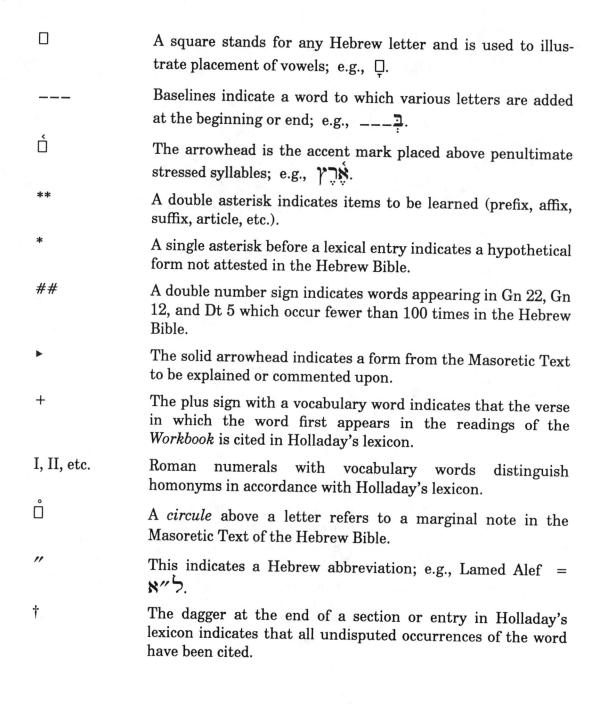

□   A square stands for any Hebrew letter and is used to illustrate placement of vowels; e.g., בַ.

---   Baselines indicate a word to which various letters are added at the beginning or end; e.g., ___בְּ.

Ȯ́   The arrowhead is the accent mark placed above penultimate stressed syllables; e.g., אֶ֫רֶץ.

**   A double asterisk indicates items to be learned (prefix, affix, suffix, article, etc.).

*   A single asterisk before a lexical entry indicates a hypothetical form not attested in the Hebrew Bible.

A double number sign indicates words appearing in Gn 22, Gn 12, and Dt 5 which occur fewer than 100 times in the Hebrew Bible.

►   The solid arrowhead indicates a form from the Masoretic Text to be explained or commented upon.

+   The plus sign with a vocabulary word indicates that the verse in which the word first appears in the readings of the *Workbook* is cited in Holladay's lexicon.

I, II, etc.   Roman numerals with vocabulary words distinguish homonyms in accordance with Holladay's lexicon.

Ȯ̊   A *circule* above a letter refers to a marginal note in the Masoretic Text of the Hebrew Bible.

″   This indicates a Hebrew abbreviation; e.g., Lamed Alef = לְ״א.

†   The dagger at the end of a section or entry in Holladay's lexicon indicates that all undisputed occurrences of the word have been cited.

CHAPTER I: GETTING STARTED

THE STORY OF THE HEBREW BIBLE

For most of you, Hebrew is the first language outside the Indo-European family of languages that you have studied. Hebrew belongs to the northwest branch of the Semitic language family along with Aramaic and other Canaanite languages, such as Ugaritic, Phoenician, Moabite, and Edomite. It was the language of the ancient Israelites and of their writings that make up the Hebrew Bible (Christian Old Testament).

A large portion of the Hebrew Bible comes from the pre-exilic and exilic periods. The Hebrew language at that time was written in what is called the Phoenician-Old Hebrew script. This script was an early form of the first alphabetic script ever devised. It contained only consonants and no vowels. We have, however, no extant biblical texts from this time. But we do have non-biblical examples of Hebrew written in this script recovered mainly in archaeological excavations in the last hundred years, such as the Gezer calender, the Moabite stone, the Siloam inscription, the Lachish and Arad letters, and many more.

In the centuries following the exile, the everyday language in Palestine slowly changed from Hebrew to Aramaic, which had become the *lingua franca* of the Ancient Near East. Although the language of most biblical writings continued to be Hebrew, the written script was slowly changed from Old Hebrew to the so-called "square script" of Aramaic, which is still the script we use for Hebrew today. In other words, while the language of most biblical writings continued to be Hebrew, the script in which it was written became the script that had evolved for Aramaic.

By the end of the first century C.E., the long process of the formation of the Hebrew Bible was about at an end. But at that time, the Hebrew Bible existed in not one but many manuscripts with various histories. It became the task of the scribes called the Sopherim to begin the long process of working toward a standard text. During the next several centuries, the Sopherim developed the earliest Masorah, that is, the tradition about the text, which aided in keeping the text free from further alteration.

Beginning as early as the fifth century C.E., the scribes we call the Masoretes (also spelled Massoretes) began their two-fold work. First, the Masorah started by the Sopherim was systematized and fully developed. Second, systems of adding vowels to the hitherto consonantal text were devised, since Hebrew was no longer widely used (except in the synagogues) and there arose the need of preserving the traditional pronunciation of the text.

By the end of the tenth century C.E., a generally accepted pointed text, that is, one with the dots and dashes that make up the vowels, had been developed in Palestine by the ben Asher family of Masoretes. This textual tradition was not always carefully preserved as copies were made in the Middle Ages. The first printed edition of the Hebrew Bible was published in 1524/25 in Venice but it was based on late and perhaps somewhat inferior manuscripts. Nevertheless, it became the *textus receptus*, i.e., the "received" or normative text, and has been the basis of most Hebrew Bibles and translations since then until a half century ago.

The third and subsequent editions of *Biblia Hebraica* (BH, BH³, or BHK), edited by Rudolf Kittel in 1937, and its recently published revised edition *Biblia Hebraica Stuttgartensia* (BHS), edited by Karl Elliger and Wilhelm Rudolph from 1967 to 1977, reproduce not the *textus receptus* but the text of a specific manuscript, Codex Leningradensis, a good copy made in 1008 C.E. from the generally accepted Masoretic Text (MT) of the ben Asher family. BHS is the standard edition of the MT used by scholars today and is the one to be used with this *Workbook*.

The text of the Hebrew Bible has had a long and varied history. Yet through the ages it has constituted the foundation of the faith of countless people and it constantly awaits the efforts of any who would learn its language in order to delve directly into its riches.

HEBREW PRONUNCIATION SYSTEMS

At least three ways of pronouncing Biblical Hebrew have evolved in the last centuries. The "Ashkenazi" pronunciation stems from Eastern European Jewry and is still used in some synagogues, especially among the Orthodox. The "Sefardi" pronunciation stems from Spanish Jewry and is used in many Conservative and Reform synagogues today and is the basis of modern Israeli pronunciation. The "academic" pronunciation was developed mainly by Christian scholars.

This *Workbook* follows a somewhat simplified form of the "Sefardi" pronunciation with the corresponding simplified transliterations of Hebrew grammatical terms. The Sefardi pronuncation is explained on pp. 3 to 11. But the pages introducing pronunciation are repeated on pp. 12 to 18 giving the standard "academic" pronunciation. For those who are using the Sefardi pronunciation, go on to the next page. For those who are using the academic pronunciation, skip to page 12. To make reference to these pages somewhat easier, the Sefardi pronunciation is marked with margin tab **1** and the academic pronunciation with margin tab **2**.

Note 3A: The Hebrew Alphabet

	Consonant	As a final consonant	Name		Sound
1.	א		Alef	אָלֶף	(not heard)
2.	בּ		Bet	בֵּית	"b" as in boy
	ב				"v" as in van
3.	גּ		Gimel	גִּמֶל	"g" as in get
	ג				(same)
4.	דּ		Dalet	דָּלֶת	"d" as in dog
	ד				(same)
5.	ה		He	הֵא	"h" as in hay
6.	ו		Vav	וָו	"v" as in van
7.	ז		Zayin	זַיִן	"z" as in zone
8.	ח		Het	חֵית	guttural "ch" (German: Bach)
9.	ט		Tet	טֵית	"t" as in tie
10.	י		Yod	יוֹד	"y" as in yes
11.	כּ		Kaf	כַּף	"k" as in keep
	כ	ךּ			guttural "ch" (German: ich)
12.	ל		Lamed	לָמֶד	"l" as in lie
13.	מ	ם	Mem	מֵים	"m" as in main
14.	נ	ן	Nun	נוּן	"n" as in noon
15.	ס		Samek	סָמֶךְ	"s" as in say
16.	ע		Ayin	עַיִן	(not heard)
17.	פּ		Pe	פֵּא	"p" as in pay
	פ	ף			"f" as in fat
18.	צ	ץ	Tsade	צָדֵי	"ts" as in rats
19.	ק		Qof	קוֹף	"q" as in baroque
20.	ר		Resh	רֵישׁ	"r" as in rat
21.	שׂ		Sin	שִׂין	"s" as in say
	שׁ		Shin	שִׁין	"sh" as in show
22.	תּ		Tav	תָּו	"t" as in tie
	ת				(same)

1

FEATURES OF THE HEBREW ALPHABET

1 1. Alef (א) and Ayin (ע) are for our purposes not pronounced. Technically, Alef is an emphasized glottal stop that one hears as the vocal chords begin to produce the sound of a vowel. The Ayin is a deep guttural sound that most English speaking people cannot duplicate.

2. The following letters can be easily confused unless care is taken to notice the distinctive features of each letter:

Bet (ב) and Kaf (כ)   Tet (ט) and Mem (מ)

Dalet (ד) and Resh (ר)   Ayin (ע) and Tsade (צ)

Vav (ו) and Zayin (ז)   Sin (שׂ) and Shin (שׁ)

Gimel (ג) and Nun (נ)   He (ה), Het (ח), and Tav (ת)

Note 4A: Begadkefat Letters

Six of the consonants (ב, ג, ד, כ, פ, and ת) may be written with a dot in the middle of the letter. This dot, called a **Dagesh**, indicates the "hard" pronunciation of the letter: ב = b, ג = g, ד = d, כ = k, פ = p, and ת = t. Without the Dagesh three of these letters have a "spirantized" sound: ב = v, כ = kh, and פ = f. The other three no longer have a spirantized sound in the Sefardi pronunciation. They retain the same hard pronunciation even without the Dagesh: ג = g, ד = d, and ת = t. These six letters are mneumonically called the **Begadkefat** letters.

Note 4B: Final Consonants

Five of the consonants (כ, מ, נ, פ, and צ) have a different written form when they end a word (ך, ם, ן, ף, and ץ). Notice that four of the five have an extension of the letter downward below the usual bottom of the letters. Final Kaf is always written with a raised vowel in it. The usual vowel is two dots: ךְ.

Note 4C: Vowel Letters

Three of the consonants (ה, ו, and י) often lose their consonantal character and combine with vowel signs (various dots and dashes) to form long vowels. When this happens, they are called **vowel letters** and not consonants. The Latin term for a vowel letter is *mater lectionis*. The use of the vowel letters will become evident as we turn to the vowel system.

THE VOWELS

The vowels that were inserted into the consonantal text by the Masoretes consist of dots and dashes called "pointing" usually placed under and to be pronounced after the consonant. Hebrew has two types of vowels. **Full vowels** can be either long or short and function like English vowels. **Reduced vowels** indicate a very short sound or even no sound at all. They are used under special circumstances to be explained later. English has no category of vowels like this.

1

Note 5A: Full Vowels

Short			**Long**		
◌ַ	Patah	"a" as in f*a*ther	◌ָ	Qamets	"a" as in f*a*ther
◌ֶ	Segol	"e" as in b*e*t	◌ֵ	Tsere	"e" as in th*ey*
◌ִ	Hireq	"i" as in h*i*t	◌ִי	Hireq Yod	"i" as in mach*i*ne
◌ָ	Qamets Hatuf	"o" as in s*o*ft	◌ֹ	Holem	"o" as in h*o*le
◌ֻ	Qibbuts	"u" as in p*u*t	◌ו	Shureq Vav	"u" as in l*u*te

Most of the above vowels are placed directly below the consonant. Notice, however, that three of the above vowels are different. The Holem is not under the consonant but above and to the left of the consonant: ◌ֹ. Also Hireq Yod and Shureq Vav are formed with a vowel letter. **REVIEW Note 4C.** The Yod and the Vav are no longer consonants and thus do not have their consonantal sound. Instead, they combine with vowel pointings to form long vowels: ◌ִי and ◌ו.

Note 5B: More Long Vowels

Additional long vowels are formed by combining vowel pointing with the three vowel letters (ה, ו, and י):

◌ָה	Qamets He	"a" as in f*a*ther	◌ֶה	Segol He	"e" as in th*ey*
◌ֹו	Holem Vav	"o" as in h*o*le	◌ֶי	Segol Yod	"e" as in th*ey*
◌ֹה	Holem He	"o" as in h*o*le	◌ֵה	Tsere He	"e" as in th*ey*
			◌ֵי	Tsere Yod	"e" as in th*ey*

Note 5C: Reduced Vowels

Simple Sheva			**Composite Shevas**		
◌ְ	Sheva	silent or very short "e"	◌ֲ	Hatef Qamets	very short "a"
			◌ֱ	Hatef Segol	very short "e"
			◌ֳ	Hatef Qamets	very short "o"

SYLLABLES

Hebrew is read from right to left, so that the vowels are placed under (or after) the consonants following which they are pronounced. Reading from right to left, the name of the first letter of the alphabet אָלֶף would be read: ←‏ אָ |, לֶ |, ף |

Note 6A: Syllables

Every word and syllable begins with a consonant. Every syllable has one vowel, either a full vowel (long or short) or a reduced vowel. A syllable may or may not end with a consonant. A syllable that ends with a vowel is an **open syllable.** One that ends with a consonant is a **closed syllable.** The word אָלֶף has one open and one closed syllable: אָ|לֶף. The word בֵּית has one closed syllable.

STRESS

Every Hebrew word has one main stress. It usually falls on the last syllable (the ultima) but may fall on the next to the last syllable (the penultima). Longer words may also have a secondary stress toward the beginning of the word. In this *Workbook*, words that have the primary stress on the ultima have no accent marking. Words that have the primary stress on the penultima are marked with an arrowhead accent above the consonant that begins the stressed syllable: אָ֫לֶף.

Note 6B: Syllables and Stress

A basic rule for unstressed syllables: **A closed unstressed syllable must have a <u>short</u> vowel.** Notice in the word אָ֫לֶף that the unstressed closed syllable has a short vowel (Segol). A corollary rule: An open unstressed syllable usually, but not always, has a long vowel or a Sheva. These rules will often help to distinguish the infrequent short vowel Qamets Hatuf (◌ָ) from the very frequent long vowel Qamets (◌ָ). These two vowels look alike.

Note 6C: Maqqef

Hebrew often employs a dash (⁻) called a **Maqqef** to connect two or more words into one phrase. When this happens, the major stress for the whole phrase is on the last word and the words before a Maqqef are unstressed. If the word before a Maqqef is a closed syllable, the vowel of that syllable must be short. **REVIEW Note 6B**. A word such as אֶת⁻ is therefore a closed unstressed syllable. Similarly, the vowel in the word כָּל⁻ must be the short vowel Qamets Hatuf.

Note 7A: Transliteration Table

Consonants: (alternatives)

Hebrew		alt
א	- ʾ	'
בּ	- b	
ב	- b	ḇ, bh, v
גּ	- g	
ג	- g	ḡ, gh
דּ	- d	
ד	- d	ḏ, dh
ה	- h	
ו	- v	w
ז	- z	
ח	- ḥ	ch
ט	- ṭ	
י	- y	
כּ	- k	
כ ך	- k	ḵ, kh, ch
ל	- l	
מ ם	- m	
נ ן	- n	
ס	- s	
ע	- ʿ	ʿ
פּ	- p	
פ ף	- f	p̄, ph
צ ץ	- ṣ	ts
ק	- q	
ר	- r	
שׂ	- ś	
שׁ	- š	
תּ	- t	
ת	- t	ṯ, th

Full Vowels:

◌ַ	- a	◌ָ	- ā
◌ֶ	- e	◌ֵ	- ē
◌ִ	- i	◌ִי	- î
◌ֹ	- o	◌	- ō
◌ֻ	- u	ו	- û

Reduced Vowels: (alternatives)

◌ְ	- e	ĕ
◌ֲ	- a	ă
◌ֱ	- e	ĕ
◌ֳ	- o	ŏ

Long Vowels with Vowel Letters:

◌ָה	- āh	â
◌ֵי	- ê	
◌ֶי	- ê	
◌ֵה	- ēh	ê
◌ֶה	- ēh	ê
ו	- ô	
◌ֹה	- ōh	ô

Other Matters: (Some terms are introduced in subsequent pages.)

1. Final consonants are not distinguished.
2. Maqqef (־) is transliterated as a dash (-).
3. Dagesh Lene is often not indicated, unless the alternative symbols are used in its absence.
4. Dagesh Forte is indicated by doubling the consonant in transliteration.
5. Only the vocal Sheva is indicated. In reconstructing the Hebrew from an English transliteration, a silent Sheva (syllable divider) must be written according to the rules in Note 10A or 17A.
6. Vowels with the vowel letters Vav and Yod are always written with a circumflex (ו = û; ◌ֵי = ê), but vowels with the vowel letter He may be written either with a circumflex or with a long vowel followed by "h" (◌ָה = â or āh).

TRANSLITERATION

The transliteration table in Note 7A is provided for use in the initial learning process of mastering the sight and sounds of the consonants and vowels. But the student should learn as soon as possible to read the Hebrew directly without relying on transliteration. There is, however, another reason for being able to use transliterated Hebrew. Many scholarly publications now use transliteration, such as the *Journal of Biblical Literature* and the *Catholic Biblical Quarterly*. Also, Holladay's *Lexicon*, to be introduced later, uses some transliteration. Unfortunately, there is no single system of transliteration, so that the most common alternatives are listed in the table.

Note 8A: Diphthongs

Certain combinations of vowels and the consonants Vav and Yod produce diphthongs. In the first two categories below the Yod remains a consonant: Examples:

1.   ַיֿ or ָיֿ   "ai" as in *ai*sle   אֵלַי
2.   וֹיֿ   "oi" as in *oi*l   גּוֹי

Vav remains a consonant in the following combinations:

3.   ַו, ָו, or ָיו   "av" and in Sl*av*   אֵלָיו
4.   ִיו   "eev" as in sl*eev*e   אָבִיו

Since the Vav and Yod remain consonants in these instances and are not vowel letters, they should be transliterated as consonants.

Note 8B: Quiescent Alef

When Alef begins a word or syllable, it is the emphasized glottal stop as the sound of the vowel begins. Technically, it does have a sound even though for our purposes it seems silent. But an Alef becomes truly silent, i.e., quiesces, when it ends a word or syllable. A quiescent Alef has no vowel under or after it, because it ends a word or syllable: גְּאַ, לֹא, יֹאמֶר. Notice that a Holem preceding a quiescent Alef is written above the upper right corner of the Alef (אֹ).

Note 8C: Final Kaf

A final Kaf always has vowel pointing, which is located up in the center of the letter. The only full vowel that can occur with a final Kaf is Qamets: ךָ, making the final syllable of that word an open syllable. When the final Kaf is the consonant that ends a word's last syllable, it helps form a closed syllable. **REVIEW Note 6A.** The Kaf then receives the reduced vowel Sheva: ךְ.   Examples: לָךְ, לֵךְ.

Exercise 1: Pronounce the following one syllable words and write the transliteration in the space to the right or on a separate sheet.

אָב	father		לֹא	no, not
אוֹר	light		מָה	what? how?
אִישׁ	man (male)		מִן	from
אַף	nose		נָא	please
בֵּן	son		נוּס	to flee, escape
בַּת	daughter		סוּס	horse
גּוּר	to sojourn		עִיר	city
גַּם	also, moreover		עֵץ	tree, piece of wood
דּוֹר	generation		פֶּה	mouth
הֵן	behold		פֶּן־	lest
זֶה	this (masc.)		צוּף	to flood
חוּץ	outside, street		צַר	enemy; distress
חֹק	rule, statute		קוֹל	voice, sound
טוֹב	good		רוּץ	to run
יָד	hand		רַךְ	weak
יֵשׁ	there is		שֶׂה	lamb, kid
כֹּה	thus; here		שִׂים	to put, set
כִּי	that; because		שׁוּב	to turn, return
כָּל־	all		שֵׁשׁ	six
לֵב	heart, mind		תָּם	upright

Exercise 2: Reconstruct the Hebrew from the following transliterations.

ʾāz	then		zōʾt	this (fem.)
ʾak	surely, only		yām	sea
ʾet-	(sign of dir. obj.)		yôm	day
bêt	house of		ᶜim	with
bîn	to understand		ᶜēt	time
gôy	nation, people		qûm	to arise, get up
dām	blood		raq	only
har	hill, mountain		śar	official, prince

Note 10A: Simple Sheva

A simple Sheva (◌ְ) may be *silent* and indicate that the consonant under which it stands has ended the syllable. Thus a silent Sheva functions as a **syllable divider**. Or a simple Sheva may be slightly *vocal* (a very short "e" sound) and indicate that the consonant under which it stands is beginning a new syllable. The rule to distinguish a silent from a vocal Sheva is:

> A Sheva is *silent* (i.e., a syllable divider) if it is not under a doubled consonant (i.e., one with a Dagesh Forte as explained below) and if it follows a *short* vowel. All other simple Shevas (and all composite Shevas) are *vocal*.

Silent Sheva: בְּנְךָ,   אַבְרָם   (syllable divider)

Vocal Sheva: בְּנוֹ,   נֵלְכָה

Note 10B: Dagesh

The Dagesh (◌ּ -- a dot within a letter) may be of two kinds:

1. **Dagesh Lene**   (the simple or weak Dagesh)
   - ▸ Occurs only in the six Begadkefat consonants (ב, ג, ד, כ, פ, ת). **REVIEW Note 4A**. Confusion arises because the Begadkefat letters can also have the Dagesh Forte, explained below.
   - ▸ Indicates the hard pronunciation of these consonants without doubling them, as a Dagesh Forte does.
   - ▸▸ Occurs only after a *silent* Sheva (syllable divider) or at the beginning of a word.

   Examples: בְּנוֹ,   אָהַבְתָּ

2. **Dagesh Forte**   (the strong or doubling Dagesh)
   - ▸ Occurs in any consonant except א, ה, ח, ע (the guttural consonants) and ר. These consonants can never be doubled.
   - ▸ Indicates the doubling of the consonant and, if a Begadkefat letter, its hard pronunciation.
   - ▸▸ Occurs only after a *full* vowel (long or short).

   Examples: נִסָּה,   אֵלֶּה

As you can see, the rules for distinguishing types of Shevas and Dageshes are interrelated. When a Sheva occurs under a consonant with a Dagesh, **always determine the type of Dagesh first** before applying the rules for the Sheva. Can you identify the Dageshes and the Shevas in this example? בְּסֻבָּךְ

Note 11A: Dagesh & Syllables

When a consonant is doubled, i.e., when it has a Dagesh Forte, one of the doubled consonants thus formed ends the preceding syllable and the other begins the following syllable. Thus the word נִסָּה has two syllables, the first *closed* and the second *open*: נִסּ|סָה. **REVIEW Note 6A.** Notice that the Dagesh Forte eliminates the need for the Sheva and for writing a second Samek.

1

Exercise 3: Pronounce and transliterate the following multi-syllable words.

אֶרֶץ	earth, land	מִדְבָּר	desert
אִשָּׁה	woman	מְלָאכָה	work, occupation
בְּרָכָה	blessing	נְאֻם	oracle
בֹּקֶר	morning	סֵפֶר	scroll
גָּדוֹל	great	עַתָּה	now
דָּבָר	word, thing	צַדִּיק	righteous
הִנֵּה	behold	קָדוֹשׁ	holy
חֲמִשִּׁים	fifty	שָׂדֶה	field
יְהוּדָה	Judah	שְׁלִישִׁי	third
כֹּהֵן	priest	שָׁלוֹם	peace
לַיְלָה	night	תּוֹרָה	torah

NAMES OF THE VOWELS

The following list gives the Hebrew names for the vowels, the full transliteration, and the simplified transliteration used in the *Workbook* in referring to the vowels. See the simplified transliteration of the consonant names in Note 3A.

פַּתַח	*pataḥ*	Patah	קָמֶץ	*qāmeṣ*	Qamets
סֶגֹל	*seḡōl*	Segol	צֵרֵי	*ṣērê*	Tsere
חִירֶק	*ḥîreq*	Hireq	חִירֶק יוֹד	*ḥîreq yôd*	Hireq Yod
קָמֶץ חָטוּף	*qāmeṣ ḥāṭûf*	Qamets Hatuf	חֹלֶם	*ḥōlem*	Holem
קִבּוּץ	*qibbûṣ*	Qibbuts	שׁוּרֶק וָו	*šûreq vāv*	Shureq Vav
	שְׁוָא	*ševā*ʾ	Sheva		

This concludes the section on Sefardi pronunciation. Pp. 12-18 introduce the academic pronunciation. **Skip to p. 19 to continue.**

Note 12A: The Hebrew Alphabet

	Consonant	As a final consonant	Name		Sound
1.	א		Aleph	אָלֶף	(not heard)
2.	בּ / ב		Beth	בֵּית	"b" as in *boy* "v" as in *van*
3.	גּ / ג		Gimel	גִּמֶל	"g" as in *get* (same)
4.	דּ / ד		Daleth	דָּלֶת	"d" as in *dog* "th" as in *they*
5.	ה		He	הֵא	"h" as in *hay*
6.	ו		Waw	וָו	"w" as in *wow!*
7.	ז		Zayin	זַיִן	"z" as in *zone*
8.	ח		Heth	חֵית	guttural "ch" (German: Ba*ch*)
9.	ט		Teth	טֵית	"t" as in *tie*
10.	י		Yodh	יוֹד	"y" as in *yes*
11.	כּ / כ	ךּ	Kaph	כַּף	"k" as in *keep* guttural "ch" (German: i*ch*)
12.	ל		Lamedh	לָמֶד	"l" as in *lie*
13.	מ	ם	Mem	מֵם	"m" as in *main*
14.	נ	ן	Nun	נוּן	"n" as in *noon*
15.	ס		Samekh	סָמֶךְ	"s" as in *say*
16.	ע		Ayin	עַיִן	(not heard)
17.	פּ / פ	ף	Pe	פֵא	"p" as in *pay* "ph" as in *phone*
18.	צ	ץ	Tsadhe	צָדֵי	"ts" as in ra*ts*
19.	ק		Qoph	קוֹף	"q" as in baro*q*ue
20.	ר		Resh	רֵישׁ	"r" as in *rat*
21.	שׂ שׁ		Sin Shin	שִׂין שִׁין	"s" as in *say* "sh" as in *show*
22.	תּ / ת		Taw	תָּו	"t" as in *tie* "th" as in pa*th*

2

FEATURES OF THE HEBREW ALPHABET

1. Aleph (א) and Ayin (ע) are for our purposes not pronounced. Technically, Aleph is an emphasized glottal stop that one hears as the vocal chords begin to produce the sound of a vowel. The Ayin is a deep guttural sound that most English speaking people cannot duplicate.

2. The following letters can be easily confused unless care is taken to notice the distinctive features of each letter:

Beth (ב) and Kaph (כ)	Teth (ט) and Mem (מ)
Daleth (ד) and Resh (ר)	Ayin (ע) and Tsadhe (צ)
Waw (ו) and Zayin (ז)	Sin (שׂ) and Shin (שׁ)
Gimel (ג) and Nun (נ)	He (ה), Heth (ח), and Taw (ת)

2

Note 13A: Begadhkephath Letters

Six of the consonants (ב, ג, ד, כ, פ, and ת) may be written with a dot in the middle of the letter. This dot, called a **Dagesh**, indicates the "hard" pronunciation of the letter: ב = b, ג = g, ד = d, כ = k, פ = p, and ת = t. Without the Dagesh five of these letters have a "spirantized" sound: ב = v or bh, ד = dh, כ = ch or kh, פ = ph, and ת = th. One letter retains the hard pronunciation even without the Dagesh: ג = g. The distinction between Gimel with or without a Dagesh is no longer made in the academic pronunciation. These six letters are mneumonically called the **Begadhkephath** letters.

Note 13B: Final Consonants

Five of the consonants (כ, מ, נ, פ, and צ) have a different written form when they end a word (ך, ם, ן, ף, and ץ). Notice that four of the five have an extension of the letter downward below the usual bottom of the letters. Final Kaph is always written with a raised vowel in it. The usual vowel is two dots: ךְ.

Note 13C: Vowel Letters

Three of the consonants (ה, ו, and י) often lose their consonantal character and combine with vowel signs (various dots and dashes) to form long vowels. When this happens, they are called **vowel letters** and not consonants. The Latin term for a vowel letter is *mater lectionis*. The use of the vowel letters will become evident as we turn to the vowel system.

THE VOWELS

The vowels that were inserted into the consonantal text by the Massoretes consist of dots and dashes called "pointing" usually placed under and to be pronounced after the consonant. Hebrew has two types of vowels. **Full vowels** can be either long or short and function like English vowels. **Reduced vowels** indicate a very short sound or even no sound at all. They are used under special circumstances to be explained later. English has no category of vowels like this.

2

Note 14A: Full Vowels

Short			Long		
◌ַ	Pathah	"a" as in h*a*t	◌ָ	Qamets	"a" as in f*a*ther
◌ֶ	Segol	"e" as in b*e*t	◌ֵ	Tsere	"e" as in th*e*y
◌ִ	Hireq	"i" as in h*i*t	◌ִי	Hireq Yodh	"i" as in mach*i*ne
◌ָ	Qamets Hatuph	"o" as in s*o*ft	◌ֹ	Holem	"o" as in h*o*le
◌ֻ	Qibbuts	"u" as in p*u*t	ו	Shureq Waw	"u" as in l*u*te

Most of the above vowels are placed directly below the consonant. Notice, however, that three of the above vowels are different. The Holem is not under the consonant but above and to the left of the consonant: ◌ֹ. Also Hireq Yodh and Shureq Waw are formed with a vowel letter. **REVIEW Note 13C.** The Yodh and the Waw are no longer consonants and thus do not have their consonantal sound. Instead, they combine with vowel pointings to form long vowels: ◌ִי and ו.

Note 14B: More Long Vowels

Additional long vowels are formed by combining vowel pointing with the three vowel letters (ה, ו, and י):

◌ָה	Qamets He	"a" as in f*a*ther	◌ֶה	Segol He	"e" as in th*e*y
◌ֹו	Holem Waw	"o" as in h*o*le	◌ֶי	Segol Yodh	"e" as in th*e*y
◌ֹה	Holem He	"o" as in h*o*le	◌ֵה	Tsere He	"e" as in th*e*y
			◌ֵי	Tsere Yodh	"e" as in th*e*y

Note 14C: Reduced Vowels

Simple Shewa		Composite Shewas	
◌ְ Shewa silent or very short "e"		◌ֲ Hateph Qamets very short "a"	
		◌ֱ Hateph Segol very short "e"	
		◌ֳ Hateph Qamets very short "o"	

SYLLABLES

Hebrew is read from right to left, so that the vowels are placed under (or after) the consonants following which they are pronounced. Reading from right to left, the name of the first letter of the alphabet אָלֶף would be read: ף | לֶ | אָ ←

Note 15A: Syllables

Every word and syllable begins with a consonant. Every syllable has one vowel, either a full vowel (long or short) or a reduced vowel. A syllable may or may not end with a consonant. A syllable that ends with a vowel is an **open syllable**. One that ends with a consonant is a **closed syllable**. The word אָלֶף has one open and one closed syllable: אָ | לֶף. The word בַּיִת has one closed syllable.

STRESS

Every Hebrew word has one main stress. It usually falls on the last syllable (the ultima) but may fall on the next to the last syllable (the penultima). Longer words may also have a secondary stress toward the beginning of the word. In this *Workbook*, words that have the primary stress on the ultima have no accent marking. Words that have the primary stress on the penultima are marked with an arrowhead accent above the consonant that begins the stressed syllable: אָלֶף.

Note 15B: Syllables and Stress

A basic rule for unstressed syllables: **A closed unstressed syllable must have a <u>short</u> vowel**. Notice in the word אָלֶף that the unstressed closed syllable has a short vowel (Segol). A corollary rule: An open unstressed syllable usually, but not always, has a long vowel or a Shewa. These rules will often help to distinguish the infrequent short vowel Qamets Hatuph (◌ָ) from the very frequent long vowel Qamets (◌ָ). These two vowels look alike.

Note 15C: Maqqeph

Hebrew often employs a dash (ـ) called a **Maqqeph** to connect two or more words into one phrase. When this happens, the major stress for the whole phrase is on the last word and the words before a Maqqeph are unstressed. If the word before a Maqqeph is a closed syllable, the vowel of that syllable must be short. **REVIEW Note 15B**. A word such as אֶת־ is therefore a closed unstressed syllable. Similarly, the vowel in the word כָּל־ must be the short vowel Qamets Hatuph.

TRANSLITERATION

> **Study the Transliteration Table in Note 7A** and read the section on transliteration at the top of p. 8.

2

Note 16A: Diphthongs

Certain combinations of vowels and the consonants Waw and Yodh produce diphthongs. In the first two categories below the Yodh remains a consonant: Examples:

1. בַיְ or בָיְ   "ai" as in a*i*sle   אֵלַי

2. וֹי   "oi" as in o*i*l   גּוֹי

Waw remains a consonant in the following combinations:

3. בֶוְ, בַוְ, or בָיו   "ow" and in w*ow*!   אֵלָיו

4. בִיו   "ee-oo"   אָבִיו

Since the Waw and Yodh remain consonants in these instances and are not vowel letters, they should be transliterated as consonants.

Note 16B: Quiescent Aleph

When Aleph begins a word or syllable, it is the emphasized glottal stop as the sound of the vowel begins. Technically, it does have a sound even though for our purposes it seems silent. But an Aleph becomes truly silent, i.e., quiesces, when it ends a word or syllable. A quiescent Aleph has no vowel under or after it, because it ends a word or syllable: נָא, לֹא, יֹאמֶר. Notice that a Holem preceding a quiescent Aleph is written above the upper right corner of the Aleph (אֹ).

Note 16C: Final Kaph

A final Kaph always has vowel pointing, which is located up in the center of the letter. The only full vowel that can occur with a final Kaph is Qamets: ךָ, making the final syllable of that word an open syllable. When the final Kaph is the consonant that ends a word's last syllable, it helps form a closed syllable. **REVIEW Note 15A.** The Kaph then receives the reduced vowel Shewa: ךְ.   Examples: לָךְ, לֵךְ.

> **Exercises 1 & 2:**   Do the exercises on p. 9 following the academic pronunciation rules. Since transliteration systems vary, make allowance for alternative ways of transcribing some letters and vowels.

Note 17A: Simple Shewa

A simple Shewa (ְ) may be *silent* and indicate that the consonant under which it stands has ended the syllable. Thus a silent Shewa functions as a **syllable divider**. Or a simple Shewa may be slightly *vocal* (a very short "e" sound) and indicate that the consonant under which it stands is beginning a new syllable. The rule to distinguish a silent from a vocal Shewa is:

A Shewa is *silent* (i.e., a syllable divider) if it is not under a doubled consonant (i.e., one with a Dagesh Forte as explained below) and if it follows a *short* vowel. All other simple Shewas (and all composite Shewas) are *vocal*.

Silent Shewa: בִּנְךָ, אַבְרָם (syllable divider)
Vocal Shewa: בְּנוֹ, נֵלְכָה

Note 17B: Dagesh

The Dagesh (ּ -- a dot within a letter) may be of two kinds:

1. **Dagesh Lene** (the simple or weak Dagesh)
   ▸ Occurs only in the six Begadhkephath consonants (ב, ג, ד, כ, פ, ת). **REVIEW Note 13A**. Confusion arises because the Begadhkephath letters can also have the Dagesh Forte, explained below.
   ▸ Indicates the hard pronunciation of these consonants without doubling them, as a Dagesh Forte does.
   ▸▸ Occurs only after a *silent* Shewa (syllable divider) or at the beginning of a word.

   Examples: בְּנוֹ, אָהַבְתָּ

2. **Dagesh Forte** (the strong or doubling Dagesh)
   ▸ Occurs in any consonant except א, ה, ח, ע (the guttural consonants) and ר. These consonants can never be doubled.
   ▸ Indicates the doubling of the consonant and, if a Begadhkephath letter, its hard pronunciation.
   ▸▸ Occurs only after a *full* vowel (long or short).

   Examples: אֵלֶּה, נִסָּה

As you can see, the rules for distinguishing types of Shewas and Dageshes are interrelated. When a Shewa occurs under a consonant with a Dagesh, **always determine the type of Dagesh first** before applying the rules for the Shewa. Can you identify the Dageshes and the Shewas in this example? בְּסִבְּךָ

Note 18A: Dagesh & Syllables

When a consonant is doubled, i.e., when it has a Dagesh Forte, one of the doubled consonants thus formed ends the preceding syllable and the other begins the following syllable. Thus the word נִסָּה has two syllables, the first *closed* and the second *open*: נִס|סָה. **REVIEW Note 15A.** Notice that the Dagesh Forte eliminates the need for the Shewa and for writing a second Samekh.

2

Exercise 3: Do the pronunciation and transliteration exercise on p. 11.

NAMES OF THE VOWELS

The following list gives the Hebrew names for the vowels and the full transliterations, along with simplified transliterations, for the academic pronunciation.

פַּתַח	*pataḥ*	Pathah	קָמֶץ	*qāmeṣ*	Qamets
סֶגֹל	*seḡōl*	Segol	צֵרֵי	*ṣērê*	Tsere
חִירֶק	*ḥîreq*	Hireq	חִירֶק יוֹד	*ḥîreq yôḏ*	Hireq Yodh
קָמֶץ חָטוּף	*qāmeṣ ḥāṭûf*	Qamets Hatuph	חֹלֶם	*ḥōlem*	Holem
קִבּוּץ	*qibbûṣ*	Qibbuts	שׁוּרֶק וָו	*šûreq vāv*	Shureq Waw
			שְׁוָא	*ševāʾ*	Shewa

For the simplified transliterations used in the rest of this *Workbook*, which are based on the Sefardi pronunciation, see Note 3A for the consonants and Notes 5A, 5B, and 5C for the vowels. There are only a few differences and they should not cause much difficulty as you use the *Workbook*.

This concludes the special section on academic pronunciation. Proceed to the next page.

USING THE WORKBOOK

The approach of this *Workbook* is inductive and analytical. It is inductive in that the vocabulary, grammar, and syntax of Hebrew will be explained only as items appear in the readings. It is analytical in that we shall take each word and phrase apart to show its components. Little by little we shall build a working knowledge of Biblical Hebrew as we bring together all of the various elements we have learned in the readings. In the end, the student should have a basic facility in studying the Hebrew Bible in its original language.

Please note the following instructions:

1. The *Workbook* is to be used back and forth, constantly reviewing those items which you have learned and fitting in new items as they occur. Do not linger too long, however, on any one item. Keep reading and rely on repeated occurrences of items to fix them better in your mind.

2. The **Notes**, which are indented and centered on the page, contain the main explanations of the grammar and syntax to be learned. Study them carefully and review them as directed. The Notes are numbered to coincide with the page number for easy reference.

3. The **Charts** give the complete overview of grammatical forms and help students organize their learning. They are located in several clusters throughout the *Workbook*. After briefly studying the format and content of the Charts, you may proceed in the *Workbook*, for there will be many references back to them. The Charts are also numbered to coincide with the page number for easy reference and each cluster has a marginal tab number.

4. Besides the Notes and Charts, every item to be learned or commented upon is introduced by a number or symbol at the left margin of the page. Look for one of these four indicators:

    a. All numbered words starting on p. 25 are to be learned as part of the student's vocabulary. Each word occurs over 100 times in the Hebrew Bible and is given in its lexicon form. **Appendix II** is an alphabetical listing of all words occurring over 100 times with cross references back to the verse where the word first occurred in our readings. You are encouraged to develop your own glossary in Appendix II by writing in the translations in the space provided.

    b. All items marked ** are to be learned. They consist of various endings and additions to words that are very important.

    c. Words marked ## occur fewer than 100 times in the Hebrew Bible and need not be learned as part of the student's vocabulary.

    d. The symbol ▶ introduces a form from the text for comment or explanation.

5. All verbs in Hebrew usually have three root consonants. It is customary to list the three consonants of verb roots without pointing. Initially, however, the pointing of the simplest, lexicon form of the verb will be given in parentheses at the right margin, so that you will know how to pronounce verbs as you learn their meanings.

6. After a while, forms will appear in the text about which nothing is said in the *Workbook*. Such forms contain only items that have already been explained and that you are expected to know.

7. The vowels especially will seem quite elusive for the time being, but little by little their changes will become clearer.

8. During the study of Genesis 22, the Hebrew of the verse or verse part discussed on that page will be printed at the top of the page for the student's convenience.

9. Also during the study of Genesis 22, five **Progress Checks** are included to assist in the early stages of the learning process.

10. Included in the **Contents** are the tab numbers which appear in the margins to mark the two systems of pronunciation, the charts of grammatical forms, and the vocabulary listing. These tabs make it easier to locate the various clusters of charts when reference is made to them.

11. The **General Index** lists all of the items of grammar and syntax explained in the *Workbook*. If you remember having been introduced to a matter but cannot find where it was, use the Index for guidance.

Exercise 4: The following page contains the Hebrew text of Genesis 22:1-19, the first reading of the *Workbook*. Pronounce and transliterate the Hebrew in the first two verses.

22 ¹ וַיְהִ֗י אַחַר֙ הַדְּבָרִ֣ים הָאֵ֔לֶּה וְהָ֣אֱלֹהִ֔ים נִסָּ֖ה אֶת־אַבְרָהָ֑ם
וַיֹּ֥אמֶר אֵלָ֖יו אַבְרָהָ֑ם וַיֹּ֥אמֶר הִנֵּֽנִי׃ ² וַיֹּ֡אמֶר קַח־נָ֠א אֶת־בִּנְךָ֨ אֶת־
יְחִֽידְךָ֤ אֲשֶׁר־אָהַ֨בְתָּ֙ אֶת־יִצְחָ֔ק וְלֶךְ־לְךָ֔ אֶל־אֶ֖רֶץ הַמֹּרִיָּ֑ה וְהַעֲלֵ֤הוּ
שָׁם֙ לְעֹלָ֔ה עַ֚ל אַחַ֣ד הֶֽהָרִ֔ים אֲשֶׁ֖ר אֹמַ֥ר אֵלֶֽיךָ׃ ³ וַיַּשְׁכֵּ֨ם אַבְרָהָ֜ם
בַּבֹּ֗קֶר וַֽיַּחֲבֹשׁ֙ אֶת־חֲמֹר֔וֹ וַיִּקַּ֞ח אֶת־שְׁנֵ֤י נְעָרָיו֙ אִתּ֔וֹ וְאֵ֖ת יִצְחָ֣ק בְּנ֑וֹ
וַיְבַקַּע֙ עֲצֵ֣י עֹלָ֔ה וַיָּ֣קָם וַיֵּ֔לֶךְ אֶל־הַמָּק֖וֹם אֲשֶׁר־אָֽמַר־ל֥וֹ הָאֱלֹהִֽים׃
⁴ בַּיּ֣וֹם הַשְּׁלִישִׁ֗י וַיִּשָּׂ֨א אַבְרָהָ֧ם אֶת־עֵינָ֛יו וַיַּ֥רְא אֶת־הַמָּק֖וֹם מֵרָחֹֽק׃
⁵ וַיֹּ֨אמֶר אַבְרָהָ֜ם אֶל־נְעָרָ֗יו שְׁבוּ־לָכֶ֥ם פֹּה֙ עִם־הַחֲמ֔וֹר וַאֲנִ֣י וְהַנַּ֔עַר
נֵלְכָ֖ה עַד־כֹּ֑ה וְנִֽשְׁתַּחֲוֶ֖ה וְנָשׁ֥וּבָה אֲלֵיכֶֽם׃ ⁶ וַיִּקַּ֨ח אַבְרָהָ֜ם אֶת־עֲצֵ֣י
הָעֹלָ֗ה וַיָּ֨שֶׂם֙ עַל־יִצְחָ֣ק בְּנ֔וֹ וַיִּקַּ֣ח בְּיָד֔וֹ אֶת־הָאֵ֖שׁ וְאֶת־הַֽמַּאֲכֶ֑לֶת
וַיֵּלְכ֥וּ שְׁנֵיהֶ֖ם יַחְדָּֽו׃ ⁷ וַיֹּ֨אמֶר יִצְחָ֜ק אֶל־אַבְרָהָ֤ם אָבִיו֙ וַיֹּ֣אמֶר אָבִ֔י
וַיֹּ֖אמֶר הִנֶּ֣נִּֽי בְנִ֑י וַיֹּ֗אמֶר הִנֵּ֤ה הָאֵשׁ֙ וְהָ֣עֵצִ֔ים וְאַיֵּ֥ה הַשֶּׂ֖ה לְעֹלָֽה׃ ⁸ וַיֹּ֨אמֶר֙
אַבְרָהָ֔ם אֱלֹהִ֞ים יִרְאֶה־לּ֥וֹ הַשֶּׂ֛ה לְעֹלָ֖ה בְּנִ֑י וַיֵּלְכ֥וּ שְׁנֵיהֶ֖ם יַחְדָּֽו׃
⁹ וַיָּבֹ֗אוּ אֶל־הַמָּקוֹם֮ אֲשֶׁ֣ר אָֽמַר־ל֣וֹ הָאֱלֹהִים֒ וַיִּ֨בֶן שָׁ֤ם אַבְרָהָם֙ אֶת־
הַמִּזְבֵּ֔חַ וַֽיַּעֲרֹ֖ךְ אֶת־הָעֵצִ֑ים וַֽיַּעֲקֹד֙ אֶת־יִצְחָ֣ק בְּנ֔וֹ וַיָּ֤שֶׂם אֹתוֹ֙ עַל־
הַמִּזְבֵּ֔חַ מִמַּ֖עַל לָעֵצִֽים׃ ¹⁰ וַיִּשְׁלַ֤ח אַבְרָהָם֙ אֶת־יָד֔וֹ וַיִּקַּ֖ח אֶת־
הַֽמַּאֲכֶ֑לֶת לִשְׁחֹ֖ט אֶת־בְּנֽוֹ׃ ¹¹ וַיִּקְרָ֨א אֵלָ֜יו מַלְאַ֤ךְ יְהוָה֙ מִן־הַשָּׁמַ֔יִם
וַיֹּ֖אמֶר אַבְרָהָ֣ם אַבְרָהָ֑ם וַיֹּ֖אמֶר הִנֵּֽנִי׃ ¹² וַיֹּ֗אמֶר אַל־תִּשְׁלַ֤ח יָֽדְךָ֙
אֶל־הַנַּ֔עַר וְאַל־תַּ֥עַשׂ ל֖וֹ מְא֑וּמָה כִּ֣י׀ עַתָּ֣ה יָדַ֗עְתִּי כִּֽי־יְרֵ֤א אֱלֹהִים֙
אַ֔תָּה וְלֹ֥א חָשַׂ֛כְתָּ אֶת־בִּנְךָ֥ אֶת־יְחִֽידְךָ֖ מִמֶּֽנִּי׃ ¹³ וַיִּשָּׂ֨א אַבְרָהָ֜ם אֶת־
עֵינָ֗יו וַיַּרְא֙ וְהִנֵּה־אַ֔יִל אַחַ֕ר נֶאֱחַ֥ז בַּסְּבַ֖ךְ בְּקַרְנָ֑יו וַיֵּ֤לֶךְ אַבְרָהָם֙ וַיִּקַּ֣ח
אֶת־הָאַ֔יִל וַיַּעֲלֵ֥הוּ לְעֹלָ֖ה תַּ֥חַת בְּנֽוֹ׃ ¹⁴ וַיִּקְרָ֧א אַבְרָהָ֛ם שֵֽׁם־הַמָּק֥וֹם
הַה֖וּא יְהוָ֣ה׀ יִרְאֶ֑ה אֲשֶׁר֙ יֵאָמֵ֣ר הַיּ֔וֹם בְּהַ֥ר יְהוָ֖ה יֵרָאֶֽה׃
¹⁵ וַיִּקְרָ֛א מַלְאַ֥ךְ יְהוָ֖ה אֶל־אַבְרָהָ֑ם שֵׁנִ֖ית מִן־הַשָּׁמָֽיִם׃ ¹⁶ וַיֹּ֕אמֶר בִּ֥י
נִשְׁבַּ֖עְתִּי נְאֻם־יְהוָ֑ה כִּ֗י יַ֚עַן אֲשֶׁ֤ר עָשִׂ֨יתָ֙ אֶת־הַדָּבָ֣ר הַזֶּ֔ה וְלֹ֥א חָשַׂ֖כְתָּ
אֶת־בִּנְךָ֥ אֶת־יְחִידֶֽךָ׃ ¹⁷ כִּֽי־בָרֵ֣ךְ אֲבָרֶכְךָ֗ וְהַרְבָּ֨ה אַרְבֶּ֤ה אֶֽת־זַרְעֲךָ֙
כְּכוֹכְבֵ֣י הַשָּׁמַ֔יִם וְכַח֕וֹל אֲשֶׁ֖ר עַל־שְׂפַ֣ת הַיָּ֑ם וְיִרַ֣שׁ זַרְעֲךָ֔ אֵ֖ת שַׁ֥עַר
אֹיְבָֽיו׃ ¹⁸ וְהִתְבָּרֲכ֣וּ בְזַרְעֲךָ֔ כֹּ֖ל גּוֹיֵ֣י הָאָ֑רֶץ עֵ֕קֶב אֲשֶׁ֥ר שָׁמַ֖עְתָּ בְּקֹלִֽי׃
¹⁹ וַיָּ֤שָׁב אַבְרָהָם֙ אֶל־נְעָרָ֔יו וַיָּקֻ֛מוּ וַיֵּלְכ֥וּ יַחְדָּ֖ו אֶל־בְּאֵ֣ר שָׁ֑בַע וַיֵּ֥שֶׁב
אַבְרָהָ֖ם בִּבְאֵ֥ר שָֽׁבַע׃

GETTING ACQUAINTED WITH THE HEBREW TEXT

Genesis 22:1-19 contains the Aqedah (עֲקֵדָה, ʿaqēdāh), the story of the "binding" of Isaac. In order to assist you at the beginning, the full Hebrew text of the story appears on the preceding page and verse portions will appear at the top of each page as we proceed through the chapter. But you should also have the text as it appears in *Biblia Hebraica Stuttgartensia* (BHS). Since subsequent readings will not be printed in the *Workbook*, the sooner you get accustomed to using BHS the better. Whether you are using the text on the previous page or BHS, **do not write in the Hebrew text**. Make a photo copy, if you wish to mark up the text, but keep the text in the *Workbook* and in the Hebrew Bible clean so that your notes do not become a crutch that inhibits your learning.

OBSERVATIONS ABOUT BHS

As you look at pp. 31 and 32 in BHS, you will notice several features that do not appear in the text on the previous page. The three most important are:

1. **Marginal notes and footnotes.** The marginal notes consist of the brief comments of the Masoretes called the *Masora parva* (Mp). They are written or abbreviated in Aramaic. A small supralinear circle (◌̊), called a *circule*, placed over a word or between words of a phrase, indicates a marginal note. The top section of the footnotes contains references to fuller listings of the Mp in the *Masora magna* (Mm). The bottom set of footnotes contains the "critical apparatus," the editor's discussion of textual matters. A small raised letter in the text (ᵃ) indicates a reference to the critical apparatus in the footnotes.

2. **Accent markings.** In the Hebrew text itself there are about thirty different Masoretic accent markings, which are written either above, below, or sometimes between the letters. They serve a) to mark the stressed syllable, b) to punctuate the sentence, and c) as musical guides. Most words will have just one accent and it will be on the last syllable. Some longer words may have a secondary accent. Remember, in this *Workbook* initially only one accent marking will be used, namely, the supralinear arrowhead (◌̀), and then only when the stress is on the penultima. **REVIEW Page 6 or 15.** A little later we will make note of a couple of uses of the Masoretic accents for punctuation.

3. **Verse numbering.** Besides the number that appears at the beginning of each verse within the text, the verse number also appears in the inside margin, if the verse begins in the middle of that line and not at the beginning of the line.

The next two pages contain charts for verb and noun endings. **Skip to p. 25,** for there will be many references back to these verb and noun charts.

Chart 23A: The Affixes*

An affix indicates the pronominal SUBJECT of a PERFECT verb. It consists of one or two letters with pointing and is attached *after* the verb root.

	singular			plural		
3m	‎ــــ	*he*	Gn 22:1	‎וـــــ	*they*	Gn 22:18
3f	‎הָـــ	*she*	Gn 12:13			
2m	‎תָּـــ	*you*	Gn 22:2	‎תֶּםـــــ	*you*	Dt 5:1
2f	‎תְּـــ	*you*		‎תֶּןـــــ	*you*	
1c	‎תִּיـــــ	*I*	Gn 22:12	‎נוּـــــ	*we*	Js 24:17

Chart 23B: The Prefixes*

A prefix indicates the pronominal SUBJECT of an IMPERFECT verb. It always consists of one letter with pointing attached *before* the verb root, and may also have one or two letters *after* the verb root, especially in the plural.

	singular			plural		
3m	‎ـــיـ	*he*	Gn 22:1	‎וـــــיـ	*they*	Gn 22:6
3f	‎ـــתـ	*she*	Gn 12:15	‎הנָـــــתـ	*they*	Js 24:7
2m	‎ـــתـ	*you*	Gn 22:12	‎וـــــתـ	*you*	Js 24:6
2f	‎יـــתـ	*you*	Gn 12:13	‎הנָـــــתـ	*you*	
1c	‎ـــאـ	*I*	Gn 22:2	‎ـــנـ	*we*	Gn 22:5

The verses refer to the first appearance of the form in the readings. The barest abbreviations are used for person, gender, and number: "3fs" = third person, feminine, singular; "1cp" = first, common (applied to both genders), plural.

* An affix may also be called an **afformative**.
  A prefix may also be called a **preformative**.

Chart 24A: Suffixes

A suffix indicates a pronominal OBJECT used in relation to a preposition, noun, or verb. It consists of one or two letters with pointing attached *at the end* of the word.

	singular			plural		
3m	וֹ___	*him, his*	Gn 22:1	ם___	*them, their*	Gn 12:5
	וֹ___	*him, his*	Gn 22:3			
	הוּ___	*him, his*	Gn 22:2	הֶם___	*them, their*	Gn 22:6
	ה___	*him, his*	Gn 12:8			
3f	הָ___	*her*	Js 24:26	ן___	*them, their*	
	הָ___	*her*	Gn 12:15	הֶן___	*them, their*	
2m	ךָ___	*you, your*	Gn 22:2	כֶם___	*you, your*	Gn 22:5
2f	ך___	*you, your*	Gn 12:12	כֶן___	*you, your*	
1c	ִי___	*me, my*	Gn 22:7	נוּ___	*us, our*	Dt 5:2
	ִנִי___	*me*	Gn 22:11			

Chart 24B: Noun/Adjective Endings

	singular		plural	
	absolute	construct	absolute	construct
m	___ Gn 22:2	___ Gn 22:2	ִים___ Gn 22:1	ֵי___ Gn 22:3
f	הָ___ Gn 22:17	ת___ Gn 22:17	וֹת___ Gn 12:3	וֹת___ Gn 12:3

	dual	
m or f	ַיִם___ Gn 22:3	ֵי___ Gn 22:3

CHAPTER II: THE STUDY OF GENESIS 22:1-19

(Gn 22:1)   וַיְהִי אַחַר הַדְּבָרִים הָאֵלֶּה ¹

GENESIS 22:1

The **first word** וַיְהִי is a verb form and has three parts: ו|י|הי. (Notice that the grammatical analysis does not necessarily coincide with the syllables in pronunciation.)

1. The Vav (ו) is the conjunction equivalent to English "and."

2. The Yod (י) is a letter that has been prefixed to the verb root to indicate the pronoun subject of the verb. It is third person, masculine, singular (3ms) and can be translated "he" or "it."

3. The last two letters (הי) belong to the verb root היה (pointed for learning as הָיָה). This is the verb "to be, become, happen." Pay no attention at this time to the pointing in the form וַיְהִי and regard the action to be past time. Thus וַיְהִי may be translated "and he was" or, as the context will suggest, "and it happened." Learn from this form the following items:

**	_ _ _ י	(prefix)	*he, it*	(3ms)
1.	היה	(verb)	*to be, become, happen*	(הָיָה)

Note 25A: Final He

The final letter ה is often dropped from the end of a word or syllable, for it is a weak letter.

The **second word** אַחַר is just one item:

2.	אַחַר	(preposition)	*after, behind*

The **third word** הַדְּבָרִים has three parts: ה|דבר־|ים

3.	_ _ _ ַ ה	(definite article)	*the*

Note 25B: Definite Article

The **definite article** is always the consonant ה but the pointing may vary. The regular pointing is _ _ _ ַ ה. Notice that the Dagesh Forte in the following letter is part of the definite article. The Dagesh Forte will always be there, unless the following letter is one that cannot be doubled. **REVIEW Note 10B** or **17B**. Hebrew has no indefinite article, so that the words "a" and "an" must be supplied as English requires.

¹וַיְהִי אַחַר הַדְּבָרִים הָאֵלֶּה וְהָאֱלֹהִים נִסָּה אֶת־אַבְרָהָם

4.　　　　דָּבָר　　(noun)　　*word, thing, event, deed*

**　　　　םי‗‗‗‗　　(noun ending)　　　　　　　　(masc. pl.)

The **fourth word** הָאֵלֶּה has two parts:　　ה|אלה

**　　　　‗‗‗‗הָ　　(definite article)　　*the*

Note 26A: Definite Article and the Gutturals

The **guttural letters** (עחהא) and　ר　cannot receive a Dagesh Forte, i.e., cannot be doubled. **REVIEW Note 10B or 17B** and **Note 25B**. When the consonant following the article is　א, ע, or ר, the vowel of the article is lengthened from a short Patah to a long Qamets to compensate for the rejected Dagesh Forte. This change of the vowel is called **compensatory lengthening**.

5.　　　　אֵלֶּה　　(demonstrative adjective)　　*these*　　(com. pl.)

Note 26B: Common Gender

Certain adjectives and especially all first person verbs have **common** gender, indicating that they serve both feminine and masculine usages.

Note 26C: Attributive Adjectives

Attribute adjectives regularly follow the noun they qualify and agree in gender, number, and definiteness. In the phrase הַדְּבָרִים הָאֵלֶּה the noun is masc. pl. (‗‗‗‗םי) and is definite, i.e., has the article (הַ‗‗‗‗). Thus the adjective which follows is com. pl. and has the article.

The phrase אַחַר הַדְּבָרִים הָאֵלֶּה may be rendered: "after these things."

Proceed now to the next words. Only new items will be listed. You are expected to recognize repeated occurrences of words and other items you have already had.

6.　　　　וְ‗‗‗‗　　(conjunction)　　*and, but, then, etc.*

Note 26D: Simple Conjunction

The simple conjunction is always the letter　ו, but the pointing may vary. The regular pointing of the simple conjunction is　‗‗‗‗וְ.

7.   אֱלֹהִים   (noun)   *gods, God*

Note 27A: Plural of Majesty

Because the word אֱלֹהִים has the masc. pl. ending ◌ִים◌, it can sometimes be translated "gods." But the same form is used to refer to the God of Israel and takes singular verbs. The ending ◌ִים◌ in this case does not refer to a numerical plural but to the so-called **plural of majesty** or excellence. The article can be used when terms applying to a whole class (gods) are restricted to particular individuals (the god, or God). Our capital "G" in "God" serves the same function as the article in הָאֱלֹהִים.

נסה   (verb)   *to test, try, tempt, prove*   (נָסָה)

      You need not understand the pointing of the form נִסָּה now.

Note 27B: Verb Aspects

Hebrew verbs do not have true tenses, such as past or future. Rather, it is the aspect or quality of the action that is foremost. The action of the verb is regarded as either complete or incomplete. The term **perfect** is used to designate a verb when its aspect is *complete* and the term **imperfect** when its aspect is *incomplete*. The time element is determined by the context or by special usages.

The two aspects are easily distinguishable because both have a letter or letters attached to the verb root that indicate the pronoun subject of the verb. The pronominal subject of the **perfect** is indicated by a letter or letters **affixed** to the verb (attached after the verb). The pronominal subject of the **imperfect** is indicated by a letter **prefixed** to the verb (attached before the verb).

It is very important to remember that the appearance of an affix or a prefix on a verb form tells you two things:

    1. the aspect of the verb, whether it is perfect or imperfect;

    2. the person, gender, and number of the verb's subject.

**   ___   (affix)   *he, it*   (3ms of the perfect)

      Turn back to see this affix in **Chart 23A**. There you will see that in the 3ms of the perfect there is no letter that is attached after the verb root to indicate the subject. In fact it is the absence of an affix in the form נָסָה that tells that it is the 3ms of the perfect.

28

וְהָאֱלֹהִים נִסָּה אֶת־אַבְרָהָם וַיֹּאמֶר אֵלָיו

Note 28A: Perfect Verbs

A perfect verb form is indicated by the presence of pronominal affixes. In the form נִסָּה the three root letters of the verb נסה appear without any affix. But the 3ms of the perfect has no affix, making it the simplest form of the verb and therefore the form used for lexical entries. In all other perfect verb forms, an affix will appear.

The perfect suggests completed action, an accomplished event. Thus in the context of a narrative, the perfect often refers to past time. Nevertheless, it is more the aspect or quality of the action than the time element that is foremost in verb forms.

8.   אֵת, אֶת־   (particle)   (untranslated sign of the definite direct object)

Note 28B: Sign of Definite Direct Object

The untranslated sign that the **definite direct object** of the verb follows has two alternative forms: אֵת and אֶת־. The word is sometimes called the "accusative" particle. אֵת usually assumes its alternative form אֶת־ with the Maqqef. **REVIEW Note 6C or 15C.** Notice that אֶת־ is a closed unstressed syllable and must have a short vowel. Thus the long vowel Tsere is changed to the short vowel Segol. **REVIEW Note 6B or 15B.** There is no sign for an indefinite direct object.

9.   אַבְרָהָם   (proper noun)   Abraham

Note 28C: Proper Nouns

All proper nouns, i.e., names of people and places, are **definite** along with all words that have the definite article. **REVIEW Notes 25B and 26A.** Because אַבְרָהָם is the definite direct object in the clause, it is preceded by אֶת־.

The phrase וְהָאֱלֹהִים נִסָּה אֶת־אַבְרָהָם yields the translation: "and God tested Abraham."

**   ־ְ־ֽ־ וַ   (conjunction)   *and, but, then*, etc.
The Vav is again the conjunction "and," but the pointing indicates a special usage of the conjunction with imperfect verb forms, as explained in the next Note.

וַיֹּאמֶר אֵלָיו אַבְרָהָם וַיֹּאמֶר הִנֵּנִי: (Gn 22:1)

Note 29A: Imperfect with Vav Consecutive

When the conjunction Vav directly precedes a verb in a narrative in which successive events are being related, it is called the **Vav consecutive**. If the verb is imperfect, i.e., one that has a prefix as in וַיֹּאמֶר, the vowel of the Vav becomes Patah and the prefix normally receives a Dagesh Forte: ‎וַיִ___. When the Vav consecutive appears with an imperfect verb form, the whole form may be called **imperfect consecutive**. The imperfect consecutive is a special form and is used in narratives to express **past time**.

10.   אמר   (verb)   *to say*   (אָמַר)

The verb form וַיֹּאמֶר is an imperfect consecutive form. It is imperfect because of the 3ms prefix Yod (‎יִ___) and it is consecutive because of the distinctive pointing of the Vav with the prefix (‎וַיִ___). Since an imperfect consecutive form is past time, the form is rendered: "and he said."

11.   אֶל־   (preposition)   *to, toward*

**   ‎ו___   (suffix)   *him, his*   (3ms)
See this suffix in **Chart 24A** and read the next Note.

Note 29B: Pronominal Suffixes

When the object of a preposition is a pronoun, that object is indicated by a letter or letters called a **suffix** attached to the end of the preposition. ‎ו___ is the first of four 3ms suffixes. The Yod in the form אֵלָיו has no semantic force here but often occurs between a preposition and a suffix; it may be called a "meaningless" Yod.

12.   הִנֵּה   (demonstrative particle)   *lo! behold! here!*

**   ‎נִי___   (suffix)   *me*   (1cs)
See this suffix in **Chart 24A**.

For the loss of the final He of הִנֵּה in the form הִנֵּנִי, **REVIEW Note 25A**. This is an idiomatic phrase: "Behold, me!" or "Here I am!"

Note 29C: Sof Pasuq

The sign : is called **Sof Pasuq** and denotes the "end of a verse."

PROGRESS CHECK #1

1. Name the vowel and tell whether it is long, short, or reduced:

    a. ◌ַ _____   h. וֹ _____

    b. ◌ְ _____   i. ◌ִי _____

    c. ◌ָ _____   j. ◌ֵ _____

    d. ◌ֱ _____   k. ◌ֻ _____

    e. ◌ּ _____   l. ◌ֳ _____

    f. ◌ֶ _____   m. וֹ _____

    g. ◌ֵי _____   n. ◌ָה _____

2. A closed unstressed syllable must have a _____ vowel.

3. Every Hebrew syllable begins with a _____.

4. Dagesh Lene is used only in these six consonants: _____

5. The vowel before a silent Sheva (syllable divider) is always _____.

6. Dagesh Forte is always preceded by a _____ vowel.

7. The simple conjunction ("and") is _____.

8. Two forms of the definite article are _____ and _____.

9. Attribute adjectives are placed _____ the noun they modify and agree with the noun in 1) _____, 2) _____, and 3) _____.

10. A prefix on a verb root indicates 1) _____
    and 2) _____.

11. Pronounce and transliterate the following phrases:

    a. וַיֵּלְכוּ שְׁנֵיהֶם יַחְדָּו

    b. וַיְבַקַּע עֲצֵי עֹלָה

    c. וְאַל־תַּעַשׂ לוֹ מְאוּמָה

12. Identify the kinds of Shevas and Dageshes in the phrases above.

² וַיֹּאמֶר קַח־נָא אֶת־בִּנְךָ אֶת־יְחִידְךָ   (Gn 22:2)

GENESIS 22:2

13.   לקח   (verb)   *to take*   (לָקַח)

קַח is the active imperative 2ms of the verb לקח: "Take!"
The initial ל of this verb often does not appear, so that the
student should learn to associate the two letters קח with
the verb לקח.

14.   נָא   (particle of entreaty)   *please! I pray!*

15.   בֵּן   (noun)   *son*

**   ךָ____   (suffix)   *you, your*   (2ms)

See this suffix in **Chart 24A**.

Note 31A: Pronominal Suffixes

The pronominal suffixes serve as possessive pronouns as well as objects
of prepositions. **REVIEW Note 29B.** Compare:

בֵּן -- "a son"

בִּנְךָ -- "your son"

אֵלָיו -- "to him"

אֵלֶיךָ -- "to you"

Note 31B: Definiteness

A noun is also definite if it has a suffix. Hence, as a definite direct
object, the word בִּנְךָ is preceded by אֶת־. **REVIEW Note 28B**.
Compare:

קַח בֵּן -- "Take a son!"

קַח אֶת־הַבֵּן -- "Take the son!"

קַח אֶת־בִּנְךָ -- "Take your son!"

קַח אֶת־יִצְחָק -- "Take Isaac!"

קַח־נָא אֶת־בִּנְךָ אֶת־יְחִידְךָ אֲשֶׁר־אָהַבְתָּ אֶת־יִצְחָק

Note 32A: Summary of Definiteness

> A word is **definite** if it:
> 1. has the article: הַבֵּן
> 2. has a suffix: בִּנְךָ
> 3. is a proper noun: אַבְרָהָם

יָחִיד   (adjective)   *only, alone*

Here the adjective is used as a substantive: "your only (one)."

Note 32B: Change of pointing

The addition of a suffix at the end of a noun (or verb) often causes a change of pointing earlier in the word, usually a shortening or reduction. Compare:

$$\text{בֵּן} \quad \text{but} \quad \text{בִּנְךָ}$$

$$\text{יָחִיד} \quad \text{but} \quad \text{יְחִידְךָ}$$

---

16.   אֲשֶׁר   (relative particle)   *who, which, that*

Very often, as here, אֲשֶׁר is equivalent to our relative pronoun "who" or "which," but it can also have some other uses, as we will see later.

---

17.   אהב   (verb)   *to love*   (אָהַב)

**   תָּ___   (affix)   *you*   (2ms of the perfect)

See this affix in **Chart 23A**.

▶   אֲשֶׁר־אָהַבְתָּ   **REVIEW Note 28A.** Context again is the best indicator of the time element in Hebrew verbs. Here either "whom you have loved" or "whom you love" is possible.

---

18.   יִצְחָק   (proper noun)   *Isaac*

The direct object of קַח־נָא is a series of short dramatic phrases culminating in the mention of the boy's name: אֶת־בִּנְךָ אֶת־יְחִידְךָ אֲשֶׁר־אָהַבְתָּ אֶת־יִצְחָק.

וְלֶךְ־לְךָ אֶל־אֶרֶץ הַמֹּרִיָּה   (Gn 22:2)

19.   הלך   (verb)   *to go, walk*   (הָלַךְ)

לֵךְ is the active imperative 2ms of the verb הלך. The initial ה of this verb often does not appear, so that the student should learn to associate the two letters לֵךְ with the verb הלך. Cf. **Word 13** above.

20.   לְ––––   (preposition)   *to, for*

Note 33A: Inseparable Prepositions

לְ is one of the three **inseparable prepositions** consisting of just one letter that is attached directly to the beginning of the word that is its object. It is regularly pointed with a Sheva. The object of the preposition in this case is just the single letter of the suffix: לְךָ.

Note 33B: Reflexive Preposition

Sometimes a form made up of the preposition לְ and a suffix points back to the subject of the verb to lay stress on the subject's action. When this occurs, the verb is usually, but not always, imperative. Thus, לֶךְ־לְךָ can be rendered: "Go for yourself!" or "You, yourself, go!" Older grammarians called this the **ethical dative**. Today it may be described as the **reflexive use of the preposition** לְ.

21.   אֶרֶץ   (noun)   *land, earth*

מֹרִיָּה   (proper noun)   *Moriah*

Note 33C: Construct Chain

Two nouns (or noun equivalents) which stand together and are regarded as conveying one idea are said to be in the construct relation and may be called a **construct chain**. The two nouns are usually connected in translation by "of," although no Hebrew word for "of" appears in the phrase. אֶרֶץ הַמֹּרִיָּה is a construct chain. The first noun (in this case אֶרֶץ) is said to be in the **construct** state and is never definite in form. **REVIEW Note 32A**. The last noun (in this case הַמֹּרִיָּה) is said to be in the **absolute** state and may or may not be definite in form. Whether the entire phrase is thought to be **definite** or **indefinite** in translation is determined by the form of the absolute. If the absolute is

וַיֹּאמֶר לֶךְ־לְךָ אֶל־אֶרֶץ הַמֹּרִיָּה וְהַעֲלֵהוּ שָׁם לְעֹלָה עַל אַחַד הֶהָרִים (Gn 22:2)

definite, the whole phrase is definite; if the absolute is indefinite, the whole phrase is indefinite. Compare:

אֶרֶץ בֵּן -- "**a** land of **a** son"

אֶרֶץ הַבֵּן --- "**the** land of **the** son"

אֶרֶץ בִּנְךָ --- "**the** land of **your** son"

אֶרֶץ אַבְרָהָם --- "**the** land of **Abraham**"

22.	עלה	(verb)	*to go up*	(עָלָה)

**	הוּ‗‗‗‗	(suffix)	*him, his*	(another 3ms)

See **Chart 24A**.

► וְהַעֲלֵהוּ
The form הַעֲלֵה is an imperative 2ms of the verb עלה, but this more complex form (because of the initial ה) is to be translated "to offer" (i.e., to cause to go up). The suffix is the direct object of the verb. The final ה of the form הַעֲלֵה has been dropped before the suffix הוּ‗‗‗‗. **REVIEW Note 25A**. The form in the text may be rendered: "and offer him."

23.	שָׁם	(adverb)	*there*
24.	עֹלָה	(noun)	*burnt offering*
25.	עַל	(preposition)	*upon, concerning*
26.	אֶחָד	(number)	*one*

Note 34A: Construct State

A noun in the construct state (**REVIEW Note 33C**) may have a change of pointing, usually a shortening, from the absolute state of the word, which is the lexicon form. The absolute form of the number "one" is אֶחָד, but the construct form is אַחַד, indicating that the word in our text is a construct in a construct chain.

Some words are pointed the same in both the construct and absolute states, such as אֶרֶץ, Word 21 above.

**	הַ‗‗‗‗	(definite article)	*the*

עַל אַחַד הֶהָרִים אֲשֶׁר אֹמַר אֵלֶיךָ: (Gn 22:2)

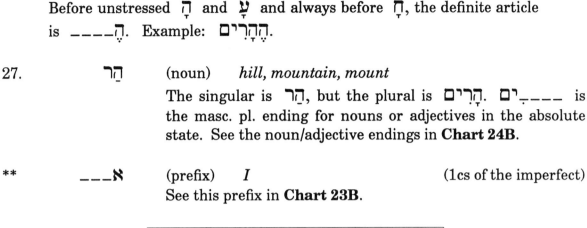

Note 35A: Definite Article

Before unstressed הָ and עָ and always before חָ, the definite article is _ _ _ _הֶ. Example: הֶהָרִים.

27.   הַר   (noun)   *hill, mountain, mount*

The singular is הַר, but the plural is הָרִים. ים_ _ _ _ is the masc. pl. ending for nouns or adjectives in the absolute state. See the noun/adjective endings in **Chart 24B**.

**   א_ _ _   (prefix)   *I*   (1cs of the imperfect)

See this prefix in **Chart 23B**.

Note 35B: First Person Imperfect

The 1cs prefix א_ _ _ and the first root consonant of the verb אמר have coalesced from the hypothetical אאמר to אֹמַר. This can happen only with this prefix and with verbs whose initial consonant א is quiescent in 1cs imperfect forms.

Note 35C: Summary of the Use of Affixes, Prefixes, and Suffixes

AFFIX	(or afformative): The technical term used to describe the letter(s) that are attached just *after* the root of a verb to signify 1) a **perfect** verb form, and 2) the pronominal **subject** of the verb.
PREFIX	(or preformative): The technical term used to describe the letter that is attached just *before* the root of a verb to signify 1) an **imperfect** verb form, and 2) the pronominal **subject** of the verb.
SUFFIX	The technical term used to describe the letter(s) that are attached to the *end* of a word to signify 1) the pronominal **object of a preposition**, 2) the pronominal **direct object of a verb**, or 3) the pronominal **possessive object of a noun** or noun equivalent.

PROGRESS CHECK #2

1. A Vav consecutive with an imperfect verb is regularly pointed _____ .

2. An imperfect consecutive form expresses _____ time.

3. In a narrative a perfect verb form usually expresses _____ time.

4. In a construct chain, the noun that appears first is called the _____ , and the noun that appears last is called the _____ .

5. If a construct chain is definite, the article may be used only with the _____ .

6. a) A verb with a Yod-prefix has the subject _____ .
   b) A verb with an Alef-prefix has the subject _____ .

7. Give the translations of the following pronominal suffixes:

   a. ךָ _____

   b. הוּ _____

   c. ו _____

8. The imperatives of הלךְ and לקח drop _____ .

9. A word is definite if it

   a. _____

   b. _____

   or c. _____

10. Pronounce and transliterate Genesis 22:3-4.

3 וַיַּשְׁכֵּם אַבְרָהָם בַּבֹּקֶר וַיַּחֲבֹשׁ אֶת־חֲמֹרוֹ (Gn 22:3)

GENESIS 22:3

| ## | שׁכם | (verb) | *to rise early* | (שָׁכַם) |

Note 37A: Word Order

Regular word order in a narrative verbal clause is first the verb, then the subject. Each verb has a pronoun subject indicated by the affix or prefix, but always expect an expressed subject which might follow. Here אַבְרָהָם is the expressed subject for the verb with the 3ms prefix. **REVIEW Note 29A** for the pointing of the Vav and its significance.

| 28. | בְּ‎–––– | (preposition) | *in, on, by, with, when* |

Another inseparable preposition. **REVIEW Note 33A.**

| 29. | בֹּקֶר | (noun) | *morning* |

Note 37B: Inseparable Prepositions and the Article

When the inseparable prepositions בְּ, לְ, or כְ appear with a word that has the article, the ה of the article disappears but the pointing of the article remains and becomes the pointing of the preposition.

Compare:

בְּבֹקֶר -- "in a morning"

הַבֹּקֶר -- "the morning"

בַּבֹּקֶר -- "in the morning"

##	חבשׁ	(verb)	*to tie, bind, gird, saddle*	(חָבַשׁ)
30.	חֲמוֹר	(noun)	*ass*
**	וֹ‎––––	(suffix)	*him, his*	(another 3ms)

See **Chart 24A**.

Note 37C: Full or Defective Writing

The vowels with the vowel letters Vav and Yod are sometimes written without the vowel letter. Without the vowel letters, the vowels are said to be written **defectively** (*scriptio defectiva*), while with the vowel letters the vowels are said to be written **fully** (*scriptio plena*). E.g, since the last vowel of חֲמוֹר is usually written fully (וֹ), this is its lexicon form. But occasionally the word occurs with its second vowel written defectively as חֲמֹר, especially if a suffix has been added.

וַיִּקַּח אֶת־שְׁנֵי נְעָרָיו

▶   וַיִּקַּח   **REVIEW Word 13.** Note what kind of Dagesh is in the Qof. Its significance will be explained below in Note 41C.

31.   שְׁנַיִם   (number)   *two*

The construct form is שְׁנֵי.

**   ַיִם‎ָ   (noun ending)   (for dual forms)

See the noun/adjective endings in **Chart 24B.**

Note 38A: Dual Number (Absolute)

Hebrew nouns and adjectives may have singular, plural, or **dual** forms. The dual ending is used

1) for things that naturally occur in pairs: יָדַיִם -- "two hands"

2) for any two of a kind: יוֹמַיִם -- "two days"

Distinguish between the absolute dual ending ַיִם and the absolute plural ending ִים.

**   ֵי   (noun ending)   (for masc. pl. or dual construct)

See the noun/adjective endings in **Chart 24B.**

Note 38B: Masc. Pl. & Dual Construct

When a masc. pl. or dual noun is in the construct state (i.e., when it is not the last word in a construct chain), the ם of the absolute ending is dropped and the ending becomes ֵי.   **REVIEW Note 33C.** Compare:

הַדְּבָרִים -- "the words"

דִּבְרֵי אַבְרָהָם -- "the words of Abraham"

32.   נַעַר   (noun)   *youth, boy, servant*

Note 38C: Masc. Pl. with Suffixes

The Yod between a noun and a suffix, as in נְעָרָיו, indicates that the noun is masc. pl. (or dual). The Yod is all that is left of the masc. pl. ending ִים. Compare:

נַעַר -- "a boy"

נְעָרִים -- "boys"

נְעָרָיו -- "his boys"

וַיִּקַּח אֶת־שְׁנֵי נְעָרָיו אִתּוֹ וְאֵת יִצְחָק בְּנוֹ   (Gn 22:3)
וַיְבַקַּע עֲצֵי עֹלָה וַיָּקָם

33.   אֶת, אֶת־   (preposition) *with*

Note 39A: Preposition אֵת־ with Suffixes

The preposition אֵת־ or אֵת becomes אֹת___ with suffixes.
Without suffixes, however, it cannot be distinguished from the sign of
the definite direct object (see **Word 8**), except by context.

▸   בְּנוֹ   What noun and what suffix?

בקע   (verb)   *to cleave, split, cut*   (בָּקַע)

Note 39B: Absence of Dagesh Forte

Before יְ (Yod-prefix with a Sheva) the Vav consecutive is simply וַ
and no Dagesh Forte appears in the prefix. Example: וַיְבַקַּע. The
same absence of the Dagesh Forte occurred at the beginning of verse 1.
Thus, וַיְהִי is imperfect consecutive, indicating past time.

34.   עֵץ   (noun)   *tree, piece of wood*

▸   עֲצֵי עֹלָה   **REVIEW Notes 33C and 38B.**

35.   קוּם   (verb)   *to rise up, arise*

Note 39C: Hollow Verbs

Some verbs really have only two root consonants, not three, but in the
lexicon form either the vowel letter Vav or Yod appears between the two
consonants. Such verbs, called **hollow verbs**, are pointed in our
vocabulary listings. Example: קוּם.

Note 39D: Qamets Hatuf

A closed unstressed syllable must have a _____ vowel. Notice
in the form וַיָּקָם that the last syllable is closed and unstressed. What
vowel, then, occurs under the Qof? This is the first occurrence of this
vowel in Genesis 22. **REVIEW Note 6B or 15B.**

HELP IN FINDING THE VERB ROOT

In the next few lines of Genesis 22, a number of **imperfect** verb forms will occur that
have only two root consonants appearing in the form. Sometimes this happens
because it is a hollow verb and has only two root consonants (**REVIEW Note 39C**).

וַיָּ֫קָם וַיֵּ֫לֶךְ אֶל־הַמָּקוֹם אֲשֶׁר־אָמַר־לוֹ הָאֱלֹהִים:

Other times verbs with three root letters lose either the first or last consonant under certain conditions. Clues for discovering the missing consonant or vowel letter are given in upcoming Notes, with the summary of all the clues in Note 43A. These rules are very helpful and will later enable you to reconstruct the verb root in order to look it up in the lexicon.

Note 40A: Missing Middle Letter

If only two root consonants appear in an imperfect verb form, i.e., one with a prefix, suspect a **hollow verb**, if the vowel of the prefix is a Qamets (◌ָ). The missing middle vowel letter will be Shureq Vav (וּ), Holem Vav (וֹ), or Hireq Yod (ִי◌). Compare:

וַיָּ֫קָם from קוּם

וַיָּבֹא from בוֹא

וַיָּ֫שֶׂם from שִׂים

Note 40B: Missing First Letter

If only two root consonants appear in an imperfect verb form, suspect a missing **first** consonant, if the vowel of the prefix is Tsere (◌ֵ). The missing consonant will regularly be Yod (י), except for the one very frequent verb הָלַךְ, in which case it is a He (ה). See **Word 19**. Compare:

וַיֵּ֫שֶׁב from יָשַׁב

יֵרֶד from יָרַד

וַיֵּ֫לֶךְ from הָלַךְ

36. מָקוֹם (noun) *place*

Note 40C: Lexicon Verb Forms

REVIEW Note 28A. The simplest form of the verb is the 3ms of the perfect, which has no affix. This is the lexicon form of verbs that have three root consonants and the form that has been appearing in the parentheses for pronunciation in the *Workbook*. The two regular vowels of the perfect 3ms are a Qamets and a Patah. The two vowels of verbs ending in He or Alef are a Qamets and a Qamets. Compare:

אָמַר -- "he said"   הָיָה -- "he was"

לָקַח -- "he took"   נָשָׂא -- "he lifted up"

אֲשֶׁר־אָמַר־לוֹ הָאֱלֹהִים: ⁴ בַּיּוֹם הַשְּׁלִישִׁי וַיִּשָּׂא אַבְרָהָם אֶת־עֵינָיו (Gn 22:3-4)

▶ לוֹ   The preposition and the 3ms suffix. The preposition has lost the Sheva because the suffix is a vowel.

Note 41A: Word Order

REVIEW Note 37A. Between the verb and the expressed subject there often is a short word or phrase. Example: אֲשֶׁר־אָמַר־לוֹ הָאֱלֹהִים.

GENESIS 22:4

37.   יוֹם   (noun)   *day*

▶   בַּיּוֹם   **REVIEW Note 37B.**

38.   שְׁלִישִׁי   (adjective)   *third*

▶   בַּיּוֹם הַשְּׁלִישִׁי   **REVIEW Note 26C.**

39.   נשא   (verb)   *to raise, lift up, bear, carry*   (נָשָׂא)

Note 41B: Assimilated Nun

It is common for an initial Nun of a verb root to be attracted by and absorbed into the following consonant, which is then doubled. Compare the same thing in English: "inlegal" becomes "illegal" and "inmune" becomes "immune." In Hebrew the **Nun** is often **assimilated** to the following consonant and is indicated by a Dagesh Forte. Example: וַיִּשָּׂא from the verb נשא.

Note 41C: Missing Initial Nun

If only two root consonants appear in an imperfect verb form, first see whether there is a Dagesh Forte in the first root consonant that appears. If so, suspect that the verb's first consonant is a **Nun** that has been assimilated. E.g., the Dagesh Forte in the Sin of וַיִּשָּׂא is the assimilated Nun from the root נשא. The one exception is the very frequent verb לקח, in which case the assimilated first consonant is ל. See **Word 13** and the form וַיִּקַּח in v. 3 above.

40.   עַיִן   (noun)   *eye*

וַיִּשָּׂא אַבְרָהָם אֶת־עֵינָיו וַיַּרְא אֶת־הַמָּקוֹם מֵרָחֹק׃

Note 42A: Feminine Gender

Parts of the body that occur in pairs are regularly feminine and have dual forms (**REVIEW Note 38A**):

עַ֫יִן	-- "eye"	עֵינַ֫יִם	-- "two eyes"
יָד	-- "hand"	יָדַ֫יִם	-- "two hands"
אֹ֫זֶן	-- "ear"	אָזְנַ֫יִם	-- "two ears"

Note 42B: Dual Construct

The dual endings suffice for both masc. and fem. nouns:

יוֹם	(ms) -- "day"	יוֹמַ֫יִם	(dual) -- "two days"
עַ֫יִן	(fs) -- "eye"	עֵינַ֫יִם	(dual) -- "two eyes"

Also, there is no distinction between masc. pl. and dual forms either in the construct state or with suffixes. **REVIEW Chart 24B.** Compare:

דְּבָרִים	-- "words" (mp)	עֵינַ֫יִם	-- "eyes" (dual)
דִּבְרֵי	-- "words of" (mp cs.)	עֵינֵי	-- "eyes of" (dual cs.)
דְּבָרָיו	-- "his words" (mp + sf.)	עֵינָיו	-- "his eyes" (dual + sf.)

41.   ראה   (verb)   *to see*   (רָאָה)

Note 42C: Missing Final He

If only two root consonants appear in an imperfect verb form, suspect a missing **final He** (ה), if the vowel of the prefix is either Hireq (◌ִ) or Patah (◌ַ). Compare:

$$\text{וַיִּ֫בֶן from בנה}$$
$$\text{וַיַּ֫רְא from ראה}$$

42.   מִן   (preposition)   *from, out of*

Note 42D: Preposition מִן

The preposition מִן may be separable or inseparable; i.e., it may be a separate word or attached to the following word. When it is inseparable, the form is regularly ‗‗‗‗ִמ. Notice the Dagesh Forte in the

וַיַּרְא אֶת־הַמָּקוֹם מֵרָחֹק: (Gn 22:4)

following consonant indicating the assimilated Nun (compare **Note 41B**). If, however, the following consonant is a guttural or ר (compare **Note 26A**), it rejects the Dagesh and the vowel of the Mem is lengthened from Hireq to Tsere. Thus the inseparable form of מִן before gutturals is ◌ֵ◌◌◌◌. Compare:

מִן־בֵּן -- "from a son"   מִן־אֶרֶץ -- "from a land"

מִבֵּן -- "from a son"   מֵאֶרֶץ -- "from a land"

רָחוֹק   (adjective or adverb)   *far, distant; afar*

▸   מֵרָחֹק   **REVIEW Note 37C.**

Note 43A: Summary of Missing Letter Clues

(90% effective)

If only two root letters appear in an **imperfect** verb form, you can reconstruct the three root letters of the lexicon form by following these steps:

FIRST, check for a Dagesh Forte in the first root consonant that appears.

1. If so, suspect a missing **initial** נ --

   (נסע) וַיִּסַּע, (נשׂא) וַיִּשָּׂא   ▸ exception: לקח

SECOND, if no Dagesh Forte, check the vowel of the prefix:

2. If a ◌ֵ, suspect a missing **initial** י --

   (ירד) וַיֵּרֶד, (ישׁב) וַיֵּשֶׁב   ▸ exception: הלך

3. If a ◌ָ, suspect a missing **middle** ו, וֹ, or ◌ִי --

   (שׂים) וַיָּשֶׂם, (בוא) וַיָּבֹא, (קום) וַיָּקָם

4. If a ◌ִ, ◌ַ, or א, suspect a missing **final** ה --

   (בנה) וָאֶבֶן, (ראה) וַיַּרְא, (בנה) וַיִּבֶן

44

PROGRESS CHECK #3

1. The letter attached directly *after* a verb root is called the _____ and tells the pronominal _____ of the verb and that the aspect of the verb is _____.

2. The letter attached directly *before* a verb root is called the _____ and tells the pronominal _____ of the verb and that the aspect of the verb is _____.

3. The masc. pl. absolute noun/adjective ending is:

4. The masc. pl. construct noun/adjective ending is:

5. The dual absolute noun/adjective ending is:

6. The dual construct noun/adjective ending is:

7. Translate the following expressions and explain all the elements. Be careful to distinguish between singular and plural, absolute and construct, and definite and indefinite forms. The definite article, suffixes, and an inseparable preposition are included in the exercise.

a.	דָּבָר	k.	דְּבַר בֵּן
b.	הַדָּבָר	l.	דְּבַר הַבֵּן
c.	בְּדָבָר	m.	דִּבְרֵי בֵּן
d.	בַּדָּבָר	n.	בְּדִבְרֵי הַבֵּן
e.	דְּבָרוֹ	o.	דְּבַר בָּנִים
f.	דְּבָרְךָ	p.	דְּבַר הַבָּנִים
g.	דְּבָרִים	q.	דִּבְרֵי בְּנוֹ
h.	הַדְּבָרִים	r.	דְּבַר בִּנְךָ
i.	דְּבָרֶיךָ	s.	בְּדִבְרֵי בָּנָיו
j.	דְּבָרָיו		

^{5} וַיֹּאמֶר אַבְרָהָם אֶל־נְעָרָיו שְׁבוּ־לָכֶם פֹּה עִם־הַחֲמוֹר (Gn 22:5)
וַאֲנִי וְהַנַּעַר נֵלְכָה עַד־כֹּה

GENESIS 22:5

43.   יָשַׁב   (verb)   *to sit, dwell, stay*   (יָשַׁב)

שְׁבוּ is the active imperative 2mp of יָשַׁב. וּ___ signifies the plural.

**   כֶם____   (suffix)   *you, your*   (2mp)
See **Chart 24A**.

Note 45A: Inseparable Prepositions

The three inseparable prepositions לְ, בְּ, and כְּ are pointed with a Qamets with most suffixes.   Example: לְךָ but לָכֶם.

▶   לָכֶם   **REVIEW Note 33B.**

פֹּה   (adverb)   *here*

44.   עִם   (preposition)   *with*

Note 45B: The Gutturals and the Definite Article

The gutturals (עחהא) and ר cannot receive a Dagesh Forte.   But unlike א, ע, and ר, the gutturals ה and ח imply the Dagesh Forte, so that the vowel before them is not lengthened.   **REVIEW Note 26A**. Notice the pointing of the article in the form הַחֲמוֹר.

Note 45C: The Gutturals

When the four guttural letters (עחהא) have a Sheva, they regularly have a **composite Sheva** and not a simple Sheva.   ר never has a composite Sheva but takes a simple Sheva.   On some occasions, however, ע and ח have a silent Sheva as a syllable divider.   Notice the composite Sheva in הַחֲמוֹר but the simple Sheva in יַחְדָּו.

Note 45D: The Conjunction Vav

When the conjunction Vav appears before a guttural with a composite Sheva, the conjunction has the corresponding short vowel.   Example: וַאֲנִי.

46

(Gn 22:5)

וַאֲנִי וְהַנַּעַר נֵלְכָה עַד־כֹּה וְנִשְׁתַּחֲוֶה וְנָשׁוּבָה אֲלֵיכֶם:

45. אֲנִי (independent personal pronoun) *I* (1cs)

** נְ___ (prefix) *we* (1cs of the imperfect)
See **Chart 23B**.

► נֵלְכָה Without the Qamets He at the end of this form, which will be explained in the next Note, the form would be נֵלֵךְ. Since this is an imperfect verb with only two root letters appearing, **REVIEW Note 43A** for the root. This is one of the exception verbs.

Note 46A: Cohortative He

הָ___ at the end of a word can indicate several things. In the form נֵלְכָה it appears at the end of an **imperfect** verb in the **first** person. In such a case, it is the sign of the **cohortative**, which expresses desire or intention and may have two uses:

a. emphatic: נֵלְכָה -- "We will **indeed** go!"

b. hortatory: נֵלְכָה -- "**Let us** go!"

Context must determine which usage is meant.

46. עַד (preposition) *until, as far as*

47. כֹּה (adverb) *thus, so; there*

48. חוה (verb) *to bow down, worship* (חוה)
This peculiar verb always as שׁת between the prefix and the root consonants. More will be said about this verb in Note 113D below.

Note 46B: The Conjunction Vav

We have become accustomed to imperfect consecutive forms indicating past time with the pointing of the Vav consecutive being ___ַו. **REVIEW Note 29A**. But if an imperfect form has the conjunction Vav with its regular pointing (___וְ), then the imperfect that follows has as its primary significance the *uncompleted* aspect and derives its time element only secondarily from the context. **REVIEW Note 27B**. Here the time is future, i.e., an as yet uncompleted action.

(Gn 22:5-6)   ⁶וַיִּקַּח אַבְרָהָם אֶת־עֲצֵי הָעֹלָה   וְנָשׁוּבָה אֲלֵיכֶם:
וַיָּשֶׂם עַל־יִצְחָק בְּנוֹ וַיִּקַּח בְּיָדוֹ אֶת־הָאֵשׁ וְאֶת־הַמַּאֲכֶלֶת
וַיֵּלְכוּ שְׁנֵיהֶם יַחְדָּו:

49.   שׁוּב   (verb)   *to turn, return*
What kind of verb do we call שׁוּב?   **REVIEW Note 39C.**
Notice that the vocabulary form of this verb is pointed.

▶   וְנָשׁוּבָה   **REVIEW Notes 46A and 46B.**

▶   אֲלֵיכֶם   **REVIEW Note 29B.**

Note 47A: Summary of the Definite Article's Pointing

The pointing of the **definite article** is as follows:

1. Before ordinary consonants: ַהּ−−−−   הַדָּבָר
2. Before the gutturals א, ע, and ר: הָ−−−−   הָעֹלָה
3. Before the gutturals ה and ח: הַ−−−−   הַחֲמוֹר
4. Before unstressed הָ and עָ
   and always before חָ:   הֶ−−−−   הֶהָרִים
5. Before stressed הָ and עָ:   הָ−−−−   הָהָר

GENESIS 22:6

▶   וַיִּקַּח   **REVIEW Note 43A.**

50.   שִׂים   (verb)   *to set, put, place*

51.   יָד   (noun)   *hand*

52.   אֵשׁ   (noun)   *fire, flame*

מַאֲכֶלֶת   (noun)   *knife*

**   יְ−−−וּ   (prefix)   *they*   (3mp of the imperfect)
See **Chart 23B.**

48

(Gn 22:6-7)

וַיֵּלְכוּ שְׁנֵיהֶם יַחְדָּו: ⁷ וַיֹּאמֶר יִצְחָק אֶל־אַבְרָהָם אָבִיו
וַיֹּאמֶר אָבִי וַיֹּאמֶר הִנֶּנִּי בְנִי

Note 48A: Prefixes

Within the prefix system of indicating the pronominal subject of imperfect verb forms, there is **always** a prefixed letter *before* the verb root. But the prefix system may also have one or two letters attached *after* the verb root, especially in plural forms. Thus the 3mp prefix is ‫וּ‬___‫יִ‬, as appears in the form ‫וַיֵּלְכוּ‬. Examine the prefixes in **Chart 23B**.

** ‫הֶם‬____ (suffix) *them, their* (3mp)
See **Chart 24A**.

Note 48B: Nouns with Suffixes

A noun with a suffix is really a little construct chain with the noun being the construct and the suffix being the absolute. Since the suffix is definite, the noun is definite in translation. **REVIEW Note 33C**. Compare:

‫בִּנְךָ‬ -- "the son of you" or "your son"

‫שְׁנֵיהֶם‬ -- "the two of them"

\#\# ‫יַחְדָּו‬ (adverb) *together, at the same time*
For the simple Sheva under the guttural Het in ‫יַחְדָּו‬, **REVIEW Note 45C**.

GENESIS 22:7

53. ‫אָב‬ (noun) *father*

Note 48C: Irregular Nouns

Several very common nouns have some irregularities in their forms. The noun ‫אָב‬ is irregular in that the Yod between it and most suffixes (‫אָבִיו‬) has no semantic force, as with some prepositions. **REVIEW Note 29B**. Here the Yod is "meaningless" and does not indicate the plural, as one would expect, based on **Note 38C**.

** ‫י‬____ (suffix) *me, my* (another 1cs)
See **Chart 24A**.

(Gn 22:7-8) וַיֹּאמֶר הִנֶּנִּי בְנִי וַיֹּאמֶר הִנֵּה הָאֵשׁ וְהָעֵצִים וְאַיֵּה הַשֶּׂה לְעֹלָה: ⁸ וַיֹּאמֶר אַבְרָהָם אֱלֹהִים יִרְאֶה־לּוֹ הַשֶּׂה לְעֹלָה בְּנִי

Note 49A: Absence of Dagesh Lene

A Dagesh Lene on occasion is omitted from the Begadkefat letters (בגדכפת) at the beginning of a word, if the preceding word ends in an open syllable with a long vowel. Notice the phrase: הִנֶּנִּי בְנִי.

Note 49B: Absence of the Verb "to be"

The verb היה is often not expressed but is understood in simple sentences. English usually requires that we supply the verb "to be" where the context suggests it. Thus the phrase הִנֵּה הָאֵשׁ may be rendered: "Behold, the fire" or "Here (is) the fire."

##	אַיֵּה	(interrogative)	*where?*
##	שֶׂה	(noun)	*lamb, kid*

GENESIS 22:8

Note 49C: Inverted Word Order

In the phrase אֱלֹהִים יִרְאֶה the subject comes before the verb. **REVIEW Note 37A.** Inverted word order may bring emphasis to the word that comes first or have other uses.

▶ יִרְאֶה — Here the meaning of the verb ראה is not simply visual action but comparable to our idiomatic use of the same verb: "to see to it," thus "to provide." The imperfect without the Vav consecutive indicates uncompleted action and may be translated as a future.

Note 49D: Euphonic Dagesh Forte

Sometimes a letter has a Dagesh Forte merely for the sake of a more fluid pronunciation, as is the case in the phrase יִרְאֶה־לּוֹ. This is called the **euphonic** or conjunctive use of the Dagesh Forte.

▶ יִרְאֶה־לּוֹ — For the use of לּוֹ, **REVIEW Note 33B.**

אֱלֹהִים יִרְאֶה־לּוֹ הַשֶּׂה לְעֹלָה בְּנִי וַיֵּלְכוּ שְׁנֵיהֶם יַחְדָּו:

⁹ וַיָּבֹאוּ אֶל־הַמָּקוֹם אֲשֶׁר אָמַר־לוֹ הָאֱלֹהִים וַיִּבֶן שָׁם אַבְרָהָם

אֶת־הַמִּזְבֵּחַ וַיַּעֲרֹךְ אֶת־הָעֵצִים וַיַּעֲקֹד אֶת־יִצְחָק בְּנוֹ

Note 50A: "Accusative" of Respect

If הַשֶּׂה were the definite direct object, we would have expected אֶת־הַשֶּׂה. This may be a so-called "accusative" of respect: "with respect to the lamb" or "regarding the lamb."

| ## | יַחְדָּו | (adverb) | *together* |

GENESIS 22:9

54.	בּוֹא	(verb)	*to go in, enter*
▶	וַיָּבֹאוּ	**REVIEW Note 43A.**
▶	אָמַר־לוֹ הָאֱלֹהִים	For the word order, **REVIEW Note 41A.**
55.	בנה	(verb)	*to build*	(בָּנָה)
▶	וַיִּבֶן	**REVIEW Note 43A.**
56.	מִזְבֵּחַ	(noun)	*altar*

Note 50B: Gutturals and Patah

The guttural letters (עחהא) usually have a preference for Patah after and even before them, although א often prefers a Segol.

Note 50C: Patah Furtive

A Patah often "sneaks in" before a final guttural, when a long stressed vowel appears before it. This is called the **Patah furtive** and is pronounced *after* the preceding vowel but *before* the final guttural. Example: מִזְבֵּחַ.

| ## | ערך | (verb) | *to arrange, set in order* | (עָרַךְ) |
| ## | עקד | (verb) | *to bind* | (עָקַד) |

The word **Aqedah**, which is often used as a title for Genesis 22, is the noun עֲקֵדָה ("binding") derived from the verb עקד.

וַיָּשֶׂם אֹתוֹ עַל־הַמִּזְבֵּחַ מִמַּעַל לָעֵצִים: (Gn 22:9)

▶   וַיָּשֶׂם   **REVIEW Note 43A**.

Note 51A: Direct Object Sign with Suffixes

The sign of the definite direct object (אֶת־ or אֵת) becomes אֹת__ with most suffixes. Examples: אֹתוֹ, אֹתְךָ. The sign of the definite direct object can therefore be distinguished from the preposition "with" (also אֶת־, אֵת) when they have suffixes. **REVIEW Note 39A**.

57.   מַעַל   (adverb)   *above, from upon*

▶   מִמַּעַל   **REVIEW Note 42D**.

▶   לָעֵצִים   **REVIEW Notes 37B and 47A**.

▶   מִמַּעַל לָעֵצִים   How might this phrase be expressed in English?

Note 51B: Summary of the Gutturals (and Resh)

The peculiarities of the guttural letters (עחהא) and Resh (ר) are as follows:

1. They cannot receive a Dagesh Forte (similarly with ר). Before א, ע, and ר, the preceding vowel is lengthened.   הָעֵץ

   ה and ח imply the Dagesh Forte, so that the preceding vowel is usually not lengthened.   הַהוּא

2. They alone take composite Shevas (sometimes exceptions: ע and ח -- יַחְדָּו)   חֲמוֹר

3. They prefer the vowel Patah before and after them (א often prefers Segol).   נַעַר

4. They often take Patah furtive after a long stressed vowel.   מִזְבֵּחַ

וַיִּשְׁלַח אַבְרָהָם אֶת־יָדוֹ וַיִּקַּח אֶת־הַמַּאֲכֶלֶת 10
לִשְׁחֹט אֶת־בְּנוֹ: 11 וַיִּקְרָא אֵלָיו מַלְאַךְ יהוה

GENESIS 22:10

| 58. | שלח | (verb) | *to send* | (שָׁלַח) |

The verb שלח usually can be translated "to send," but because of its object יָד in this context, the verb has the idiomatic meaning "to stretch forth, extend."

| ## | מַאֲכֶלֶת | (noun) | *knife* | |

| ## | שחט | (verb) | *to slaughter, kill* | (שָׁחַט) |

Note 52A: Infinitive Construct

Hebrew has two kinds of infinitives, one called the infinitive absolute (explained below in Note 63B) and the other called the infinitive construct, such as the form לִשְׁחֹט. The **infinitive construct** is a verbal noun which often functions very much like our English infinitive. The form שְׁחֹט (without the preposition לְ) is the infinitive construct: "to slaughter." It is very common but not necessary for the infinitive construct to be accompanied by a preposition: לִשְׁחֹט -- "to slaughter." The *rule of thumb* is: **a verb form with a preposition is usually the infinitive construct.**

Note 52B: Inseparable Prepositions

When the inseparable prepositions, which are regularly pointed with a simple Sheva, come before a consonant with another simple Sheva, the vowel of the preposition becomes Hireq. Example: שְׁחֹט + לְ = לִשְׁחֹט.

GENESIS 22:11

| 59. | קרא | (verb) | *to call, proclaim, read aloud* | (קָרָא) |

| ► | וַיִּקְרָא אֵלָיו... | For the word order, **REVIEW Note 41A.** | |

| 60. | מַלְאָךְ | (noun) | *messenger, angel* | |

| 61. | יהוה | (proper noun) | *Yahweh, Adonai,* Lord | |

11 (Gn 22:11) וַיִּקְרָא אֵלָיו מַלְאַךְ יהוה מִן־הַשָּׁמַיִם וַיֹּאמֶר
אַבְרָהָם אַבְרָהָם וַיֹּאמֶר הִנֵּנִי:

Note 53A: The Tetragrammaton

The distinctive name of the God of Israel consisted of the four consonants יהוה, commonly referred to as the "Tetragrammaton." Since this word was not to be pronounced (out of respect for the name) when the Masoretes pointed the consonantal text, it was usually read as the word אֲדֹנָי meaning "Lord." In pointing the text, then, they placed the vowels of אֲדֹנָי with the consonants of the name יהוה, to remind the reader to say "Adonai" instead of pronouncing the Tetragrammaton. The resulting form in the text was יְהֹוָה, which was never intended to be pronounced as it looked. Nevertheless, some early translators transliterated this concocted term as "Jehovah" (JeHoVaH), a form that has the consonants of one word (יהוה) and the vowels of another (אֲדֹנָי).

Biblia Hebraica Stuttgartensia points יהוה as יְהוָה with vowels that have been explained as those of the Aramaic word שְׁמָא meaning "the name." The Tetragrammaton will appear unpointed in the *Workbook* as can be seen in the text at the top of the page.

In any case, do not try to pronounce the Tetragrammaton as pointed in the text. Instead, follow Jewish practice and read "Adonai." In translating into English, one may use the term "Yahweh" (the way scholars believe the name was pronounced in early times) or the term "Lord," following the practice of most standard translations. Incidentally, the standard translations usually tell the reader that the word "Lord" is being substituted for the Tetragrammaton by using upper case letters: Lord.

▶ מַלְאַךְ יהוה   **REVIEW Note 33C.**

62.   שָׁמַיִם   (noun)   *sky, heavens*
Although in form the word שָׁמַיִם appears to have a dual ending, it probably was not originally so, and no "two-ness" should be read into the word's meaning. But the lexicon form is שָׁמַיִם.

מִן־הַשָּׁמַיִם   **REVIEW Note 42D.**

54

PROGRESS CHECK #4

1. What are the four guttural letters?

2. What additional letter often acts like a guttural?

3. What vowel do most of the gutturals prefer before and after them?

4. Translate the following prepositions with nouns or suffixes:

a.	בְּךָ	f.	עִם בְּנֵיכֶם	
b.	לָהֶם	g.	עַד מְקוֹמִי	
c.	עָלָיו	h.	מִן־הָאֵשׁ	
d.	אֲלֵיכֶם	i.	מֵאֶרֶץ הֶהָרִים	
e.	אֶת־עֵצוֹ			

5. Translate the following *imperfect* verb forms. This exercise gives you practice in recognizing the root of verbs that have only two root letters appearing, in identifying the various prefixes, and in distinguishing the Vav conjunction from the Vav consecutive.

a.	וַיָּשֶׂם	f.	יַעֲלוּ	
b.	וַנָּבֹא	g.	וַנִּבֶן	
c.	אֵלֵךְ	h.	וְיִקְחוּ	
d.	וַיָּקוּמוּ	i.	*וַתֵּשֶׁב	
e.	*וְתִשָּׂא	j.	**וָאָבֹא	

*   The prefix in e. and i. has not yet been introduced. See the prefixes in Chart 23B for the possible translations of this prefix.

** Can you explain the pointing of the Vav consecutive here on the analogy of the pointing of the article before most gutturals? See Notes 47A and 51B.

INTRODUCTION TO THE HEBREW VERB STEMS

Verbs in English and Hebrew have some things in common. A verb in both may be indicative, imperative, an infinitive, or a participle. But over the next several verses, a dimension of the Hebrew verbal system will be introduced which has no direct parallel in English. We have already seen a couple of differences. First, Hebrew has no "tenses" as such (past or future) but rather the two aspects, perfect and imperfect. These two aspects generally serve for what in English we call the indicative. Second, the pronominal subjects of perfect and imperfect verb forms appear as affixed or prefixed letters.

But the greatest difference is in what we call "voice" in English. The Hebrew verb may be simply active or passive, as in English, but beyond these two, Hebrew develops five more "voices." These seven "voices" are commonly called **stems** in Hebrew grammar and each one has a distinctive Hebrew name and particular significances. The stems are distinguished in form by various pointings within the verb and/or by the addition of preformatives as stem signs. Initially, only the crucial "clue" pointing and the key stem signs will be given, for they are sufficient to identify most forms. But the fully pointed form of a standard model verb will also be given as an example.

Hebrew grammarians have traditionally employed the verb קטל as a model verb to illustrate the forms and meanings of the various stems. It has the double disadvantage, however, of only occurring three times in the Hebrew Bible and of having a very nasty meaning ("to kill"). But it has the double advantage of having three root letters that never change or cause changes, as the Begadkefat letters, the vowel letters, and the gutturals do, and of yielding translations that can illustrate well the meanings of the various stems. Therefore, we will retain the verb קטל as the model verb, in spite of its unfortunate meaning.

GENESIS 22:12

63.   אַל   (adverb)   *no, not*

**   _ _ _תִּ   (prefix)   *you*   (2ms of the imperfect)
See **Chart 23B**. Notice that a Tav serves as two prefixes. The 2ms is the more frequent.

Note 55A: Simple Prohibition

Although there are distinctive imperative forms in Hebrew to express positive command, **simple prohibition** (negative command) does not use the imperative but אַל with a form of the verb called the "jussive," as in the phrase אַל־תִּשְׁלַח. The **jussive** expresses desire or intention

¹²וַיֹּ֗אמֶר אַל־תִּשְׁלַ֤ח יָֽדְךָ֙ אֶל־הַנַּ֔עַר וְאַל־תַּ֥עַשׂ ל֖וֹ מְא֑וּמָה
כִּ֣י עַתָּ֣ה יָדַ֗עְתִּי

in the 2nd and 3rd persons, just as the cohortative does in the 1st person (**REVIEW Note 46A**). The form of the jussive very often coincides with the imperfect, as it does here. But the jussive can have distinctive forms, usually a somewhat shorter form than the imperfect. Jussive forms always use the prefixes as pronominal subjects. 2nd person jussives with אַל may be rendered: "Do not . . . ."

64.	עשׂה	(verb)	*to do, to make, act, perform*	(עָשָׂה)
▶	וְאַל־תַּ֥עַשׂ	**REVIEW Notes 43A and 55A.**		
##	מְא֑וּמָה	(noun)	*anything, something*	

Codex Leningradensis, which BHS reproduces (see p. 2 above), has a Dagesh in the second Mem of מְא֑וּמָה, but other manuscripts do not.

65.	כִּי	(conjunction)	*that; for, because*

Note 56A: The Conjunction כִּי

The three most common uses of the frequently used conjunction כִּי are to introduce:

1. **indirect discourse** after verbs of seeing, hearing, knowing, telling, remembering, etc.: "She saw *that* it was good."
2. **causal clauses**: "He went there *because* he was told."
3. **direct discourse**, in which case it equals our quotation marks: She said, " . . . ."

Observe the context carefully to determine which usage is intended. כִּי also has some other less frequent meanings, such as "if" and "when" in conditional clauses, "surely" in oaths or for emphasis, or a strong "but."

66.	עַתָּה	(adverb)	*now*	
67.	ידע	(verb)	*to know*	(יָדַע)
**	־ְ־ִּ֗תִי	(affix)	*I*	(1cs of the perfect)

See **Chart 23A.**

▶	יָדַ֗עְתִּי	The perfect aspect indicates "completed" action. But what time element suits this context best?

כִּי עַתָּה יָדַ֫עְתִּי כִּי־יְרֵא אֱלֹהִים אַתָּה   (Gn 22:12)

**   קָ□□□   (the clue pointing of the Qal perfect)

Note 57A: Qal Perfect

The most common of the "stems" of the verb is the simple active, called the **Qal** stem. The regular pointing of the model verb in the Qal perfect 3ms is קָטַל -- "he killed." **REVIEW Note 40C.** The clue pointing is the Qamets under the first root consonant. Several Qal perfect verb forms have already appeared:

אָמַר -- "he said"

אָהַ֫בְתָּ -- "you loved" or "you love"

יָדַ֫עְתִּי -- "I knew" or "I know"

▶   כִּי   **REVIEW Note 56A.**

68.   ירא   (verb) *to fear, be awed*   (יָרֵא)

יְרֵא is the active (Qal) participle (masc. sg.) used as a construct. Participles are verbal adjectives.

Note 57B: Stative Verbs

A few verbs which describe a condition or a state and not an action are called **stative verbs** and usually have a Tsere as their second vowel in the lexicon form (Qal perfect 3ms):

יָרֵא -- "he was afraid"

כָּבֵד -- "it was heavy"

טָמֵא -- "he was unclean"

▶   יְרֵא אֱלֹהִים   This construct chain has the participle יְרֵא as the construct and the noun אֱלֹהִים as the absolute. The phrase could be definite, "the fearer of God," if אֱלֹהִים refers specifically to the God of Israel. But it may also be an indefinite phrase: "a fearer of deity," hence, "a devout person."

69.   אַתָּה   (independent personal pronoun) *you*   (2ms)

Note 57C: Nominal Clause

A clause in which the subject and predicate are connected by the verb "to be" is called a **nominal clause**. In Hebrew nominal clauses, the verb היה is often understood but not expressed and should be included in

(Gn 22:12) כִּי־יְרֵא אֱלֹהִים אַתָּה וְלֹא חָשַׂכְתָּ אֶת־בִּנְךָ אֶת־יְחִידְךָ מִמֶּנִּי:

translation. **REVIEW Note 49B.** Here the phrase יְרֵא אֱלֹהִים אַתָּה is such a nominal clause. The normal word order is subject-predicate, but inversion emphasizes the predicate. Compare:

יִצְחָק נַֽעַר -- "Isaac (is) a boy"

נַֽעַר יִצְחָק -- "Isaac (is), in fact, a boy"

70.   לֹא   (adverb)   *no, not*

Note 58A: The Negative Adverb

The ordinary negative adverb is לֹא. It is also used to express the negative with perfect and imperfect verb forms. On the other hand, אַל (Word 63) is limited to special usages, such as in simple prohibition with the jussive. **REVIEW Note 55A.**

\#\#   חָשַׂךְ   (verb)   *to withhold, keep back*   (חָשַׂךְ)

▶   חָשַׂכְתָּ   **REVIEW Note 57A.**

\#\#   יָחִיד   (adjective)   *only, alone*

Note 58B: Preposition מִן

When the preposition מִן has a suffix, another מ appears between it and most of the suffixes. In some instances, it appears that מִן is reduplicated before the suffixes, as in מִמֶּנִּי.

Note 58C: Summary of the Preposition מִן

1. As a separate word: מִן   מִן־מָקוֹם

2. Inseparably, before ordinary consonants: מִ__ַ__   מִמָּקוֹם

3. Inseparably, before the gutturals and ר :   מֵ____   מֵאֶרֶץ

4. With most suffixes, מִן is reduplicated (at least in part); i.e., another מ appears between it and most suffixes: מִמֶּנִּי -- "from me"; מִמְּךָ -- "from you" (sg.); but מִכֶּם -- "from you" (pl.).

¹³ וַיִּשָּׂא אַבְרָהָם אֶת־עֵינָיו וַיַּרְא וְהִנֵּה־אַיִל אַחַר נֶאֱחַז   (Gn 22:13)
בַּסְּבַךְ בְּקַרְנָיו וַיֵּלֶךְ אַבְרָהָם וַיִּקַּח אֶת־הָאַיִל

GENESIS 22:13

▶   וַיִּשָּׂא   **REVIEW Note 43A**.

Note 59A: Qal Stem

Almost all of the imperfect verbs we will meet for a while that appear with only two root consonants are Qal stem, such as וַיִּשָּׂא.   The *rule of thumb* is: If the "missing letter rules" of Note 43A work, the stem of the verb is **Qal**.

▶   עֵינָיו   **REVIEW Note 38C**.

▶   וַיַּרְא   **REVIEW Note 43A** for the *root* and **Note 59A** for the *stem*.

71.   אַיִל   (noun)   *ram*

**   נ☐☐☐   (Nifal stem sign)

Note 59B: Nifal Stem

In order to make a simple active (Qal) verb passive, a Nun is attached before the root as a stem sign. This simple passive stem is called the **Nifal** stem. Compare these perfect forms:

Qal pf.   לָקַח -- "he took"   אָהַבְתָּ -- "you loved"

Nifal pf.   נִלְקַח -- "he was taken"   נֶאֱהַבְתָּ -- "you were loved"

אחז   (verb)   *to seize, grasp, catch*   (אָחַז)

    נֶאֱחַז is a Nifal (passive) form because of the Nun stem sign. This form is the Nifal perfect 3ms of אחז. The expressed subject is אַיִל.

סְבַךְ   (noun)   *thicket*

▶   בַּסְּבַךְ   **REVIEW Note 37B**.

קֶרֶן   (noun)   *horn*

▶   בְּקַרְנָיו   **REVIEW Note 38C**.

(Gn 22:13-14) וַיַּעֲלֵהוּ לְעֹלָה תַּחַת בְּנוֹ: ¹⁴ וַיִּקְרָא אַבְרָהָם שֵׁם־הַמָּקוֹם

הַהוּא יהוה יִרְאֶה אֲשֶׁר יֵאָמֵר הַיּוֹם

▶ וַיַּעֲלֵהוּ — This is an imperfect consecutive 3ms with a 3ms suffix (ה____וּ) as the object, from the verb עלה. But its stem is neither Qal nor Nifal and will not be introduced until Note 65A below. In the meantime, translate "and offered him" and proceed. An imperative form of this same verb occurred in Gn 22:2.

72.　　תַּחַת　　(preposition)　*under, instead of*

GENESIS 22:14

**　　יְ◻◻◻　　(the clue pointing of the Qal imperfect)

Note 60A: Qal Imperfect

In an imperfect form with all three root consonants present, a Hireq under the prefix and a Sheva under the first root consonant is the infallible sign of the **Qal imperfect**. The model verb in this form is יִקְטֹל -- "he will kill."

73.　　שֵׁם　　(noun)　*name*

74.　　הוּא　　(3ms independent personal pronoun and sg. demonstrative adjective)　*he; that*

Note 60B: Demonstrative Adjectives

The 3rd person independent personal pronouns serve also as the demonstrative adjectives "that" (sg.) and "those" (pl.). When הוּא is a pronoun ("he, it"), it is comparable to אֲנִי ("I") and אַתָּה ("you"). When הוּא is an adjective ("that"), it follows the usage of other adjectives.

▶　　הַמָּקוֹם הַהוּא　　**REVIEW Note 26C**.

▶　　יִרְאֶה　　**REVIEW Note 60A**.

**　　יִ◻◻◻　　(the clue pointing for the Nifal imperfect)

אֲשֶׁר יֵאָמֵר הַיּוֹם בְּהַר יְהוָה יֵרָאֶה׃   (Gn 22:14-15)

15 וַיִּקְרָא מַלְאַךְ יְהוָה אֶל־אַבְרָהָם שֵׁנִית מִן־הַשָּׁמָיִם׃

Note 61A: Nifal Imperfect

The **Nifal imperfect** would have both the stem sign of the Nifal (נ☐☐☐) and a prefix. But the hypothetical form יְנ☐☐☐ becomes יִ☐ָ☐☐, since the Nun is assimilated to the first root consonant and appears as a Dagesh Forte. The hypothetical form of the model verb (Nif. impf. 3ms) would be יִנְקָטֵל, but it becomes יִקָּטֵל -- "he will be killed." Compare:

Qal impf.	יִשְׁלַח	-- "he will send	
Nifal impf.	יִשָּׁלַח	-- "he will be sent"	

תִּקְרָא	-- "you will call"
תִּקָּרֵא	-- "you will be called"

But in the form יֵאָמֵר the Alef rejects the Dagesh and the Hireq under the prefix is lengthened to a Tsere. **REVIEW Note 51C.** The clue pointing of the Nifal imperfect for verbs with an initial guttural root letter is יֵ☒☐☐.

▶ הַיּוֹם The article with יוֹם would literally be translated "the day," but the phrase has the same force as English "today."

▶ יֵרָאֶה **REVIEW Note 61A.** ראה in the Nifal can be translated "to be seen" or most often "to appear."

▶ בְּהַר יְהוָה יֵרָאֶה Can you see more than one way to understand the grammatical relationship of the words in this phrase?

GENESIS 22:15

75.   שֵׁנִי   (adjective)   *second*

Note 61B: שֵׁנִי, שֵׁנִית

שֵׁנִי is the masc. sg. and שֵׁנִית is the fem. sg. The final ת is a feminine ending. Here the fem. form of the adjective is used as an adverb of time: "a second (time)."

Note 61C: Pausal Forms

Every verse has two main accents that serve as punctuation. The first is called the **Atnah** (☐) and appears somewhere in the middle of every verse on a stressed syllable and serves to divide the verse into two logical parts. It is equivalent to a comma, semi-colon, or period,

מִן־הַשָּׁמַיִם: ¹⁶ וַיֹּאמֶר בִּי נִשְׁבַּעְתִּי נְאֻם־יהוה

כִּי יַעַן אֲשֶׁר עָשִׂיתָ אֶת־הַדָּבָר הַזֶּה

depending on the context. The other accent is the **Silluq** (ֽ) and always appears in the last word of every verse on the stressed syllable. Words having either of these accents are said to be **in pause** and the vowel in such pausal forms is usually lengthened. Thus, שָׁמָיִם is the pausal form of שָׁמַיִם (notice the change from a short to a long vowel in the stressed syllable). אַבְרָהָם already has a long vowel on the syllable with the Atnah, so that its pausal form remains the same. Now that pausal forms have been introduced, the supralinear stress mark (ֹ) will not be used in the *Workbook* with words in pause, since such forms have either an Atnah or a Silluq on the stressed syllable.

GENESIS 22:16

▶   בִּי   The preposition בְּ and the 1cs suffix.

76.   שׁבע   (verb)   *to swear, take an oath*   (שָׁבַע)
                 The basic meanings of this verb are in the Nifal stem.

▶   נִשְׁבַּעְתִּי   **REVIEW** Note 59B. What stem is this form?

Note 62A: Verbs whose Basic Stem is not Qal

Some verbs may not appear in the Qal stem but have their simple active or basic meaning in another stem. In this case, שׁבע does not appear in the Qal but in the Nifal, where its meaning nevertheless is simple active and not passive.

77.   נְאֻם   (noun)   *utterance, oracle*

▶   נְאֻם יהוה   A parenthetical expression in this sentence. In prophetic literature, this phrase is often translated "says the Lord," but literally it is a construct chain. Notice the Atnah. **REVIEW Note 61C.**

יַעַן   (preposition)   *on account of, because of*

Note 62B: Prepositions used as Conjunctions

אֲשֶׁר often follows a preposition to make it serve as a conjunction. In such cases, אֲשֶׁר is usually not translated. Thus the entire phrase כִּי יַעַן אֲשֶׁר may be rendered: "because."

כִּי יַעַן אֲשֶׁר עָשִׂיתָ אֶת־הַדָּבָר הַזֶּה וְלֹא חָשַׂכְתָּ (Gn 22:16-17)
אֶת־בִּנְךָ אֶת־יְחִידֶךָ: ¹⁷ כִּי־בָרֵךְ אֲבָרֶכְךָ

Note 63A: Verbs Ending in He

Verbs that in biblical Hebrew end in He ended in Yod in an earlier stage of the language. This original Yod remains as the third root letter in some perfect forms, such as in עָשִׂיתָ. Notice, however, that the Yod is here a vowel letter, not a consonant. The root is עשׂה. **REVIEW Note 57A** for the stem.

78.	זֶה	(demonstrative adjective)	*this*	(masc. sg.)
		The plural of זֶה is אֵלֶּה, Word 6 above.		
##	חָשַׂךְ	(verb)	*to withhold*	
##	יָחִיד	(adjective)	*only*	(Notice the pausal form)

GENESIS 22:17

▶	כִּי	**REVIEW Note 56A.** Here is one of the less frequent usages of כִּי: "surely" in oaths.
79.	ברך	(verb) *to bless* (בָּרַךְ)
		The common meaning of this verb is in the Piel stem.
▶	בָרֵךְ	This is the Piel infinitive absolute, to be explained in Notes 63B and 64A below. For the absence of the Dagesh Lene in the Bet (כִּי־בָרֵךְ), **REVIEW Note 49A.**

Note 63B: Infinitive Absolute

Hebrew has two kinds of infinitives. The infinitive construct functions very much like an English infinitive. **REVIEW Note 52A.** But the **infinitive absolute**, which never has a preposition or suffix attached to it, most closely corresponds to the English **adverb.** Two of the most common uses of the infinitive absolute occur when it appears with another form of the same verb.

1. If an infinitive absolute *precedes* a verb of the same root, it indicates **emphasis**.
2. If it *follows* a verb of the same root, it indicates **repeated** or **continuous action.**

We will use a verb in the Qal stem to illustrate (הָלוֹךְ is the inf. abs.). Notice how an English **adverb** translates the inf. abs.:

1. הָלוֹךְ הָלַךְ -- "walking, he walked" or "he certainly walked"
2. הָלַךְ הָלוֹךְ -- "he walked, walking" or "he walked continually"

64

כִּי־בָרֵךְ אֲבָרֶכְךָ וְהַרְבָּה אַרְבֶּה אֶת־זַרְעֲךָ

**   ☐☐☐   (Piel stem sign)

Note 64A: Piel Stem

A third stem besides Qal (simple active) and Nifal (simple passive) is
Piel. The Piel stem, which has a Dagesh Forte to double the middle
root consonant, serves to extend the meaning of the verb in some way or
to give it a special nuance. Some examples in English will show the
various ways in which the Piel modifies the Qal meaning:

Qal	**Piel**
to be great	to magnify
to be finished	to finish
to break	to shatter
to ask	to beg
to learn	to teach

The Piel has often been described as the "intensive" stem, but that
description only accounts for a small portion of the occurrences. Since
the Piel has multiple functions, one must consult the lexicon to know
just what the Piel meaning of a verb might be. Only for the sake of
convenience will the term "intensive" be used of the Piel in the
Workbook, but the quotation marks around "intensive" will caution the
student of the inadequacy of the term.

**   יְ☐☐☐   (the clue pointing of the Piel imperfect)

Note 64B: Piel Imperfect

A Dagesh Forte in the middle root consonant is characteristic of all Piel
forms. The **Piel imperfect** has a Sheva under the prefix (☐ under the
א-prefix) and a Dagesh Forte in the middle root consonant, if possible.
The Piel impf. 3ms of the model verb is יְקַטֵּל -- "he massacred." For
the form אֲבָרֶכְךָ, **REVIEW Note 51B** to explain the composite Sheva
under the Alef and the absence of the Dagesh Forte in the Resh. What
is ךָ____?

►   בָרֵךְ אֲבָרֶכְךָ   This, then, is the Piel infinitive absolute and the Piel impf.
1cs with a 2ms suffix. The imperfect derives its time element
from the context. Here it is future, the promise as yet
unfulfilled. The phrase can be rendered: "I will surely bless
you."

**   ☐☐☐ה   (Hifil stem sign)

כִּי־בָרֵךְ אֲבָרֶכְךָ וְהַרְבָּה אַרְבֶּה אֶת־זַרְעֲךָ (Gn 22:17)

Note 65A: Hifil Stem

A fourth pattern that Hebrew verbs follow besides the Qal (simple active), Nifal (simple passive), and Piel ("intensive" active) is the **Hifil**, which has a He directly before the root as its stem sign. The Hifil is the **causative active** stem. Some examples in English can illustrate the uses of the Hifil:

Qal	Hifil
to be many	to cause to be many, to multiply
to be holy	to cause to be holy, to sanctify
to see	to cause to see. to show
to go up	to cause to go up, to bring or lead up
	to offer up (a sacrifice)

80.   רבה   (verb)   *to be many, great* (Qal)   (רָבָה)
    to multiply, increase (Hifil)

▶   הַרְבָּה   This is the Hifil infinitive absolute. It is Hifil because of the He, but as of now you do not know what makes this form an inf. abs. **REVIEW Note 63B.**

Note 65B: Vowel Classes

Hebrew vowels are grouped into three classes, whereas we think of five classes of vowels in English. To learn the Hebrew vowel classes, it is simplest to relate them to English vowels:

1. The **first class** includes the "a" vowels:

    ◌ַ, ◌ָ, ◌ָה, and ◌ֲ

2. The **second class** includes the "e" and "i" vowels:

    ◌ֶ, ◌ֵ, ◌ִ, ◌ִי, ◌ֵה, ◌ֶי, ◌ֵי, and ◌ֱ

3. The **third class** includes the "o" and "u" vowels:

    ◌ֹ, ◌ֻ, ◌ֹ, וּ, וֹ, ◌ֹה, and ◌ָ

See the vowel charts on pp. 5 and 14.

**   יַ◌ִ◌ים (the clue pointing of the Hifil imperfect)

Note 65C: Hifil Imperfect

The Hifil imperfect should have both the He to indicate the Hifil and a prefix. But the He is elided and the prefix stands immediately before the root. The **Hifil imperfect** has a Patah under the prefix and a 2nd

וְהַרְבָּה אַרְבֶּה אֶת־זַרְעֲךָ כְּכוֹכְבֵי הַשָּׁמַיִם וְכַחוֹל אֲשֶׁר עַל־שְׂפַת הַיָּם

class vowel after the 2nd root consonant. The clue pointing has a Hireq Yod, but other 2nd class vowels may appear. The Hifil impf. 3ms of the model verb is יַקְטִיל -- "he caused to kill."

▶ אַרְבֶּה — The Hifil impf. 3ms of רבה. The Patah under the prefix is the single determining clue for the Hifil in this form.

Note 66A: Verbs Ending in He

A verb whose root ends in He regularly has Segol He at the end in imperfect forms of all stems. Thus it is merely coincidental that the Hifil form אַרְבֶּה has a 2nd class vowel after the 2nd root consonant. Compare:

Qal   **Hifil**

תִּרְבֶּה -- "you will be many"   תַּרְבֶּה -- "you will multiply"

▶ וְהַרְבָּה אַרְבֶּה — This phrase may be translated: "and I will greatly multiply."

81. זֶרַע — (noun) *seed, offspring*

82. כְּ־־־־ — (preposition) *as, like*
This is the third and last of the inseparable prepositions. What are the other two?

כּוֹכָב — (noun) *star*

▶ כְּכוֹכְבֵי — What does the Tsere Yod ending indicate? **REVIEW Note 38B.**

חוֹל — (noun) *sand*

▶ וְכַחוֹל — **REVIEW Notes 37B and 47A.**

83. שָׂפָה — (noun) *lip, speech, edge*

** הָ־־־ — (noun/adjective ending)   (fem. sg. absolute)

** תָ־־־ — (noun/adjective ending)   (fem. sg. construct)
See the noun/adjective endings in **Chart 24B.**

אֲשֶׁר עַל־שְׂפַת הַיָּם וְיִרַשׁ זַרְעֲךָ אֵת שַׁעַר אֹיְבָיו: ‏(Gn 22:17-18)

‏18 וְהִתְבָּרֲכוּ

Note 67A: Feminine Nouns

Some nouns in Hebrew are feminine but have no distinctive fem. sg. ending, e.g., אֶרֶץ. Other nouns have the distinctive fem. sg. ending ה ָ ‏___, when they appear in the absolute state. When in the construct state, fem. sg. nouns with the ה ָ ‏___ ending have the ת ַ ‏___ ending. The ת is the old original fem. ending. **REVIEW Note 61B.** Thus שְׂפַת is the fem. sg. construct form of שָׂפָה.

84.   יָם   (noun)   *sea*

▸ אֲשֶׁר עַל־שְׂפַת הַיָּם   **REVIEW Note 49B.**

85.   ירשׁ   (verb)   *to possess, inherit*   (יָרַשׁ)

▸   וְיִרַשׁ   The missing letter rules should not be applied here, for this form is written defectively (**REVIEW Note 37C**) for וְיִירַשׁ, which is the same as וְיִירַשׁ. The latter form has the clue pointing of the Qal imperfect. **REVIEW Note 60A.** Is this form imperfect consecutive? **REVIEW 46B.**

86.   שַׁעַר   (noun)   *gate*

87.   אֹיֵב   (noun)   *enemy*

GENESIS 22:18

**   הִתְ□□□   (Hitpael stem sign)

Note 67B: Hitpael Stem

The fifth and final stem that appears in this chapter is the **Hitpael**. It is the **reflexive** or **reciprocal** stem, but it may have other nuances as well. Again the lexicon must be consulted for specific meanings. Here are some English examples:

Qal	Piel	Hitpael
to be holy	to consecrate	to consecrate oneself
to be great	to magnify, praise	to magnify oneself, boast
to see		to look at one another
to go		to go back and forth
to become rich		to pretend to be rich

(Gn 22:18) ‏¹⁸וְהִתְבָּרֲכוּ בְזַרְעֲךָ כֹּל גּוֹיֵי הָאָרֶץ עֵקֶב אֲשֶׁר שָׁמַעְתָּ בְּקֹלִי:‎

The Hitpael verb stem sign is ‏□□□הִתְ‎, with He Tav before the root and a Dagesh Forte to double the middle root letter, if possible. The Hitpael perf. 3ms of the model verb is ‏הִתְקַטֵּל‎ -- "he killed himself."

| ** | ‏וּ___‎ | (affix) | *they* | (3cp of the perfect) |

See **Chart 23A**.

Note 68A: Common Gender

All first person verbs are **common** gender; i.e., the form is the same for both masc. and fem. usages. The only place outside the first person where there is a common gender is in the 3cp of the perfect: ‏וּ___‎.

Note 68B: Perfect Consecutive

Imperfect consecutive forms have a distinctive pointing of the Vav (‏וַ_‏___‎). Hebrew also has a corresponding **perfect consecutive**, but it has no distinctive pointing of the Vav, which is pointed the same as the simple Vav conjunction (‏וְ____‎). Context must decide whether a form is the perfect consecutive or merely the perfect with the simple Vav conjunction. Perfect consecutives, being the counterpart of the imperfect consecutives, have a **present** or **future** time element.

▸ ‏וְהִתְבָּרֲכוּ‎   This is the Hitpael perfect consecutive 3cp of ‏ברך‎ : "and they will bless themselves."

▸ ‏בְזַרְעֲךָ‎   For the absence of the Dagesh Lene in the Bet, **REVIEW Note 49A**.

88.   ‏כֹּל‎   (noun)   *all, every, any*

Note 68C: ‏כָּל־‎ , ‏כֹּל‎

‏כֹּל‎ (also written ‏כָּל־‎ with the Maqqef -- **REVIEW Note 6C or 15C**) is properly a noun meaning "entirety." But it corresponds to the English usage of the adjective "all, every."

89.   ‏גּוֹי‎   (noun)   *nation, people*

▸   ‏גּוֹיֵי‎   What does the Tsere Yod ending indicate?

▸ ‏כֹּל גּוֹיֵי הָאָרֶץ‎   This phrase is the expressed subject of ‏וְהִתְבָּרֲכוּ‎. **REVIEW Note 41A** for the word order in this whole clause.

עֵקֶב אֲשֶׁר שָׁמַעְתָּ בְּקֹלִי: ‏¹⁹ וַיָּשָׁב אַבְרָהָם אֶל־נְעָרָיו ‏(Gn 22:18-19)
וַיָּקֻמוּ וַיֵּלְכוּ יַחְדָּו אֶל־בְּאֵר שָׁבַע
וַיֵּשֶׁב אַבְרָהָם בִּבְאֵר שָׁבַע:

##	עֵקֶב	(preposition and conjunction)	*because of, because*
▶	עֵקֶב אֲשֶׁר	**REVIEW** Note 62B.	
90.	שׁמע	(verb) *to hear, listen to, obey*	‏(שָׁמַע)
91.	קוֹל	(noun) *voice, sound*	

Note 69A: The Verb שׁמע

Hebrew idiom uses בְּ after the verb שׁמע, as in the phrase שָׁמַעְתָּ
בְּקֹלִי. The English idiom may use no preposition ("to hear") or the
preposition "to" ("to listen to"). For the stem of this form, **REVIEW**
Note 57A.

| ▶ | בְּקֹלִי | Written defectively for בְּקוֹלִי. **REVIEW** Note 37C. What is the יִ‎_‎_‎_‎_? |

GENESIS 22:19

▶	וַיָּשָׁב	For the vowel under the Shin, **REVIEW** Note 39D.
▶	וַיָּשָׁב	For the root of this and the following three verbs, **REVIEW** Note 43A.
▶	וַיָּקֻמוּ	
▶	וַיֵּלְכוּ	
▶	וַיֵּשֶׁב	
##	יַחְדָּו	(adverb) *together*
##	בְּאֵר שֶׁבַר	(proper noun) *Beersheba*
▶	בְּאֵר שָׁבַע	For the change of pointing, **REVIEW** Note 61C.
▶	בִּבְאֵר שָׁבַע	**REVIEW** Note 52B for the Hireq under the Bet.

PROGRESS CHECK #5

1. Distinguish the following pairs of similarly looking or sounding words:

a.	עַתָּה and אַתָּה		f.	שָׁם and שֵׁם		
b.	ירא and ראה		g.	עלה and עלה		
c.	וַיֵּשֶׁב and וַיָּשָׁב		h.	שְׁנַיִם and שָׁמַיִם		
d.	אֹתוֹ and אִתּוֹ		i.	אֶחָד and אַחַר		
e.	היה and חוה		j.	לקח and הלך		

2. Practice translating these "non-biblical" sentences:

a) וַיִּקַּח יִצְחָק אֶת־הָעֵצִים הָאֵלֶּה:

b) בַּבֹּקֶר הַשֵּׁנִי וַיִּבְנוּ אֶת־הַמִּזְבֵּחַ:

c) וַיֹּאמֶר אַבְרָהָם אֲלֵיהֶם וַיֹּאמֶר אֵשֵׁב עִם בְּנִי:

d) וַיְהִי בַּיּוֹם הַהוּא וַיָּשֻׁבוּ הַנְּעָרִים אֶל־אֶרֶץ אֲבִיהֶם:

e) עַתָּה יָדַעְתָּ כִּי בֶּן־אָבִי אָנִי:

f) וָאֶקַּח אֶת־שְׁנֵי הַמַּלְאָכִים אִתִּי וַנֵּלֶךְ לַיָּם:

g) וַיְבָרֶךְ יהוה אֶת־אַבְרָהָם וַיַּרְבֶּה אֶת־זַרְעוֹ:

h) נִלְקַח יִצְחָק אֶל־אַחַד הָרֵי הָאָרֶץ:

3. Practice analyzing and translating the following verb forms. All stems are Qal.

a.	וַתֵּשֶׁב	g.	וַתִּקַּח	
b.	אֶשְׁלַח	h.	יִשְׂאוּ	
c.	וַנִּבֶן	i.	עָשָׂה	
d.	יִרֵא	j.	וַנֵּלֶךְ	
e.	וְיֹאמֶר	k.	וַתֵּרֶא	
f.	קָרָאתִי	l.	עָלִיתָ	

Note 71A: Summary of the Hebrew Verb

The meaning of a Hebrew verb can be modified according to several distinct patterns called "stems." The modifications are accomplished by changes of pointing within the verb and/or by the addition of preformatives as stem signs.

Theoretically, nine stems would be possible. The translations given here are based on theoretical meanings of the model verb קטל in the various stems, for this verb only occurs in the Qal stem in the Hebrew Bible.

	simple	"intensive"	causative
active	to kill	to massacre	to cause someone to kill
passive	to be killed	to be massacred	to be caused to kill
reflexive	to kill oneself	to massacre oneself	to cause someone to kill himself

Actually, only seven stems figure in biblical Hebrew, except for a few instances. The old simple passive forms have practically disappeared, so that now one stem does service for both simple passive and simple reflexive. The "intensive" reflexive often does not have an "intensive" force. And no causative reflexive survives. The actual picture, then, is this:

	simple	"intensive"	causative
active	Qal: to kill	Piel: to massacre	Hifil: to cause someone to kill
passive	Nifal: to be killed	Pual: to be massacred	Hofal: to be caused to kill
reflexive		Hitpael: to kill oneself	--------

Only five of these stems occur very often, namely, the five we encountered in Genesis 22: Qal, Nifal, Piel, Hitpael, and Hifil. The two passive stems Pual and Hofal are very infrequent.

SYNOPSIS OF THE MODEL VERB

On the following two pages a synopsis of the model verb קטל appears together with the clue pointing and the reference to the passage where an analogous form first occurs in the readings of the *Workbook*. Since at the start it is difficult to memorize the clue pointing in the abstract, the student should make constant reference back to this synopsis until the basic clue pointing is learned.

72

Chart 72: Synopsis of the Model Verb

	Qal	Qal passive	Nifal	Piel
(stem sign →)			נ□□□	□□□
Perfect 3ms	קָטַל □□ָ Gn 22:12		נִקְטַל נִ□□□ Gn 12:16	קִטֵּל □□ִ Gn 12:4
Imperfect 3ms	יִקְטֹל יִ□□ָ Gn 22:14		יִקָּטֵל יִ□□ָ Gn 22:14	יְקַטֵּל יְ□□□ Gn 22:17
Imperative 2ms	קְטֹל □□ְ Dt 5:1		הִקָּטֵל	קַטֵּל □□ַ Dt 5:16
Infinitive Absolute	קָטוֹל □וֹ□ָ Gn 12:9		הִקָּטֹל נִקְטֹל	קַטֹּל קַטֵּל □□ַ 2 Sm 12:14
Infinitive Construct	קְטֹל □□ְ Js 24:10		הִקָּטֵל הִ□□ָ 2 Sm 11:20	קַטֵּל □□ַ Js 24:9
Participle ms	קֹטֵל □□וֹ Dt 5:1	קָטוּל □וּ□ָ Dt 5:15	נִקְטָל נִ□□ָ Ps 51:19	מְקַטֵּל מְ□□□ Gn 12:3

4

Synopsis of the Model Verb

Pual	Hitpael	Hifil	Hofal	
קֻטַּל	הִתְקַטֵּל	הִקְטִיל	הָקְטַל	(← stem sign)
	התְ◻◻◻	ה◻◻◻	הָ◻◻◻	
קֻטַּל	הִתְקַטֵּל	הִקְטִיל	הָקְטַל	Perfect 3ms
	הִתְ◻◻◻	ה◻◻ִים		
	Gn 22:18	Gn 12:11		
יְקֻטַּל	יִתְקַטֵּל	יַקְטִיל	יָקְטַל	Imperfect 3ms
יְ◻◻ַ◻	יִתְ◻◻◻	יַ◻◻ִים	יָ◻◻ַ◻	
Gn 2:1	Dt 5:21	Gn 22:17	Dt 5:9	
	הִתְקַטֵּל	הַקְטֵל		Imperative 2ms
		הַ◻◻ֵ◻		
		2 Sm 11:25		
קֻטֹּל	הִתְקַטֵּל	הַקְטֵל	הָקְטֵל	Infinitive Absolute
		הַ◻◻ֵ◻		
		2 Sm 12:2		
קֻטַּל	הִתְקַטֵּל	הַקְטִיל	הָקְטַל	Infinitive Construct
		הַ◻◻ִים		
		Dt 5:5		
מְקֻטָּל	מִתְקַטֵּל	מַקְטִיל	מָקְטָל	Participle ms
	מִתְ◻◻◻	מ◻◻ִים		
	2 Sm 11:4	Js 24:17		

4

NAMES OF THE STEMS

The names of the stems, except for Qal (קַל -- "light, swift"), derive from the verb פָּעַל ("to do"), which was used in early grammars of Hebrew as a model verb. Each stem beyond the Qal is named according to the pointing of the perfect 3ms form of this verb in that stem. Thus, "Nifal" is merely the transliteration of נִפְעַל, which is the perfect 3ms of the simple passive/reflexive stem. If you look at the synopsis in Chart 72 and substitute the root letters פעל for the model verb קטל in the perfect 3ms forms, you will have the names of the Hebrew stems:

נִפְעַל -- Nifal

פִּעֵל -- Piel

פֻּעַל -- Pual

הִתְפַּעֵל -- Hitpael

הִפְעִיל -- Hifil

הָפְעַל -- Hofal

MORE ON THE VERB STEMS

Although every verb by form falls into the category of one of the seven stems, the relationship between that stem and the verb's meaning is not always predictable. For one thing, very few verbs actually occur in all seven stems. In fact it is said that only six of about 1400 verbs do. Most verbs occur in only three or four stems at most. Thus a verb may not occur in the Qal at all and so may have a simple meaning in the Piel or Hifil. In such cases, the particular modification of a stem may not be reflected in the meaning of that verb. For instance, there are verbs that occur only in the Piel or Hifil but do not exhibit any obvious "intensive" or causative meanings. Consequently, a lexicon must be consulted constantly for the range of meanings of a verb in a given stem.

THE USE OF A LEXICON WITH THE WORKBOOK

If exegesis of biblical texts is one of the primary goals of learning biblical Hebrew, then it is essential that the student learn to use a good lexicon and not rely on textbook glossaries or pocket dictionaries. Only a lexicon that categorizes meanings based on references to biblical passages is equipped to be of service in the task of exegesis. It is now time for the student to begin to use a lexicon as we proceed through the *Workbook*. In Genesis 22 all the new words were listed and translations provided. Now for the next two readings from Genesis 12 and Deuteronomy 5 all the new words will still be listed, but the student is expected to use a Hebrew-English lexicon to determine appropriate translations.

THE STANDARD LEXICONS

The two most widely used large and comprehensive Hebrew-English lexicons are:

1. F. Brown, S. R. Driver, and C. A. Briggs, *A Hebrew and English Lexicon of the Old Testament* (1907). This exhaustive lexicon, known as Brown-Driver-Briggs or BDB, is based on the lexicon of W. Gesenius, the father of Hebrew lexicography, as translated into English by Edward Robinson from 1836 to 1854. BDB has been the most widely used lexicon in the English speaking world this century, but it has two drawbacks. First, because it has not been revised since its publication eighty years ago, it does not reflect the advances made in Hebrew lexicography this century. Second, it is very difficult for beginners to use, since all words are listed under the verb root from which the word is derived and not simply alphabetically.

2. L. Koehler and W. Baumgartner, *Lexicon in Veteris Testamenti Libros* (1953). This more recent lexicon, known as Koehler-Baumgartner or KB, takes account of the advances in Hebrew lexicography during the first half of this century. Although it has been used mainly in the German speaking world, all the translations are given in both German and English. A new third edition of KB has recently been completed in three volumes (1967, 1974, 1983), but the editors decided to eliminate the English translations, making this lexicon useful only for those who know German. This third edition appears under the title *Hebräisches und aramäisches Lexikon zum Alten Testament*.

STUDENT LEXICONS

Beginning students now have two lexicons that are useful for the exegetical study of the Hebrew Bible:

1. BDB has been reissued as *The New Brown-Driver-Briggs-Gesenius Hebrew and English Lexicon* (1979). It has been prepared by Jay P. Green, Sr., and is published by Hendrickson Publishers. It has reproduced BDB in a reduced page size but has added an alphabetical list of all Hebrew words with a page and column reference back to BDB. It is now possible for beginners to look up a word in the alphabetical index and then find the entry for the word in the main body of the lexicon.

2. William Holladay has prepared *A Concise Hebrew and Aramaic Lexicon of the Old Testament* (1971), published by Eerdmans. It is based on the Koehler-Baumgartner lexicon, including the first two volumes of the third edition. Holladay includes every Hebrew word but has somewhat abridged the entries. This is the most up-to-date lexicon available. The use of Hebrew script for the beginning of every entry and of transliteration in the body of the entry gives the student practice in both forms of rendering Hebrew today.

USE OF HOLLADAY'S LEXICON

Although either the new BDB or Holladay's lexicon may be used effectively in learning Hebrew, the latter will be incorporated into the rest of the *Workbook*. Holladay is somewhat more manageable and easier to use for the beginner, and it reflects more recent developments in the study of the Hebrew language.

A few words should be said about the use of Holladay. Read the "Introduction" and note the list of "Abbreviations." Except for a paragraph in the "Introduction," Holladay does not include a complete chart for transliteration. Refer to Note 7A above for help in using Holladay's system. When looking up a Hebrew word, you will find it by applying the alphabetical principle only to the consonants and vowel letters, since the vowel pointing does not figure in the alphabetical arrangement. E.g., the hollow verbs קוּם, שִׂים, and בּוֹא appear alphabetically with the vowel letter but without the pointing: קום, שׂים, and בוא.

Let us take two examples of words from Genesis 12 to see what kinds of information can be gleaned from a lexical entry.

1. Look up the word בַּיִת (Word 92). The entry begins on p. 38 of Holladay. The Roman numeral I before the word indicates that another word has the same spelling. Such other words are listed after this entry with successive Roman numerals. Next we are told that the word בַּיִת occurs at least 2000 times in the Hebrew Bible. Then a number of commonly occurring (or sometimes rarely occurring) forms are given in Hebrew characters. Notice the form of the construct, construct with suffixes, plural, etc. Next scan the whole semantic section of the entry and notice the bold-face words. These are the most important translations. The basic translation may be remembered as "house," but the specific translation "palace" or "temple" may be required in some contexts. The Hebrew forms and phrases in this section are transliterated. Be aware that the translations given after such transliterations are of the whole phrase in context and not simply a translation of the word בַּיִת. A few representative passages are listed for each category of translation.

2. A second example is the verb גדל (Word 94) on p. 56 of the lexicon. The entry is broken down into the various stems in which the verb appears (Hitpael is listed last). Under each stem, some common forms are listed, followed by basic translations for that stem. The basic meaning of this verb in the Qal is "to be or become great." But the verb appears in Gn 12:2 in the Piel stem. Notice that Gn 12:2 is actually listed for translation 4 under the Piel. In this context in this stem the word may be translated "praise." Notice further that the symbol † occurs after the paragraph on the Hitpael. This means that all of the occurrences of this verb in the Hitpael in the Hebrew Bible have been listed -- four of them.

Make constant reference to the lexicon, even for words that you have already learned. Often the semantic range of a word is far wider than the one or two simple translations you have learned.

CHAPTER III: THE STUDY OF GENESIS 12:1-20

For all subsequent readings in the *Workbook*, the student is to refer to the Hebrew text as printed in *Biblia Hebraica Stuttgartensia*, since the text will no longer be printed at the top of each page.

All new words are listed either with a number (to be learned as a vocabulary word) or with ## (not to be learned as a vocabulary word). But no translations are given. The student is to look up each word in the lexicon and write in the basic definitions of the word in the space provided.

The symbol + indicates that Holladay lists this verse in the lexical entry for this word. The Roman numerals refer to Holladay's way of distinguishing homonyms.

GENESIS 12:1

▸   אַבְרָם   "Abram," the name of Abraham until Gn 17. It is an alternative form of Word 9.

▸   לֶךְ־לְךָ   **REVIEW Word 19** and **Note 33B.**

▸   מֵאַרְצְךָ   **REVIEW Note 58C.**

Note 77A: Segolate Nouns

Many nouns have two Segols as vowels and have the stress on the first syllable: אֶרֶץ. Such words are called **Segolate nouns**. When suffixes are added to the sg., the pointing becomes ‗□□ֶ□ :

$$\text{נַפְשִׁי} \quad -- \quad \text{"my life" from} \quad \text{נֶפֶשׁ}$$
$$\text{מֵאַרְצְךָ} \quad -- \quad \text{"from your land" from} \quad \text{אֶרֶץ}$$

Note 77B: The Conjunction Vav

Before בּ, מ, פּ, and consonants that have a simple Sheva, the Vav conjunction is ‗‗‗‗וּ. This is the one exception to the rule that all syllables begin with a consonant. Example: וּמִמּוֹלַדְתְּ.

מוֹלֶדֶת   +

92.   בַּיִת   I

What is the sg. construct form? The word almost always occurs as a construct or with suffixes.

78

(Gn 12:1-2)

▶ אָבִיךָ   **REVIEW Note 48C**.

▶ אַרְאֶךָּ   It is only coincidental that the missing letter rules of Note 43A work on this verb form, for the stem is not Qal. The Patah under the prefix suggests what stem? **REVIEW Note 65B**. The final He of the root has been lost because of the presence of the suffix. Regard ךָ simply as the 2ms suffix for now. Look up this verb and note its meaning in this stem. +

GENESIS 12:2

▶ וְאֶעֶשְׂךָ   The final He of the root has again been lost because of the suffix. Is this imperfect consecutive? **REVIEW Note 46B**. The events here are not thought of as successive but perhaps simultaneous or with emphasis.

Note 78A: א Prefix

The 1cs prefix א regularly has Segol under it in the Qal rather than a Hireq as the other prefixes do. Compare:

יִקְטֹל -- "he will keep"

אֶקְטֹל -- "I will keep"

93. גָּדוֹל

לְגוֹי גָּדוֹל   **REVIEW Note 26C**.

▶ וַאֲבָרֶכְךָ   A Sheva (here a composite Sheva because of the guttural) under the prefix suggests what stem? **REVIEW Note 64B**. For the pointing of the Vav conjunction, **REVIEW Note 45D**.

94. גדל   +

▶ וַאֲגַדְּלָה   What stem is this? Look up the meanings in this stem. + What does the final He indicate? **REVIEW Note 46A**.

▶ שְׁמֶךָ   This is the pausal form of שִׁמְךָ. **REVIEW Note 61C**. Cf. בִּנְךָ from בֵּן in Gn 22:2.

▶ וֶהְיֵה   An unsual usage of היה. The form is the Qal imperative 2ms with the Vav conjunction. It may not intend a command ("and be a blessing") but may relate a consequence following the cohortative ("so that you may be a blessing").

בְּרָכָה   I

GENESIS 12:3

▶ וַאֲבָרְכָה   What stem is this? Is the Vav consecutive or conjunctive?
           What does the final He indicate?

**   מְ◻◻◻   (sign of some participles)

Note 79A: Sign of the Participle

In all the stems except the Qal and Nifal, the sign of the **participle** is
מְ◻◻◻. The clue pointing of the prefix in imperfect forms also appears
under the Mem in the participle of the same stem. See **Chart 72** and
compare the impf. and part. of the various stems. The Piel participle of
the model verb is מְקַטֵּל -- "massacring." Notice the characteristic
Sheva of the Piel under the Mem in the form מְבָרְכֶיךָ.

Note 79B: Use of Participles

Participles are verbal adjectives. They do not have person, but they do
have gender and number. They take the noun/adjective endings.
Participles, especially if they are definite, are usually translated with a
relative clause: "the one who..." (sg.) or "those who..." (pl.).

קלל   +

▶ וּמְקַלֶּלְךָ   Why the pointing of the Vav? **REVIEW Note 77B**. What
           stem? Note the meaning in this stem. +

ארר

▶ אָאֹר   Do not apply the missing letter rules.

Note 79C: Verbs with Reduplicated 2nd Root Letter

We have seen that hollow verbs have only two root consonants.
REVIEW Note 39C. Another type of verb that has only two root
consonants reduplicates the second consonant, e.g., קלל and ארר.
This class of verbs is often difficult to recognize, unless the reduplication
is evident, as is the case in מְקַלֶּלְךָ but not in אָאֹר.

▶ וְנִבְרְכוּ   Since this form has an affix (וּ‎___), the Nun cannot be a
           prefix but must be the sign of the stem. **REVIEW Note 59B**.
           Is this perfect consecutive? **REVIEW Note 68B**. Since the
           similar passage in Gn 22:18 had the Hitpael for this same
           verb, would this Nifal form more likely have its passive or
           reflexive/reciprocal force? Cf. Holladay, p. 49. +

80

(Gn 12:3-4)

95.　　מִשְׁפָּחָה　　+

**　　וֹת＿＿＿　　(noun/adjective ending)　　(fem. pl., abs. and const.)
　　　　　　　　　See **Chart 24B**.

Note 80A: Feminine Endings

The distinctive feminine sg. noun/adjective endings are ה＿＿＿ for
the absolute and ת＿＿＿ for the construct. The fem. pl. ending
וֹת＿＿＿ serves for both abs. and const. forms. Compare:

הַמִּשְׁפָּחָה -- "the family" (abs. sg.)

מִשְׁפַּחַת -- "the family of" (const. sg.)

הַמִּשְׁפָּחוֹת -- "the families" (abs. pl.)

מִשְׁפְּחוֹת -- "the familes of" (const. pl.)

96.　　אֲדָמָה　　I

GENESIS 12:4

97.　　כַּאֲשֶׁר

Notice that כַּאֲשֶׁר is the preposition כְּ with אֲשֶׁר. For
the use of אֲשֶׁר with prepositions to form conjunctions,
REVIEW Note 62B.

**　　קִּ◻◻　　(the clue pointing of the Piel perfect)

Note 80B: Piel Perfect

Piel perfect verb forms have a Hireq under the first root consonant and
a Dagesh Forte to double the middle consonant, if possible. The Piel
perfect 3ms of the model verb is קִטֵּל -- "he massacred." See the verb
synopsis in **Chart 72**.

98.　　דבר　　II　+

Notice that דבר appears most frequently in the Piel stem
where it has a simple active meaning. In fact, there are no
occurrences of a pf. or impf. form of this verb in the Qal stem.

▶　　אִתּוֹ　　**REVIEW Note 39A**. Cf. Note 51A.

| ## | לוֹט | II |

► בֶּן־... The construct form of בֵּן. The idiom begun by this word is unlike English. How would we render this phrase? See I בֵּן in Holladay, meaning 8, and the comments on the next few words below.

99. חָמֵשׁ

100. שָׁנָה (noun)
According to the distinctive Qamets He ending, what gender is שָׁנָה? **REVIEW Notes 67A** and **80A**. Yet what is its plural?

Note 81A: Numbers

A number may appear before its noun. The numbers 2 through 10 take a *plural* noun after them, but the numbers 11 through 19 and the compounds of 10 (20, 30, 40, etc.) take a *singular* noun after them.

101. שִׁבְעִים Listed under I שֶׁבַע in the lexicon.

Note 81B: Numbers

The plural forms of the numbers 3 through 9 designate the number multiplied by 10:

The plural of שָׁלֹשׁ ("3") is שְׁלֹשִׁים ("30").

The plural of חָמֵשׁ ("5") is חֲמִשִׁים ("50").

The plural of שֶׁבַע ("7") is שִׁבְעִים ("70").

102. יָצָא

What is the infinitive construct?

Note 81C: Qal Infinitive Construct

The Qal infinitive construct of verb roots with certain weak consonants (always initial Nun and usually initial Yod) are formed by dropping the initial weak consonant and attaching תֶ__ at the end. Compare:

יָשַׁב -- inf. cs. is שֶׁבֶת

יָצָא -- inf. cs. is צֵאת

נָשָׂא -- inf. cs. is שְׂאֵת

82

(Gn 12:4-5)

▶   בְּצֵאתוֹ   **REVIEW Note 52A** for the "rule of thumb."

Note 82A: Infinitive Construct

A preposition with an infinitive construct (a verbal noun) followed by a suffix or absolute noun is a common way Hebrew expresses a subordinate clause. The object of the preposition is a construct chain with the inf. cs. serving as the construct and a suffix or noun serving as the absolute. Translate such a phrase literally first and then render it into English, where a full subordinate clause is usually required.

Here, for example, בְּצֵאתוֹ would literally be "in his going out" (or "in the going out of him"), but we would say "when he went out."

\#\#   חָרָן   I

GENESIS 12:5

\#\#   שָׂרַי

103.   אִשָּׁה

What is the sg. cs. form? What is the sg. form with a sf.? Note the unusual pl. form.

Note 82B: Feminine Nouns with Suffixes

Nouns with the feminine ending הָ____ assume the old feminine ending ת before all suffixes:

אִשָּׁה -- "a woman, wife"

אִשְׁתּוֹ -- "his wife"

104.   אָח   II

Note 82C: Irregular Nouns

Like the noun אָב, the noun אָח shows some irregularities. The Yod that appears in the sg. forms of אָח with suffixes is again meaningless, as it is in the form אָחִיו. It does not indicate the pl. as with other nouns. **REVIEW Note 48C.**

▶   כָּל-   **REVIEW Note 68C.**

##	רְכוּשׁ	+

**	◻ּ____	(suffix) *them, their* (3mp)

See **Chart 24A**.

##	רכשׁ	+

105.	נֶ֫פֶשׁ	+

The word נֶ֫פֶשׁ was often rendered "soul" in older translations, but it should be carefully distinguished from any Greek idea of "soul." Note the semantic range of the word in the lexicon. Learn: "breath, life, person, self." What does it mean in the present context?

▶   עָשׂוּ   The final He of the root has been lost. What stem is it?

Note 83A: Inseparable Prepositions

The inseparable prepositions take a Qamets when they appear before a stressed syllable: לָלֶ֫כֶת. Cf. לָכֶם in Gn 22:5.

Note 83B: Qal Infinitive Construct

By reference to the "missing letters rules" of Note 43A, we can see that the verb לקח acts like verbs that begin with Nun and הלך like verbs that begin with Yod. Similarly, the Qal inf. cs. of these two verbs follows the pattern of verbs with initial Nun or Yod by dropping the first letter and adding a Tav at the end. **REVIEW Note 81C**. Compare:

לקח -- inf. cs. is קַ֫חַת

הלך -- inf. cs. is לֶ֫כֶת

**	הָ____	(He directive) *to, toward*

Note 83C: He Directive

"Direction toward" can be indicated by adding Qamets He to the end of a word: אַ֫רְצָה. This **He directive** can even appear on a construct form within a construct chain, as it does here. It may be compared to the suffix "-wards" in English, e.g., "backwards" or "skywards." The Latin name is *He locale*.

106.	כְּנַ֫עַן

84

(Gn 12:6-7)

GENESIS 12:6

107. עבר   I +

Note 84A: Verbs with a Guttural First Consonant

A Patah under the prefix in the form וַיַּעֲבֹר might suggest the Hifil stem. **REVIEW Note 65C**. But a Patah appears under the prefix in a Qal imperfect when the first root consonant is a guttural, which prefers the Patah. **REVIEW Note 51B**. The vowel after the 2nd root consonant must then determine the stem, for the Qal regularly has Holem (a 3rd class vowel) and the Hifil regularly has a 2nd class vowel. Compare:

Qal	Hifil
יִקְטֹל	יַקְטִיל
יַעֲבֹר	יַעֲבִיר

##	שְׁכֶם	II
##	אֵלוֹן	I +
##	מוֹרֶה	IV +
##	כְּנַעֲנִי	+
108.	אָז	

GENESIS 12:7

▶   וַיֵּרָא   Do not apply the missing letter rules but see the following Note.

Note 84B: Imperfect Consecutive

Besides the special pointing of the Vav (וַ____), **imperfect consecutive** forms may have two other features:

1. They may have a shortened form. E.g., with verbs ending in He, the He falls away, as in וַיֵּרָא. This loss of the He is called **apocopation**. In other verbs, a vowel change may occur.

2. The stress may move toward the beginning of the verb. E.g., יֵלֵךְ but וַיֵּלֶךְ in v. 4 above.

▶ וַיֵּרָא This is an apocopated impf. consec. form, but the stress remains on the last syllable. The unapocopated form is יֵרָאֶה. **REVIEW Note 61A** for the stem. How is ראה translated in this stem?

109. נתן

▶ אֶתֵּן For the Segol under the prefix, **REVIEW Note 78A**. For the root, **REVIEW Note 43A**.

110. זֹאת

This is the fem. sg. of זֶה. The pl. is אֵלֶּה.

▶ הָאָרֶץ הַזֹּאת **REVIEW Note 26C**.

Note 85A: Inseparable Prepositions with יהוה

Both the inseparable prepositions and the conjunction have a Patah before יהוה, for it is to be read as לַאדֹנָי. **REVIEW Note 53A** for this reading and **Note 45D** for the same pointing of the conjunction.

Note 85B: Participles

Another *rule of thumb*: **A verb form with the article is the participle**.

▶ הַנִּרְאֶה This is a masc. sg. participle. What root and stem? How is a definite participle translated? **REVIEW Note 79B**.

Note 85C: Summary of Inseparable Prepositions

1.	They are regularly pointed with a Sheva:	לְךָ, בְּיָד
2.	Before a simple Sheva they take Hireq:	לִשְׁחֹט
3.	Before a composite Sheva they take the corresponding short vowel:	כַּאֲשֶׁר
4.	Before יְ they take Hireq and the Sheva under the Yod falls away:	לִיהוּדָה
5.	With אֱלֹהִים they take a Tsere:	לֵאלֹהִים
6.	With יהוה they take a Patah:	לַיהוה
7.	Before a stressed syllable they take Qamets:	לָכֶם

	Note 86A: Summary of the Simple Vav Conjunction	
1.	It is regularly pointed with a Sheva:	וְיָד
2.	Before a simple Sheva or ב, מ, and פ it is וּ :	וּבֵין
3.	Before a composite Sheva it takes the corresponding short vowel:	וַאֲנִי
4.	Before יְ it takes Hireq and the Sheva under the Yod falls away:	וִיהוּדָה
5.	With אֱלֹהִים it takes a Tsere:	וֵאלֹהִים
6.	With יהוה it takes a Patah:	וַיהוה
7.	Before a stressed syllable it often takes Qamets:	וָרַע

GENESIS 12:8

##	עתק	+
▸	וַיַּעְתֵּק	What stem? The impf. is יַעְתִּיק, but the impf. consec. is וַיַּעְתֵּק. For the somewhat shortened form of the latter, **REVIEW Note 84B**.
▸	הָהָרָה	What is the initial He? What is the final He? For the latter **REVIEW Note 83C**.
##	קֶדֶם	

	Note 86B: Preposition מִן	

מִן with reference to position may be translated "on, on the side of" or it may not need to be translated at all. The phrase מִקֶּדֶם לְ____ may be translated: "east of . . . ."

111. בֵּית־אֵל

	Note 86C: Hebrew Proper Nouns	

Holladay does not always give the English form of Hebrew proper nouns. In such cases, transliterating may help but you may also have to check in a standard translation for the English spelling.

112.   נטה   +

Note 87A: Verbs with Loss of Two Root Letters

When a verb loses two of its three root letters, as in the form וַיֵּט, the one consonant that remains is always the middle one. Such verbs always end in He and begin either with Yod or Nun.

113.   אֹהֶל   I

**   ה____   (suffix)   *him, his*   (another 3ms)

See **Chart 24A**.

Note 87B: Qamets Hatuf

The vowel ָ is a Qamets Hatuf in a closed unstressed syllable or in an open syllable before the composite Sheva ֲ. Compare:

וַיָּ֫קָם but יָקוּם

כָּל־ but כֹּל

אָהֳלָה but אֹהֶל

▶   אָהֳלָה   The Atnah (ָ) helps to punctuate this verse.

▶   מִיָּם   **REVIEW Note 86B**. What "sea" is meant here and what direction is intended?

עַי

Notice that this place name always has the article: הָעַי.

GENESIS 12:9

114.   נסע

**   קָטוֹ□   (the pointing of the Qal infinitive absolute)

Note 87C: Qal Infinitive Absolute

The Qal inf. abs. is pointed with a Qamets under the first root consonant and a Holem Vav after the second. The form of the model verb is קָטוֹל. See **Chart 72**.

88

▸ הָלוֹךְ וְנָסוֹעַ   **REVIEW** Note **50C** for the Patah furtive. **REVIEW** Note **63B** for the forms and usage. These two inf. absolutes here denote continuous or repeated action. They give a vivid picture of Abram's movement as he proceeds nomad-fashion toward the Negeb. He goes south and encamps for a time, then sets out once more, etc., progressing steadily toward the Negeb. A translation such as "journeyed by stages" suits what the Hebrew intends rather well.

115.   נֶגֶב

▸   הַנֶּגְבָּה   **REVIEW** Note **83C** for the final Qamets He.

VERB PARSING

As you have gathered by now, the analysis of verbs is a very important part of learning and understanding the Hebrew language. From this point on, all the verb forms should be analyzed (parsed), so that you can develop the skill of seeing the relationship between the grammatical description of a form and its possible translations.

On the next page a guide for parsing verbs is provided. Students should prepare blank parsing sheets and fill in the appropriate terms for each form until verb analysis becomes second nature.

Note 89A: Verb Parsing Guide

The following format may be used to parse verb forms. The examples are taken from Gn 12:10.

Form	Root	Stem	Branch	PGN	Other features	Translation
וַיְהִי	היה	Qal	impf. consec.	3ms	Vav consec.	and there was
וַיֵּרֶד	ירד	Qal	impf. consec.	3ms	Vav consec.	and he went down
לָגוּר	גור	Qal	inf. cs.	----	לְ prep.	to sojourn

Here are the possible elements that could be involved when parsing a Hebrew verb form:

1. **FORM**   This is the form in which the verb appears in the text.

2. **ROOT**   The three root consonants of the lexicon form.

3. **STEM**   Qal, Nifal, Piel, Pual, Hitpael, Hifil, and Hofal.

3. **BRANCH (STATE or ASPECT)**

    perfect   infinitive absolute
    imperfect   infinitive construct
    perfect consecutive   participle
    imperfect consecutive   cohortative
    imperative   jussive

5. **PERSON, GENDER, NUMBER**   1, 2, 3
    masc., fem., com.
    sg., pl.

6. **OTHER FEATURES**   Vav conjunction
    Vav consecutive
    preposition
    article
    suffix (PGN)

7. **TRANSLATION**   The translation of the form *in its context.*

GENESIS 12:10

Note 90A: The Verb הָיָה

The verb הָיָה is irregular in many of its forms. The stem, however, is almost always Qal (rarely Nifal). Thus the common form וַיְהִי is Qal. The Sheva under the prefix does *not* indicate the Piel, as in other verb forms.

116.	רָעָב	+
117.	ירד	+
118.	מִצְרַיִם	
119.	גּוּר	I +
	לָגוּר	What is the "rule of thumb" regarding a verb form with a preposition? **REVIEW Note 52A.** For the pointing of the preposition, **REVIEW Note 85C.**

Note 90B: Hollow Verbs

The lexicon form of most verbs is the Qal pf. 3ms. **REVIEW Note 40C.** But the lexicon form of the **hollow verb** is the Qal inf. const., since all three root letters appear in this form and do not in the 3ms pf.

##	כָּבֵד	I +

Note 90C: Predicate Adjectives

A **predicate adjective** used in a nominal clause agrees with its noun in gender and number, but never has the article. Compare:

הַדָּבָר הַזֶּה -- "this word"

זֶה הַדָּבָר -- "this is the word"

הַדָּבָר זֶה -- "this is, indeed, the word"

▶ כָּבֵד הָרָעָב   **REVIEW Note 57C.**

GENESIS 12:11

120.	קרב	+
**	הֵסִים	(the clue pointing of the Hifil perfect)

```
Note 91A:  Hifil Perfect
```

The **Hifil perfect** always has the stem sign ‎ הָ‏_ _ _ before the root.
The Hifil pf. 3ms of the model verb is ‎ הִקְטִיל‏ -- "he caused (someone)
to kill." Notice the 2nd class vowel after the 2nd root letter. **REVIEW
Note 65B.** Consult the lexicon for the Hifil definitions of ‎ קרב‏.

►	‎ לָבוֹא‏	**REVIEW Note 90B.**
►	‎ אִשְׁתּוֹ‏	**REVIEW Note 82B.**
##	‎ יָפֶה‏	+
►	‎ יְפַת‏	For the ‎ ‏_ _ _ תָ ending, **REVIEW Note 67A.**
121.	‎ מַרְאֶה‏	+

```
Note 91B:  Nouns Beginning with  מ
```

Many nouns are formed from verb roots by adding ‎ מ‏_ _ _ to the
beginning of the root. Compare:

‎ מָקוֹם‏ ("place") from ‎ קוּם‏ ("to arise")

‎ מִזְבֵּחַ‏ ("altar") from ‎ זבח‏ ("to sacrifice")

‎ מַרְאֶה‏ ("appearance") from ‎ ראה‏ ("to see")

122.	‎ אַתְּ‏	(independent personal pronoun) + (2fs)
►	‎ אִשָּׁה...אַתְּ:‏	**REVIEW Note 57C.**

GENESIS 12:12

►	‎ וְהָיָה‏	What determines whether this form is perfect consecutive? **REVIEW Note 68B.**
**	‎ ‏_ _ _ _ ךְ	(suffix) *you, your* (2fs) See **Chart 24A.**
►	‎ אֹתָךְ‏	**REVIEW Note 51A.**
►	‎ מִצְרִים‏	*Egyptians* (not listed in Holladay)
►	‎ אִשְׁתּוֹ זֹאת‏	**REVIEW Notes 57C and 90C.**
123.	‎ הרג‏	
124.	‎ חיה‏	+

▶　　　　　יְחַיּוּ　　Notice carefully the clues for the stem of this form. What stem is indicated by the Sheva under the prefix and the Dagesh Forte in the middle root consonant? See the lexicon for the meaning in this stem.

Note 92A: Simultaneous Action

When **simultaneous** rather than consecutive events are being narrated, the consecutive pattern is broken by inverted word order, so that the clause does not begin with a verb in the consecutive form. Example:

וְהָרְגוּ אֹתִי וְאֹתָךְ יְחַיּוּ׃ .

GENESIS 12:13

**　　　　ת___ִי　　(prefix)　*you*　　　　　　(2fs)
See **Chart 23B**.

Note 92B: Imperatives

The imperative is in form like the imperfect without the initial part of the prefix. All imperatives are 2nd person. Compare:

תִּקְטֹל　--　"you will kill" (Qal impf. 2ms)

קְטֹל　--　"kill!" (Qal impv. 2ms)

If the prefix has a letter or letters at the end of the verb, as is the case with the 2fs and most pl. prefixes, the end part of the prefix remains in imperative forms. Thus, ___ִי remains of the full prefix ת___ִי in the Qal impv. 2fs form אִמְרִי .

The imperative forms לֶךְ and קַח in Gn 22:2 are in the same way like the imperfect forms without the initial prefix: וַיֵּלֶךְ and וַיִּקַּח.

125.　　אָחוֹת

126.　　לְמַעַן　　+　Listed under מַעַן in the lexicon.

127.　　יטב　　+　*to be good*
　　　　　(The lexicon is not clear on the basic meaning.)

▶　　　　יִיטַב　　We might expect this form to be pointed יְיִטַב , but the Sheva as a syllable divider has fallen away. What stem is this form?

Note 93A: Verbs with Initial Yod

There are two types of verbs that have Yod as their first root letter. The first type loses the initial Yod of the root in impf. forms (e.g., יֵשֵׁב and ירד). The second type (less frequent) retains the initial Yod of the root in impf. forms (e.g., ירשׁ and יטב). Compare:

תֵּשֵׁב -- "you will sit" (from יֵשֵׁב)

תִּיטַב -- "you will be good" (from יטב)

Note 93B: English Subjunctive

Hebrew has no subjective forms. We must translate with the English subjunctive when the context suggests it. In the present context, the phrase לְמַעַן יִיטַב לִי may be translated: "in order that it might go well with me."

##	בַּעֲבוּר	Listed under I עֲבוּר in the lexicon.	
**	הָ__	(affix) *she, it*	(3ms of the perfect)
		See **Chart 23A**.	

Note 93C: 3fs Perfect Forms

The Qal pf. 3fs of the model verb is קָטְלָה -- "she killed." But when a verb with He as the final root consonant is 3fs, there is a double feminine termination, using both the old ת and the הָ__. Compare:

עָלָה -- "he went up" עָשָׂה -- "he did"

עָלְתָה -- "she went up" עָשְׂתָה -- "she did"

Note 93D: Feminine Nouns

Many feminine nouns do not have any distinct fem. endings. Usually the context will show what gender such a noun is, especially if the word has an adjective modifying it or is the subject of a verb with a prefix or affix. In the present context, נֶפֶשׁ is known to be fem. because the verb וְחָיְתָה has the 3fs affix.

▶	נַפְשִׁי	**REVIEW Note 77A**.
##	בִּגְלָל	Listed under II גָּלָל in the lexicon. +

▶ כְּבוֹא אַבְרָם   What is the "rule of thumb" regarding a verb form with a preposition? Literally, this phrase would be rendered: "as the going in of Abram." But how would we best translate this phrase? **REVIEW Note 82A**.

▶ יָפָה   The fem. of the adjective יָפֶה ("handsome, beautiful") as in v. 11 above.

128.   הִיא   (independent personal pronoun)   (3fs)

Note 94A: 3fs Pronoun הִיא

הִיא is the fem. form of the pronoun הוּא (Word 74 above). The fem. form, however, is ordinarily written הִוא in the Pentateuch but is always to be pronounced as הִיא .

129.   מְאֹד   (adverb)

GENESIS 12:15

**   הָ____   (suffix)   *her*   (3fs)
                   See **Chart 24A**.

Note 94B: Mappiq

When final He is a consonant and not a vowel letter, a dot called a **Mappiq** is placed in the He (ה). The dot is therefore not a Dagesh. The He of the 3fs suffix has a Mappiq: הָ____ .

▶ אֹתָהּ   **REVIEW Note 51A**.

130.   שַׂר   +

131.   פַּרְעֹה   +

132.   הלל   II +

▶ וַיְהַלְלוּ   What stem? The clue pointing is the Sheva under the prefix.

Note 94C: Implied Dagesh Forte

Dagesh Forte is often omitted but said to be implied in certain consonants which have a Sheva. Such is the case with the middle consonant Lamed in the 3mp Piel form וַיְהַלְלוּ . With an implied

Dagesh, the Sheva under the Lamed is vocal. The 3ms Piel form normally has the Dagesh (יְהַלֵּל). For the absence of the Dagesh in the prefix which has a Sheva, **REVIEW Note 39B**.

**   ת___   (prefix)   *she, it*   (3fs of the imperfect)

Note 95A: ת Prefix

In **Chart 23B,** notice that the prefixes of the 2ms and 3fs of the imperfect are identical (ת___). Context alone can distinguish the two.

Note 95B: Qal Passive

There is confusion among scholars about how a form such as וַתֻּקַּח should be analyzed. It is clear that it is passive: "and she was taken." But what stem is it? Holladay lists the form as a Pual (the passive of a Piel) but allows that it might be regarded as a Qal passive. In the latter case, it is argued that the old Qal passive has largely disappeared from biblical Hebrew, since its function is carried by the Nifal, which was originally only simple reflexive. Yet the Qal passive participle is not uncommon and a few other forms of the Qal passive stem may survive. וַתֻּקַּח may be one of these other forms.

Note 95C: Phrases without Prepositions

Some phrases in Hebrew stand without any preposition that relates them to the rest of the clause. Such is the case with בֵּית פַּרְעֹה. English, however, usually requires a preposition. These phrases in Hebrew may express place, manner, motion toward, time, respect, and the like.

GENESIS 12:16

▶   הֵיטִיב   Notice the stem sign and the 2nd class vowel (הֵ◻ִי◻). What is the root? Branch? Who is the implied subject?

בַּעֲבוּר   The same word appears in v. 13 above.

Note 95D: No Verb "to have"

Hebrew has no verb "to have." Possession is indicated by the verb הָיה (expressed or understood) followed by the preposition לְ. The phrase

96

וַיְהִי־לוֹ would literally be "and there was to him," but it may be translated "and he had."

133.	צֹאן	
134.	בָּקָר	
135.	עֶבֶד	I +
##	שִׁפְחָה	
▸	וּשְׁפָחֹת	The fem. pl. ending ֹות____ is written defectively. **REVIEW 37C**.
##	אָתוֹן	+
##	גָּמָל	+

GENESIS 12:17

136.	נגע	+
##	נֶגַע	+
▸ נְגָעִים גְּדֹלִים		**REVIEW Note 95C**.
▸	עַל	May have the force of "because of."
▸	דְּבַר	The sg. const. of דָּבָר. **REVIEW Note 34A**.
▸	אֵשֶׁת	**REVIEW Word 103**.

GENESIS 12:18

137.	מָה	+

> ## Note 96A: מָה Interrogative

The interrogative particle מָה is pointed very much like the article (**REVIEW Note 47A**), often including the Dagesh Forte in the following consonant. מָה frequently has זֶה or זֹאת following it, as in the phrase מַה־זֹּאת, in which case it may be translated by the phrase "what is this?" or simply "what?"

▸	עָשִׂיתָ	**REVIEW Note 63A**.

▸   לִי   **REVIEW Note 49D**.

138.   לָ֫מָּה   +

See under מָה (D) 3. in the lexicon.

139.   נגד

Notice that this verb is not used in the Qal but has its simple meaning in which stem?

▸   הִגַּ֫דְתָּ   What is the Dagesh Forte in the Gimel?

▸   הִוא   **REVIEW Note 94A**.

GENESIS 12:19

▸   אִשְׁתְּךָ   **REVIEW Word 103**.

▸   קַח וָלֵ֑ךְ   **REVIEW Note 92B**.

GENESIS 12:20

140.   צוה

Notice that this verb is not used in the Qal but has its simple meaning in which stem?

▸   וַיְצַו   The Vav of the root צוה is never a vowel letter but always a consonant. Thus, this verb is not a hollow verb. Because of the apocopated form (**REVIEW Note 84B**), no Dagesh Forte appears in the Vav, for it is now the final consonant. The Sheva under the prefix is sufficient to indicate the stem.

141.   אִישׁ   I

What is the plural?

▸   אֲנָשִׁים   Remember that an *indefinite* direct object is not preceded by אֶת־.

▸   וַיְשַׁלְּחוּ   What significance does the use of this stem convey? See the lexicon. +

▸   וְאֶת־כָּל־אֲשֶׁר־לוֹ   **REVIEW Note 95D**.

NOUN PARADIGMS

The following pages contain three sets of charts to help you analyze various noun types and their forms when suffixes are added:

1. Nine **model nouns** are listed in all their forms:

   a. Three model nouns:

   סוּס   A masc. noun *without* changes when suffixes are added.

   דָּבָר   A masc. noun *with* changes when suffixes are added.

   תּוֹרָה   The model fem. noun.

   b. Three Segolate nouns (stressed first syllable and Segol as the second vowel):

   מֶלֶךְ   A Segolate noun with Segol as the first vowel.

   סֵפֶר   A Segolate noun with Tsere as the first vowel.

   בֹּקֶר   A Segolate noun with Holem as the first vowel.

   c. Three other common types of nouns:

   עַיִן

   חֹק

   מַרְאֶה

5

2. Sixteen **irregular nouns** are listed but only in the forms that occur in the Hebrew Bible. Study this list, so that you can refer to these charts whenever you suspect you are dealing with any of these common nouns that have irregularities in at least some of their forms:

אָב -- "father"	בֵּן -- "son"	מַיִם -- "water"
אָח -- "brother"	בַּת -- "daughter"	עִיר -- "city"
אָחוֹת -- "sister"	יוֹם -- "day"	פֶּה -- "mouth"
אִישׁ -- "man"	יָם -- "sea"	רֹאשׁ -- "head"
אִשָּׁה -- "woman"	כְּלִי -- "vessel"	שֵׁם -- "name"
בַּיִת -- "house"		

3. A chart of the **numerals** is provided to help clarify the forms and uses of the Hebrew numbers.

Chart 99: Model Nouns

SINGULAR	"horse"	"word"	"torah"
absolute	סוּס	דָּבָר	תּוֹרָה
construct	סוּס	דְּבַר	תּוֹרַת
w. 1cs suffix	סוּסִי	דְּבָרִי	תּוֹרָתִי
2ms	סוּסְךָ	דְּבָרְךָ	תּוֹרָתְךָ
2fs	סוּסֵךְ	דְּבָרֵךְ	תּוֹרָתֵךְ
3ms	סוּסוֹ	דְּבָרוֹ	תּוֹרָתוֹ
3fs	סוּסָהּ	דְּבָרָהּ	תּוֹרָתָהּ
1cp	סוּסֵנוּ	דְּבָרֵנוּ	תּוֹרָתֵנוּ
2mp	סוּסְכֶם	דְּבַרְכֶם	תּוֹרַתְכֶם
2fp	סוּסְכֶן	דְּבַרְכֶן	תּוֹרַתְכֶן
3mp	סוּסָם	דְּבָרָם	תּוֹרָתָם
3fp	סוּסָן	דְּבָרָן	תּוֹרָתָן
PLURAL			
absolute	סוּסִים	דְּבָרִים	תּוֹרוֹת
construct	סוּסֵי	דִּבְרֵי	תּוֹרוֹת
w. 1cs suffix	סוּסַי	דְּבָרַי	תּוֹרוֹתַי
2ms	סוּסֶיךָ	דְּבָרֶיךָ	תּוֹרוֹתֶיךָ
2fs	סוּסַיִךְ	דְּבָרַיִךְ	תּוֹרוֹתַיִךְ
3ms	סוּסָיו	דְּבָרָיו	תּוֹרוֹתָיו
3fs	סוּסֶיהָ	דְּבָרֶיהָ	תּוֹרוֹתֶיהָ
1cp	סוּסֵינוּ	דְּבָרֵינוּ	תּוֹרוֹתֵינוּ
2mp	סוּסֵיכֶם	דְּבְרֵיכֶם	תּוֹרוֹתֵיכֶם
2fp	סוּסֵיכֶן	דְּבְרֵיכֶן	תּוֹרוֹתֵיכֶן
3mp	סוּסֵיהֶם	דְּבְרֵיהֶם	תּוֹרוֹתֵיהֶם
3fp	סוּסֵיהֶן	דְּבְרֵיהֶן	תּוֹרוֹתֵיהֶן

5

Chart 100: Segolate Nouns

SINGULAR	"king"	"scroll"	"morning"
absolute	מֶֽלֶךְ	סֵֽפֶר	בֹּֽקֶר
construct	מֶֽלֶךְ	סֵֽפֶר	בֹּֽקֶר
w. 1cs suffix	מַלְכִּי	סִפְרִי	בָּקְרִי
2ms	מַלְכְּךָ	סִפְרְךָ	בָּקְרְךָ
2fs	מַלְכֵּךְ	סִפְרֵךְ	בָּקְרֵךְ
3ms	מַלְכּוֹ	סִפְרוֹ	בָּקְרוֹ
3fs	מַלְכָּהּ	סִפְרָהּ	בָּקְרָהּ
1cp	מַלְכֵּֽנוּ	סִפְרֵֽנוּ	בָּקְרֵֽנוּ
2mp	מַלְכְּכֶם	סִפְרְכֶם	בָּקְרְכֶם
2fp	מַלְכְּכֶן	סִפְרְכֶן	בָּקְרְכֶן
3mp	מַלְכָּם	סִפְרָם	בָּקְרָם
3fp	מַלְכָּן	סִפְרָן	בָּקְרָן

PLURAL

	"king"	"scroll"	"morning"
absolute	מְלָכִים	סְפָרִים	בְּקָרִים
construct	מַלְכֵי	סִפְרֵי	בָּקְרֵי
w. 1cs suffix	מְלָכַי	סְפָרַי	בְּקָרַי
2ms	מְלָכֶֽיךָ	סְפָרֶֽיךָ	בְּקָרֶֽיךָ
2fs	מְלָכַֽיִךְ	סְפָרַֽיִךְ	בְּקָרַֽיִךְ
3ms	מְלָכָיו	סְפָרָיו	בְּקָרָיו
3fs	מְלָכֶֽיהָ	סְפָרֶֽיהָ	בְּקָרֶֽיהָ
1cp	מְלָכֵֽינוּ	סְפָרֵֽינוּ	בְּקָרֵֽינוּ
2mp	מַלְכֵיכֶם	סִפְרֵיכֶם	בָּקְרֵיכֶם
2fp	מַלְכֵיכֶן	סִפְרֵיכֶן	בָּקְרֵיכֶן
3mp	מַלְכֵיהֶם	סִפְרֵיהֶם	בָּקְרֵיהֶם
3fp	מַלְכֵיהֶן	סִפְרֵיהֶן	בָּקְרֵיהֶן

Chart 101: More Model Nouns

SINGULAR	"eye"	"statute"	"appearance"
absolute	עַיִן	חֹק	מַרְאֶה
construct	עֵין	חָק־	מַרְאֵה
w. 1cs suffix	עֵינִי	חֻקִּי	מַרְאִי
2ms	עֵינְךָ	חֻקְּךָ	מַרְאֲךָ
2fs	עֵינֵךְ	חֻקֵּךְ	מַרְאֵךְ
3ms	עֵינוֹ	חֻקּוֹ	מַרְאֵהוּ
3fs	עֵינָהּ	חֻקָּהּ	מַרְאָהּ
1cp	עֵינֵנוּ	חֻקֵּנוּ	מַרְאֵנוּ
2mp	עֵינְכֶם	חֻקְּכֶם	מַרְאֲכֶם
2fp	עֵינְכֶן	חֻקְּכֶן	מַרְאֲכֶן
3mp	עֵינָם	חֻקָּם	מַרְאָם
3fp	עֵינָן	חֻקָּן	מַרְאָן

PLURAL	(Dual)		
absolute	עֵינַיִם	חֻקִּים	מַרְאִים
construct	עֵינֵי	חֻקֵּי	מַרְאֵי
w. 1cs suffix	עֵינַי	חֻקַּי	מַרְאַי
2ms	עֵינֶ֫יךָ	חֻקֶּ֫יךָ	מַרְאֶ֫יךָ
2fs	עֵינַ֫יִךְ	חֻקַּ֫יִךְ	מַרְאַ֫יִךְ
3ms	עֵינָיו	חֻקָּיו	מַרְאָיו
3fs	עֵינֶ֫יהָ	חֻקֶּ֫יהָ	מַרְאֶ֫יהָ
1cp	עֵינֵ֫ינוּ	חֻקֵּ֫ינוּ	מַרְאֵ֫ינוּ
2mp	עֵינֵיכֶם	חֻקֵּיכֶם	מַרְאֵיכֶם
2fp	עֵינֵיכֶן	חֻקֵּיכֶן	מַרְאֵיכֶן
3mp	עֵינֵיהֶם	חֻקֵּיהֶם	מַרְאֵיהֶם
3fp	עֵינֵיהֶן	חֻקֵּיהֶן	מַרְאֵיהֶן

5

Chart 102: Irregular Nouns

SINGULAR

	"father"	"brother"	"sister"	"man"
absolute	אָב	אָח	אָחוֹת	אִישׁ
construct	אֲבִי	אֲחִי	אֲחוֹת	אִישׁ
w. 1cs suffix	אָבִי	אָחִי	אֲחוֹתִי	אִישִׁי
2ms	אָבִיךָ	אָחִיךָ	אֲחוֹתְךָ	
2fs	אָבִיךְ	אָחִיךְ	אֲחוֹתֵךְ	אִישֵׁךְ
3ms	אָבִיו	אָחִיו	אֲחוֹתוֹ	אִישׁוֹ
3fs	אָבִיהָ	אָחִיהָ	אֲחוֹתָהּ	אִישָׁהּ
1cp	אָבִינוּ	אָחִינוּ	אֲחוֹתֵנוּ	
2mp	אֲבִיכֶם	אֲחִיכֶם		
2fp	אֲבִיכֶן			
3mp	אֲבִיהֶם	אֲחִיהֶם	אֲחוֹתָם	
3fp	אֲבִיהֶן			

PLURAL

5

	"father"	"brother"	"sister"	"man"
absolute	אָבוֹת	אַחִים		אֲנָשִׁים
construct	אֲבוֹת	אֲחֵי		אַנְשֵׁי
w. 1cs suffix	אֲבוֹתַי	אַחַי	אַחְיוֹתַי	אֲנָשַׁי
2ms	אֲבוֹתֶיךָ	אַחֶיךָ		אֲנָשֶׁיךָ
2fs	אֲבוֹתַיִךְ	אַחַיִךְ	אֲחוֹתַיִךְ	
3ms	אֲבוֹתָיו	אֶחָיו	אַחְיוֹתָיו	אֲנָשָׁיו
3fs		אַחֶיהָ		אֲנָשֶׁיהָ
1cp	אֲבוֹתֵינוּ	אַחֵינוּ		אֲנָשֵׁינוּ
2mp	אֲבוֹתֵיכֶם	אֲחֵיכֶם	אֲחוֹתֵיכֶם	
2fp				
3mp	אֲבוֹתֵיהֶם / אֲבוֹתָם	אֲחֵיהֶם	אֲחִיוֹתֵיהֶם	אַנְשֵׁיהֶם
3fp				אַנְשֵׁיהֶן

Chart 105: Irregular Nouns

SINGULAR	"city"	"mouth"	"head"	"name"
absolute	עִיר	פֶּה	רֹאשׁ	שֵׁם
construct	עִיר	פִּי	רֹאשׁ	שֵׁם
w. 1cs suffix	עִירִי	פִּי	רֹאשִׁי	שְׁמִי
2ms	עִירְךָ	פִּיךָ	רֹאשְׁךָ	שִׁמְךָ
2fs				שְׁמֵךְ
3ms	עִירוֹ	פִּיו, פִּיהוּ	רֹאשׁוֹ	שְׁמוֹ
3ms	עִירָהּ	פִּיהָ	רֹאשָׁהּ	שְׁמָהּ
1cp		פִּינוּ	רֹאשֵׁנוּ	שְׁמֵנוּ
2mp		פִּיכֶם	רֹאשְׁכֶם	שִׁמְכֶם
2fp				
3mp	עִירָם	פִּיהֶם	רֹאשָׁם	שְׁמָם
3fp		פִּיהֶן	רֹאשָׁן	

PLURAL	"city"	"mouth"	"head"	"name"
absolute	עָרִים	פִּיוֹת	רָאשִׁים	שֵׁמוֹת
construct	עָרֵי		רָאשֵׁי	שְׁמוֹת
w. 1cs suffix	עָרַי			
2ms	עָרֶיךָ			
2fs	עָרַיִךְ			
3ms	עָרָיו		רָאשָׁיו	
3fs	עָרֶיהָ		רָאשֶׁיהָ	
1cp	עָרֵינוּ		רָאשֵׁינוּ	
2cp	עָרֵיכֶם		רָאשֵׁיכֶם	
2fp				
3mp	עָרֵיהֶם		רָאשֵׁיהֶם	שְׁמוֹתָם
3fp			רָאשֵׁיהֶן	שְׁמוֹתָן

5

Chart 106: The Numerals

The Cardinals (1-10)

	with masculine nouns		with feminine nouns	
	abs.	const.	abs.	const.
1	אֶחָד	אַחַד	אַחַת	אַחַת
2	שְׁנַיִם	שְׁנֵי	שְׁתַּיִם	שְׁתֵּי
3	שְׁלֹשָׁה	שְׁלֹשֶׁת	שָׁלֹשׁ	שְׁלֹשׁ
4	אַרְבָּעָה	אַרְבַּעַת	אַרְבַּע	אַרְבַּע
5	חֲמִשָּׁה	חֲמֵשֶׁת	חָמֵשׁ	חֲמֵשׁ
6	שִׁשָּׁה	שֵׁשֶׁת	שֵׁשׁ	שֵׁשׁ
7	שִׁבְעָה	שִׁבְעַת	שֶׁבַע	שְׁבַע
8	שְׁמֹנָה	שְׁמֹנַת	שְׁמֹנֶה	שְׁמֹנֶה
9	תִּשְׁעָה	תִּשְׁעַת	תֵּשַׁע	תְּשַׁע
10	עֲשָׂרָה	עֲשֶׂרֶת	עֶשֶׂר	עֶשֶׂר

The Ordinals (1st-10th)

	masc.	fem.
1st	רִאשׁוֹן	רִאשֹׁנָה
2nd	שֵׁנִי	שֵׁנִית
3rd	שְׁלִישִׁי	שְׁלִישִׁית
4th	רְבִיעִי	רְבִיעִית
5th	חֲמִישִׁי	חֲמִישִׁית
6th	שִׁשִּׁי	שִׁשִּׁית
7th	שְׁבִיעִי	שְׁבִיעִית
8th	שְׁמִינִי	שְׁמִינִית
9th	תְּשִׁיעִי	תְּשִׁיעִית
10th	עֲשִׂירִי	עֲשִׂירִית

The Cardinals (11-19)

	with masculine nouns	with feminine nouns
11	עַשְׁתֵּי עָשָׂר, אַחַד עָשָׂר	עַשְׁתֵּי עֶשְׂרֵה, אַחַת עֶשְׂרֵה
12	שְׁנֵים עָשָׂר, שְׁנֵי עָשָׂר	שְׁתֵּים עֶשְׂרֵה, שְׁתֵּי עֶשְׂרֵה
13	שְׁלֹשָׁה עָשָׂר	שְׁלֹשׁ עֶשְׂרֵה
14	אַרְבָּעָה עָשָׂר	אַרְבַּע עֶשְׂרֵה
15	חֲמִשָּׁה עָשָׂר	חֲמֵשׁ עֶשְׂרֵה

(Numbers 16-19 follow the same pattern.)

The Larger Cardinals (20-10,000)

20	עֶשְׂרִים	300	שְׁלֹשׁ מֵאוֹת
21	אֶחָד וְעֶשְׂרִים	400	אַרְבַּע מֵאוֹת
30	שְׁלֹשִׁים	500	חֲמֵשׁ מֵאוֹת
40	אַרְבָּעִים	600	שֵׁשׁ מֵאוֹת
50	חֲמִשִּׁים	700	שְׁבַע מֵאוֹת
60	שִׁשִּׁים	800	שְׁמֹנֶה מֵאוֹת
70	שִׁבְעִים	900	תְּשַׁע מֵאוֹת
80	שְׁמֹנִים	1000	אֶלֶף, אֶלֶף אֶחָד
90	תִּשְׁעִים	2000	שְׁנֵי אֲלָפִים
100	מֵאָה, מֵאָה אַחַת	3000	שְׁלֹשֶׁת אֲלָפִים
200	שְׁתֵּי מֵאוֹת	10,000	רְבָבָה, עֲשֶׂרֶת אֲלָפִים

Chart 105: Irregular Nouns

SINGULAR	"city"	"mouth"	"head"	"name"
absolute	עִיר	פֶּה	רֹאשׁ	שֵׁם
construct	עִיר	פִּי	רֹאשׁ	שֵׁם
w. 1cs suffix	עִירִי	פִּי	רֹאשִׁי	שְׁמִי
2ms	עִירְךָ	פִּיךָ	רֹאשְׁךָ	שִׁמְךָ
2fs				שְׁמֵךְ
3ms	עִירוֹ	פִּיו, פִּיהוּ	רֹאשׁוֹ	שְׁמוֹ
3ms	עִירָהּ	פִּיהָ	רֹאשָׁהּ	שְׁמָהּ
1cp		פִּינוּ	רֹאשֵׁנוּ	שְׁמֵנוּ
2mp		פִּיכֶם	רֹאשְׁכֶם	שִׁמְכֶם
2fp				
3mp	עִירָם	פִּיהֶם	רֹאשָׁם	שְׁמָם
3fp		פִּיהֶן	רֹאשָׁן	

PLURAL				
absolute	עָרִים	פִּיוֹת	רָאשִׁים	שֵׁמוֹת
construct	עָרֵי		רָאשֵׁי	שְׁמוֹת
w. 1cs suffix	עָרַי			
2ms	עָרֶיךָ			
2fs	עָרַיִךְ			
3ms	עָרָיו		רָאשָׁיו	
3fs	עָרֶיהָ		רָאשֶׁיהָ	
1cp	עָרֵינוּ		רָאשֵׁינוּ	
2cp	עָרֵיכֶם		רָאשֵׁיכֶם	
2fp				
3mp	עָרֵיהֶם		רָאשֵׁיהֶם	שְׁמוֹתָם
3fp			רָאשֵׁיהֶן	שְׁמוֹתָן

The Cardinals (1-10)

	with masculine nouns abs.	const.	with feminine nouns abs.	const.
1	אֶחָד	אַחַד	אַחַת	אַחַת
2	שְׁנַיִם	שְׁנֵי	שְׁתַּיִם	שְׁתֵּי
3	שְׁלֹשָׁה	שְׁלֹשֶׁת	שָׁלֹשׁ	שְׁלֹשׁ
4	אַרְבָּעָה	אַרְבַּעַת	אַרְבַּע	אַרְבַּע
5	חֲמִשָּׁה	חֲמֵשֶׁת	חָמֵשׁ	חֲמֵשׁ
6	שִׁשָּׁה	שֵׁשֶׁת	שֵׁשׁ	שֵׁשׁ
7	שִׁבְעָה	שִׁבְעַת	שֶׁבַע	שְׁבַע
8	שְׁמֹנָה	שְׁמֹנַת	שְׁמֹנֶה	שְׁמֹנֶה
9	תִּשְׁעָה	תִּשְׁעַת	תֵּשַׁע	תְּשַׁע
10	עֲשָׂרָה	עֲשֶׂרֶת	עֶשֶׂר	עֶשֶׂר

The Ordinals (1st-10th)

	masc.	fem.
1st	רִאשׁוֹן	רִאשֹׁנָה
2nd	שֵׁנִי	שֵׁנִית
3rd	שְׁלִישִׁי	שְׁלִישִׁית
4th	רְבִיעִי	רְבִיעִית
5th	חֲמִישִׁי	חֲמִישִׁית
6th	שִׁשִּׁי	שִׁשִּׁית
7th	שְׁבִיעִי	שְׁבִיעִית
8th	שְׁמִינִי	שְׁמִינִית
9th	תְּשִׁיעִי	תְּשִׁיעִית
10th	עֲשִׂירִי	עֲשִׂירִית

The Cardinals (11-19)

	with masculine nouns	with feminine nouns
11	אַחַד עָשָׂר, עַשְׁתֵּי עָשָׂר	אַחַת עֶשְׂרֵה, עַשְׁתֵּי עֶשְׂרֵה
12	שְׁנֵי עָשָׂר, שְׁנַיִם עָשָׂר	שְׁתֵּי עֶשְׂרֵה, שְׁתֵּים עֶשְׂרֵה
13	שְׁלֹשָׁה עָשָׂר	שְׁלֹשׁ עֶשְׂרֵה
14	אַרְבָּעָה עָשָׂר	אַרְבַּע עֶשְׂרֵה
15	חֲמִשָּׁה עָשָׂר	חֲמֵשׁ עֶשְׂרֵה

(Numbers 16-19 follow the same pattern.)

5

The Larger Cardinals (20-10,000)

20	עֶשְׂרִים	300	שְׁלֹשׁ מֵאוֹת
21	אֶחָד וְעֶשְׂרִים	400	אַרְבַּע מֵאוֹת
30	שְׁלֹשִׁים	500	חֲמֵשׁ מֵאוֹת
40	אַרְבָּעִים	600	שֵׁשׁ מֵאוֹת
50	חֲמִשִּׁים	700	שְׁבַע מֵאוֹת
60	שִׁשִּׁים	800	שְׁמֹנֶה מֵאוֹת
70	שִׁבְעִים	900	תְּשַׁע מֵאוֹת
80	שְׁמֹנִים	1000	אֶלֶף, אֶלֶף אֶחָד
90	תִּשְׁעִים	2000	שְׁנֵי אֲלָפִים
100	מֵאָה, מֵאָה אַחַת	3000	שְׁלֹשֶׁת אֲלָפִים
200	שְׁתֵּי מֵאוֹת	10,000	רְבָבָה, עֲשֶׂרֶת אֲלָפִים

CHAPTER IV: THE STUDY OF DEUTERONOMY 5:1-22

The format of the study of Deuteronomy 5 will be the same as for Genesis 12. Follow the text of BHS. All new words will be listed, but you are to look them up in the lexicon for their basic definitions.

DEUTERONOMY 5:1

142.	מֹשֶׁה	(proper noun)
143.	יִשְׂרָאֵל	(proper noun)
▶	אֲלֵהֶם	Written defectively for אֲלֵיהֶם.
**	קְֿ͏ּ◻◻◻	(the pointing of the Qal imperative 2ms)

Note 107A: Qal Imperative

The **Qal imperative** 2ms of the model verb is קְטֹל -- "kill!" **REVIEW Note 92B** and see the verb synopsis in **Chart 72**.

144.	חֹק
145.	מִשְׁפָּט
146.	אָנֹכִי

This is an alternative form of the 1cs independent personal pronoun אֲנִי. Cf. Word 45.

**	◻◻◻	(the clue pointing of the Qal active participle)

Note 107B: Qal Active Participle

A Holem between the first and second root consonants is the sign of the **Qal active participle**. The form of the model verb (masc. sg.) is קֹטֵל -- "killing." See **Chart 72**.

Note 107C: Noun/Pronoun Plus Participle

A noun or pronoun followed by a participle is the closest Hebrew comes to expressing present tense. This construction denotes *present continuous action* relative to the time of the context. The phrase אָנֹכִי דֹּבֵר in this context would be rendered: "I (am) speaking." This phrase is also a **nominal clause** with the verb הָיָה understood. **REVIEW Note 57C.**

▶   דִּבֶּר   The pf. and impf. of the verb דבר are regularly in the Piel stem. See **Word 98**. But the verb appears a few times as a participle in the Qal. +

147.   אֹזֶן

               See **Chart 100** for the form of this type of Seogolate noun.

148.   למד

               Learn both the Qal and Piel translations.

**   ‐‐‐תֶּם   (affix)   *you*   (2mp of the perfect)
                     See **Chart 23A**.

Note 108A: Added Syllable Causes Vowel Reduction

The addition of a *stressed* syllable to the end of a word is likely to cause a *reduction* of a vowel toward the beginning of the word. **REVIEW Note 32B.** This is especially true if a long vowel appears in an open syllable two or more syllables before the main stress. A Qamets in this position is reduced to a Sheva. Compare the kinds of added syllables that receive the main stress:

1. the noun/adjective endings: דְּבָרִים from דָּבָר

2. most suffixes: אָזְנֵיכֶם from אֹזֶן

3. the 2mp affix (not affixes in general):   לְמַדְתֶּם from לָמַד

Thus the form וּלְמַדְתֶּם is Qal pf., for the clue Qamets of the Qal pf. under the first root consonant is present in the form of the reduced vowel Sheva caused by the stressed affix. The 2fp affix is also stressed.

149.   שָׁמַר

               This verb has a wider semantic range than any one English word can capture. Learn several meanings.

▶   וּשְׁמַרְתֶּם   **REVIEW Note 108A.**

▶   לַעֲשֹׂתָם   Written defectively for לַעֲשׂוֹתָם. This is a verb form with a preposition and a suffix. What form of the verb does the "rule of thumb" tell you it is? What suffix is it?

| Note 109A: Verbs Ending in He |

Verbs whose final root letter is He have תֹ__ as the ending of their
infinitive construct. Compare:

עָשָׂה -- "he did"   עֲשׂוֹת -- "to do"

DEUTERONOMY 5:2

**   נוּ____   (suffix)   *us, our*   (1cp)
                     See **Chart 24A**.

150.   כרת

| Note 109B: Prepositions with Suffixes |

Several common prepositions, including עִם, אֶת, and תַּחַת, have a
Dagesh Forte in the final consonant before a suffix. Compare:

עִמִּי -- "with me"   תַּחְתֶּיךָ -- "instead of you"
עִמָּנוּ -- "with us"   אִתִּי -- "with me"

151.   בְּרִית

חֹרֵב

DEUTERONOMY 5:3

▶   אֲבוֹתֵינוּ   See **Chart 102** for the form of this irregular noun.

▶   אֶת־אֲבוֹתֵינוּ   **REVIEW Note 39A**.

▶   כִּי   Here a strong contrast is denoted by the word כִּי : "but."
                     REVIEW Note 56A. The following clause has several short,
                     choppy phrases for emphasis.

152.   אֲנַחְנוּ   (independent personal pronoun)   +

פֹה

| Note 109C: כֹּל, כָּל־ with Suffixes |

The word כֹּל, כָּל־ with suffixes becomes כֻּל__.

153.   חַי   II

DEUTERONOMY 5:4

154.   פָּנִים   +

See under * פָּנֶה in the lexicon.

▶   פָּנִים בְּפָנִים   How does the English idiom differ?

155.   תָּוֶךְ

What is the construct form?

DEUTERONOMY 5:5

156.   עָמַד

▶   אָנֹכִי עֹמֵד   REVIEW Notes 107B and C.

157.   בֵּין

See under * בֵּין in the lexicon.

158.   עֵת

▶   בָּעֵת הַהִוא   REVIEW Notes 94A and 60B.

**   הַסְּפִרִים   (the clue pointing of the Hifil infinitive construct)

Note 110A: Hifil Infinitive Construct

The **Hifil infinitive construct** of the model verb is הַקְטִיל -- "to cause to kill." See **Chart 72**.

▶   לְהַגִּיד   Note the assimilated nun for the root and the clue pointing for the stem. This verb has a simple meaning in this stem.

Note 110B: Assimilated Nun

A Dagesh Forte in the first root consonant that appears in a verb form is an assimilated Nun. If only two root letters are present, the Nun is the initial Nun of the root. But if all three root letters are present, the Nun is the sign of the Nifal stem. A Dagesh Forte can only serve one purpose in a particular form. It cannot be both a missing root letter and the stem sign.

▶   יְרֵאתֶם   REVIEW Note **108A** for the Sheva and Note **57B** for the Tsere. What stem is this verb form?

Note 111A: פָּנִים with Prepositions

The construct form of פָּנִים combines with prepositions to form idiomatic expressions. The most common ones are these:

לִפְנֵי -- "before, in the presence of"

מִפְנֵי -- "from before, from the presence of, because of"

עַל־פְּנֵי -- "before, upon"

▶ עֲלֵיהֶם **REVIEW Notes 63A and 108A.**

▶ לֵאמֹר What form of the verb with a preposition is this? Without the preposition, the inf. const. of this verb would be אֱמֹר, but with the preposition, the Alef quiesces. Cf. לֵאלֹהִים in **Note 85C**.

Note 111B: Infinitive Construct

An infinitive construct can be translated in two ways depending on the context. E.g., לֵאמֹר might be translated either "to say" or "saying." It is very common for לֵאמֹר to introduce direct quotations and to be translated "saying."

DEUTERONOMY 5:6

The Decalogue has a double accentuation pattern due to differing traditions of verse division. The Masoretes maintained both traditions by giving some words two accents on the stressed syllable. Notice, for example, that the last word of v. 6 has both the Atnah (□) to mark the middle of a verse and the Silluq (□) to mark the end of the verse: עֲבָדִים.

▶ אָנֹכִי יהוה אֱלֹהֶיךָ This is a nominal clause, but the verb הִיה could be inserted at two places, yielding slightly different meanings.

Note 111C: Relative Particle

אֲשֶׁר is a relative particle that very often is equivalent to the English relative pronoun. But it has broader usages as well. Many times, after rendering the אֲשֶׁר clause literally, we must rephrase it into good English. Here, for example, the 1st person verb הוֹצֵאתִיךָ follows in the Hebrew, but English would require a 3rd person verb.

Note 112A: Verbs with Initial Yod

The verb form הוֹצֵאתִ֫יךָ has several identifiable elements. After stripping away the He as the sign of the Hifil, the affix as the pronominal subject, and the suffix as the object, it would appear that this verb's root was וצא. As a matter of fact, it was originally just that in an earlier stage of the language, but in biblical Hebrew the root of this type of verb has become **יצא** with an **initial Yod**. But the original Vav appears either as a consonant or as a vowel letter in most stems other than Qal. In the Hifil, such initial Yod verbs whose original first root letter was Vav have a Holem Vav (וֹ), or defectively just a Holem, in the position of the first root letter.

▶   עֲבָדֶ֫ים   Cf. מֶ֫לֶךְ in **Chart 100** for the pointing of this Segolate noun. Notice the double accents that are typical of the Decalogue.

DEUTERONOMY 5:7

▶   לֹא יִהְיֶה־לְךָ ◄   **REVIEW Note 95D**.

159.   אַחֵר   +

▶   עַל־פָּנָ֫י   **REVIEW Note 111A**.

Note 112B: Plural Nouns with 1cs Suffix

The 1cs suffix (י ָ) when added to a masc. pl. noun becomes
י ַ . The Hireq becomes a Patah. See **Chart 99** and compare:

דְּבָרִי   --   "my word"

דְּבָרַי   --   "my words"   (דְּבָרָ֫י in pause)

▶   עַל־פָּנָ֫י   This form has double pointing to take account of the two patterns of accentuation in the Decalogue. In one pattern, עַל־פָּנַי is *out of pause* and has a Patah Yod as the suffix with this plural noun. In the other pattern, עַל־פָּנָי is *in pause* and has a Qamets Yod as the suffix. The form in the text (עַל־פָּנָ֫י) retains both forms by adding the Patah after the Qamets, but only one vowel is to be pronounced.

DEUTERONOMY 5:8

Note 113A: Categorical Prohibition

We have seen that אַל with the jussive is simple prohibition: "Do not!"
REVIEW Note 55A. But לֹא with the imperfect is the strong
categorical prohibition: "You shall not!" The commandments are all
in the latter form.

Note 113B: Verbs with Initial Guttural and Final He

The Qal imperfect and Hifil imperfect of verbs that begin with a
guttural and end in He are identical. Both have a Patah under the
prefix because of the guttural first root letter and both have Segol He at
the end, since a final root letter He regularly has a Segol. **REVIEW
Note 66A.** In other words, the Qal impf. form תַּעֲשֶׂה appears to have
the clue pointing of the Hifil (Patah under the prefix and a 2nd class
vowel after the 2nd root consonant), but the presence of the initial
guttural and the final He makes the Qal have the same pointing as the
Hifil. Context alone can distinguish the two. Compare:

תַּעֲלֶה -- "you will go up" (Qal)

תַּעֲלֶה -- "you will bring, lead up" (cause to go up) (Hifil)

פֶּסֶל

תְּמוּנָה   (+ Ex 20:4)

160.   מַיִם

See **Chart 104** for the forms of this irregular noun.

Note 113C: שָׁמַיִם and מַיִם

The two nouns שָׁמַיִם and מַיִם, which appear to have dual endings
in the absolute state, are better understood as deriving from some old
plural termination. Thus there is no inherent "two-ness" in the meaning
of the words.

DEUTERONOMY 5:9

Note 113D: The Verb חוה

REVIEW Word 48. There is some disagreement as to how the form
תִּשְׁתַּחֲוֶה is to be explained. Older lexicons and some scholars today

derive it from the root שׁחה with a Tav "infix." Many others now take it from the root II חוה with a Shin-Tav as the sign of a unique stem (Eshtafal). Holladay curiously lists both roots. It appears that the verb חוה retains features of an earlier stage in the language.

161.	עבד	+
**	יָחֳסַם	(clue pointing of the Hofal imperfect)

Note 114A: Hofal Imperfect

The infrequent **Hofal stem** is the causative passive (the passive of the Hifil). The Hofal imperfect 3ms of the model verb is יָקְטַל -- "he will be caused to kill." Notice that the vowel of the prefix is Qamets Hatuf. See **Chart 72.**

▶	תָּעָבְדֵם	The stem is Hofal. See the lexicon for a suggested translation of the verb עבד in this stem. What is the final Mem?
162.	אֵל	V
##	קַנָּא	(+ Ex 20:5)
163.	פקד	
▶	פֹּקֵד	**REVIEW Note 107B.**
164.	עָוֹן	
		Notice carefully the placement of the Holem in this word. The Vav is a consonant followed by a Holem vowel. The distinction between וֹ and ֹו is not made in Holladay.
▶	אָבוֹת	See **Chart 102.**
##	שִׁלֵּשִׁים	+
##	רִבֵּעַ	+ **REVIEW Note 50C.**
165.	שׂנא	(+ Ex 20:5)
▶	לְשֹׂנְאָי	**REVIEW Note 107B.** This is a participle as the object of the preposition לְ (not an inf. const. as the "rule of thumb" might suggest). For the suffix, **REVIEW Note 112B.** Note that this is a pausal form with two accents. How are definite participles translated? **REVIEW Note 79B.**

DEUTERONOMY 5:10

166. חֶסֶד II (+ Ex 20:6)

167. אֶלֶף II

▸ אֲלָפִים See **Chart 100** for the Segolate nouns.

▸ לְאֹהֲבַי Cf. the form לְשֹׂנְאַי in v. 9.

168. מִצְוָה

A noun from the verb צוה. **REVIEW Note 91B**. The Vav in מִצְוָה is always a consonant and never a vowel letter.

▸ מִצְוֹתָו Written defectively for מִצְוֹוֹתָו. **REVIEW Note 80A**.

Note 115A: Written One Way, To Be Read Another

Although the Masoretes preserved the final Vav as it was *written* in the form מִצְוֹתָו, they included a marginal note (see the tiny letters מצותי in the margin above a Qof) that the form is to be *read* as מִצְוֹתָי. Written in the text is a 3ms suffix, but it should be read as a 1cs suffix. Cf. Ex 20:6. The vowels in the text actually go with the consonants in the margin!

DEUTERONOMY 5:11

\#\# שָׁוְא (+ Ex 20:7)

\#\# נקה

▸ יְנַקֶּה Note the clue pointing for the stem and the possible translations in this stem.

▸ אֵת אֲשֶׁר The אֲשֶׁר-clause is the direct object.

DEUTERONOMY 5:12

▸ שָׁמוֹר **REVIEW Notes 63B** and **87C**.

Note 115B: Infinitive Absolute

Besides the uses of the **infinitive absolute** in Note 63B, it may also stand alone. Then it merely puts forward emphatically the idea of the verb. Context must determine its particular force. Often it takes the place of an imperative, as the context here would suggest.

116

(Dt 5:12-13)

169.   שַׁבָּת   (+ Ex 20:8)

170.   קדשׁ   (+ Ex 20:8)

Note 116A: Piel Forms

An additional clue for the Piel: A Piel form has a Hireq under the first root consonant in perfect forms, but in all other branches it has a **Patah** under the first root letter. See **Chart 72**. Compare these Piel forms:

דִּבֶּר	(pf.)	יְנַקֶּה	(impf.)
צִוָּה	(pf.)	לְקַדְּשׁוֹ	(inf. cs.)
שִׁלַּח	(pf.)	כַּבֵּד	(impv.)

Note 116B: Consonantal Vav

A Vav with any pointing after it (even a Sheva) must be a consonant and cannot be a vowel letter. In the form צִוְּךָ the Vav has a Dagesh Forte (it is not the Shureq Vav vowel). What root, stem, and branch?

DEUTERONOMY 5:13

171.   שֵׁשׁ   +

What is the fem. sg. const.?

Note 116C: Numbers 3 - 10

The numbers 3 through 10 *disagree* in gender with the noun they modify; i.e., a fem. form of the number is used with masc. nouns and vice versa. See the numbers in **Chart 106**. A number may stand as a construct before the noun or as an absolute either before or after it. Compare:

שֵׁשֶׁת בָּנִים -- "six sons" (the number is fem.)

שֵׁשׁ בָּנוֹת -- "six daughters" (the number is masc.)

▸   יָמִים   Learn not to confuse the plurals of יָם and יוֹם. The plural of יָם is יַמִּים and the plural of יוֹם is יָמִים. See **Chart 104**.

Note 117A: Use of Consecutive Forms

Successive actions in the same time frame that follow from an *imperfect* verb are continued by the **perfect consecutive**. Such is the case in the phrase תַּעֲבֹד וְעָשִׂיתָ.

Conversely, successive actions that follow from a *perfect* verb are continued by the **imperfect consecutive**.

172.   מְלָאכָה

DEUTERONOMY 5:14

##	שְׁבִיעִי	
▸	וְיוֹם הַשְּׁבִיעִי שַׁבָּת	A nominal clause including a construct chain.
173.	בַּת	

        See **Chart 103** for the forms of this irregular noun. Notice the plural and the form with suffixes.

▸	וְעַבְדְּךָ־	See **Chart 100** for the Segolate nouns.
##	אָמָה	
##	שׁוֹר	
▸	וַחֲמֹרְךָ	Written defectively for וַחֲמוֹרְךָ.
174.	בְּהֵמָה	+
##	גֵּר	
175.	נוּחַ	I

Note 117B: Compound Subjects

Whenever there is a compound subject (a series of two or more), the verb is usually singular. The subject of the verb is grammatically only the first noun of the series. In the phrase יָנוּחַ עַבְדְּךָ וַאֲמָתְךָ, the verb is 3ms to coincide with the first of the two subjects.

176.   כְּמוֹ

Note 117C: Preposition כְּ

The preposition ____ כְּ with most suffixes becomes __ כְּמוֹ.

DEUTERONOMY 5:15

177.	זכר	+
▶	וַיֹּצִאֲךָ	Written defectively for וַיּוֹצִיאֲךָ. **REVIEW Note 112A**.
##	חָזָק	
▶	בְּיָד חֲזָקָה	**REVIEW Note 42A**. Notice the gender of the adjective.
##	זְרֹוֹעַ	
**	סָפוּם	(the pointing of the Qal passive participle)

Note 118A: Qal Passive Participle

In an earlier stage of the language there was a Qal passive stem. But in biblical Hebrew the simple passive has been largely assumed by the Nifal. **REVIEW Note 95B**. The most common survival of the original Qal passive is the participle. The **Qal passive participle** of the model verb is קָטוּל -- "killed." See **Chart 72**. The form נְטוּיָה illustrates the reduction of the Qamets in the clue pointing to a Sheva because of the added Qamets He ending (**REVIEW Note 108A**) and the retention of an original Yod as a last root letter in verbs that end in He (**REVIEW Note 63A**). Remember that participles are verbal adjectives.

178.	כֵּן	II
▶	עַל־כֵּן	An idiom: "therefore" or "this is why."
▶	לַעֲשׂוֹת	**REVIEW Note 109A**.

DEUTERONOMY 5:16

**	סַסֵס	(the clue pointing of the Piel imperative)

Note 118B: Piel Imperative

The Piel imperfect 2ms of the model verb is תְּקַטֵּל -- "you will slaughter"), so that the **Piel imperative** 2ms is קַטֵּל -- "slaughter!" **REVIEW Note 92B** and see **Chart 72**. Notice the Patah under the first root consonant in Piel forms other than perfect. **REVIEW Note 116A**.

179.   כבד   (+ Ex 20:12)

A stative verb whose Qal pointing is כָּבֵד. **REVIEW Note 57B.**

Note 119A: Stative Verbs in the Piel

Verbs with a stative meaning in the Qal are **factive** in the Piel. Compare:

Qal		**Piel**	
מָלֵא	-- "he was full"	מִלֵּא	-- "he made full, he filled"
טָמֵא	-- "he was unclean"	טִמֵּא	-- "he made unclean, he defiled"
כָּבֵד	-- "he was heavy"	כִּבֵּד	-- "he made heavy, he honored"

▸   אָבִיךָ   **REVIEW Note 48C** and see **Chart 102.**

180.   אֵם

▸   אִמֶּךָ   For the accent in this pausal form, see **Note 119C** below.

▸   צִוְּךָ   **REVIEW Notes 116A** and **B.**

ארך

▸   יַאֲרִיכֻן   Written defectively for יַאֲרִיכוּן. Before parsing the verb, see the following Note for the final Nun. **REVIEW Note 93B.**

Note 119B: Paragogic Nun

Over 300 times in the Hebrew Bible, mainly in the older literature, the 2nd and 3rd masc. pl. prefixes of the imperfect appear with an added final Nun: תָ___וּן (2mp) and יָ___וּן (3mp). This is called the **paragogic Nun**. It may once have denoted emphasis, but it usually has no significance.

▸   יָמֶיךָ   See **Chart 104.**

▸   יִיטַב   **REVIEW Word 127** and **Note 93A.**

Note 119C: Pausal Forms

Pausal forms occur when a word has one of the main accents of the sentence. **REVIEW Note 61C.** Besides the Atnah (◌) and the Silluq (◌), another major accent that occasionally takes pausal forms is the

120

(Dt 5:16-21)

Zaqef Qaton (◌ֽ). This accent usually divides each verse half into halves. Compare:

לְךָ -- "to you" (2ms)

לָךְ -- "to you" (2fs)

לָֽךְ, לָ֫ךְ, or לָ֤ךְ -- "to you" (2ms in pause)

DEUTERONOMY 5:17-20

##	רצח	
##	נאף	(+ Ex 20:14)
##	גנב	
181.	ענה	I
▶	תַּעֲנֶה	**REVIEW Note 113B.**
182.	רֵעַ	II
▶	בְּרֵעֲךָ	An adversative use of בְּ : "against."
##	עֵד	+
##	שָׁוְא	+

> **Note 120A: Construct Chains**

Hebrew has relatively few adjectives. The construct chain, however, often expresses what in English would be an adjectival phrase. Examples:

עֵד שָׁוְא -- "a witness of falsehood" = "a false witness"

אִישׁ אֱלֹהִים -- "a man of God" = "a godly man"

יוֹם הַשְּׁבִיעִי -- "day of the seventh" = "the seventh day"

DEUTERONOMY 5:21

##	חמד	(+ Ex 20:17)
▶	אֵשֶׁת	See **Chart 103.**

**   יִתְ◻◻◻   (the clue pointing of the Hitpael imperfect)

Note 121A: Hitpael Imperfect

The Hitpael imperfect should have both the stem sign ‗‗‗הִתְ and the prefix. But the He of the stem sign falls away and the prefix stands with the Tav before the verb root as ‗‗‗יִתְ (3ms). Thus a verb form with a Tav between the prefix and the root is a Hitpael. Like the Piel, the Hitpael also has a Dagesh Forte to double the middle root consonant. The **Hitpael imperfect** 3ms of the model verb is יִתְקַטֵּל -- "he will kill himself." See **Chart 72**.

##	אוה	
183.	שָׂדֶה	
▶	שָׂדֵהוּ	The He of the noun has fallen away before הוּ‗‗‗‗. Cf. מַרְאֶה in **Chart 101**.
##	אָמָה	
##	שׁוֹר	
▶	וְכֹל אֲשֶׁר לְרֵעֶךָ ◀	**REVIEW Note 95D**.

DEUTERONOMY 5:22

184.	קָהָל	
##	עָנָן	I
##	עֲרָפֶל	
▶	קוֹל גָּדוֹל	**REVIEW Note 95C**.
185.	יסף	
186.	כתב	
▶	שְׁנֵי	See **Chart 106** for the numbers.
##	לוּחַ	
▶	לֻחֹת	Written defectively in two places.

187.   אֶבֶן

▸   לֻחֹת אֲבָנִים   **REVIEW Note 120A.**

▸   וַיִּתְּנֵם   If Mem is the suffix, what is the root?

Note 122A: Prepositions with Suffixes

As we have seen, many prepositions have a "meaningless" Yod before the suffixes (**REVIEW Note 29B**).   Actually, these prepositions attach suffixes on the analogy of plural nouns, since the prepositions were themselves originally nouns.   Compare:

דְּבָרָיו	--	"his words"	אֵלָיו	--	"to him"
דְּבָרַי	--	"my words"	אֵלַי	--	"to me"
עֵינֵיכֶם	--	"your eyes"	בֵּינֵיכֶם	--	"between you"

The 1cs suffix with plural nouns (י ַ ּ) becomes י ָ ּ in pausal forms, as is the case also in the form אֵלָי.

PRONOUNS AND PREPOSITIONS

On the next pages are charts of the independent personal pronouns, the demonstrative adjectives, and a dozen of the most common prepositions with suffixes. The sign of the definite direct object is given twice, once as the objective forms of the personal pronouns in Chart 124A and again for comparison with the preposition אֶת־ in Chart 125.

Chart 123A: Independent Personal Pronouns

	As the Subject			As the Object
				(sign of definite direct object with suffixes)
1cs	אָנֹכִי, אֲנִי	*I*	1cs	אֹתִי	*me*
2ms	אַתָּה	*you*	2ms	אֹתְךָ	*you*
2fs	אַתְּ	*you*	2fs	אֹתָךְ	*you*
3ms	הוּא	*he, it*	3ms	אֹתוֹ	*him, it*
3fs	הִיא	*she, it*	3fs	אֹתָהּ	*her, it*
1cp	אֲנַ֫חְנוּ	*we*	1cp	אֹתָ֫נוּ	*us*
2mp	אַתֶּם	*you*	2mp	אֶתְכֶם	*you*
2fp	אַתֵּן	*you*	2fp	אֶתְכֶן	*you*
3mp	הֵ֫מָּה, הֵם	*they*	3mp	אֶתְהֶם, אֹתָם	*them*
3fp	הֵ֫נָּה, הֵן	*they*	3fp	אֶתְהֶן, אֹתָן	*them*

Chart 123B: Demonstrative Adjectives/Pronouns

6

	"this, these"			"that, those"
				Third person subjective personal pronouns serve also as the demonstrative adjective/pronoun "that, those."
ms	זֶה	*this*	ms	הוּא	*that*
fs	זֹאת	*this*	fs	הִיא	*that*
cp	אֵ֫לֶּה	*these*	mp	הֵ֫מָּה, הֵם	*those*
			fp	הֵ֫נָּה, הֵן	*those*

Chart 124: Prepositions with Suffixes

Preposition	בְּ	לְ	כְּ	מִן
w. 1cs suffix	בִּי	לִי	כָּמֹונִי	מִמֶּֽנִּי
2ms	בְּךָ	לְךָ	כָּמֹוךָ	מִמְּךָ
2fs	בָּךְ	לָךְ	כָּמֹוךְ	מִמֵּךְ
3ms	בֹּו	לֹו	כָּמֹוהוּ	מִמֶּֽנּוּ
3fs	בָּהּ	לָהּ	כָּמֹוהָ	מִמֶּֽנָּה
1cp	בָּֽנוּ	לָֽנוּ	כָּמֹונוּ	מִמֶּֽנּוּ
2mp	בָּכֶם	לָכֶם	כָּכֶם	מִכֶּם
2fp	בָּכֶן	לָכֶן	כָּכֶן	מִכֶּן
3mp	בָּהֶם, בָּם	לָהֶם	כָּהֶם	מֵהֶם
3fp	בָּהֶן	לָהֶן	כָּהֵֽנָּה, כָּהֵן	מֵהֵֽנָּה, מֵהֶן

Preposition	אֶל־	עַל	עַד	עִם
w. 1cs suffix	אֵלַי	עָלַי	עָדַי	עִמָּדִי, עִמִּי
2ms	אֵלֶיךָ	עָלֶיךָ	עָדֶיךָ	עִמְּךָ
2fs	אֵלַיִךְ	עָלַיִךְ	עָדַיִךְ	עִמָּךְ
3ms	אֵלָיו	עָלָיו	עָדָיו	עִמֹּו
3fs	אֵלֶיהָ	עָלֶיהָ	עָדֶיהָ	עִמָּהּ
1cp	אֵלֵֽינוּ	עָלֵֽינוּ	עָדֵֽינוּ	עִמָּֽנוּ
2mp	אֲלֵיכֶם	עֲלֵיכֶם	עֲדֵיכֶם	עִמָּכֶם
2fp	אֲלֵיכֶן	עֲלֵיכֶן	עֲדֵיכֶן	עִמָּכֶן
3mp	אֲלֵיהֶם	עֲלֵיהֶם	עֲדֵיהֶם	עִמָּם
3fp	אֲלֵיהֶן	עֲלֵיהֶן	עֲדֵיהֶן	עִמָּן

6

Chart 125: Prepositions with Suffixes

Preposition	בֵּין	אַחַר, אַחֲרֵי	תַּחַת
w. 1cs suffix	בֵּינִי	אַחֲרַי	תַּחְתַּי
2ms	בֵּינְךָ	אַחֲרֶיךָ	תַּחְתֶּיךָ
2fs	בֵּינֵךְ	אַחֲרַיִךְ	תַּחְתַּיִךְ
3ms	בֵּינוֹ	אַחֲרָיו	תַּחְתָּיו
3fs	בֵּינָהּ	אַחֲרֶיהָ	תַּחְתֶּיהָ
1cp	בֵּינֵינוּ	אַחֲרֵינוּ	תַּחְתֵּינוּ
2mp	בֵּינֵיכֶם	אַחֲרֵיכֶם	תַּחְתֵּיכֶם
2fp	בֵּינֵיכֶן	אַחֲרֵיכֶן	תַּחְתֵּיכֶן
3mp	בֵּינֵיהֶם	אַחֲרֵיהֶם	תַּחְתֵּיהֶם
3fp	בֵּינֵיהֶן	אַחֲרֵיהֶן	תַּחְתֵּיהֶן

Preposition "with"

אֵת, אֶת־

w. 1cs suffix	אִתִּי	with me
2ms	אִתְּךָ	with you
2fs	אִתָּךְ	with you
3ms	אִתּוֹ	with him, it
3fs	אִתָּהּ	with her, it
1cp	אִתָּנוּ	with us
2mp	אִתְּכֶם	with you
2fp	אִתְּכֶן	with you
3mp	אִתָּם	with them
3fp	אִתָּן	with them

Definite Direct Object Sign

אֵת, אֶת־

	אֹתִי	me
	אֹתְךָ	you
	אֹתָךְ	you
	אֹתוֹ	him, it
	אֹתָהּ	her, it
	אֹתָנוּ	us
	אֶתְכֶם	you
	אֶתְכֶן	you
	אֹתָם, אֶתְהֶם	them
	אֹתָן, אֶתְהֶן	them

6

THE CLASSIFICATION OF HEBREW VERBS

Hebrew verbs are classified for purposes of analysis according to the strength or weakness of their root letters. A verb is considered *weak* if it has one or more of the following characteristics that produce changes in various forms:

1. the guttural consonants (אההחע)
2. initial or middle Resh
3. initial Yod or Nun
4. the vowel letters (הוי)

If a verb has none of these letters, it is called a *strong* verb, such as the model verb קטל. The Begadkefat consonants are all strong letters. Strong verbs have regular pointing in all their forms. Most verbs in Hebrew, however, are weak.

Weak verbs are classified by designating 1) the weak letter and 2) its position in the verb. On the analogy of the verb פעל (used in very early Hebrew grammar as a model verb), the *first* root consonant of any verb is called its **Pe** letter, the *middle* letter its **Ayin** letter, and the *final* letter its **Lamed** letter. For example, a verb such as עמד is classified as a **Pe guttural** verb, since its only weak letter is the guttural Ayin, which appears as its Pe letter, i.e., the first letter. Some verbs are doubly weak. For example, a verb such as יצא is classified as a **Pe Yod, Lamed Alef** verb, since it begins with a Yod and ends with the guttural Alef.

The following list contains some of the usual classifications of Hebrew verbs with a couple of examples. Not all of the logical possibilities, however, are enumerated as classes of verbs. Also, some verbs may exhibit features of two or more of these enumerated classes:

1. **The Strong Verb**
   Verbs without any weak letters: קדשׁ ,כתב ,דבר

2. **Pe Guttural**
   Verbs with a guttural or Resh as their first letter: עבד, הרג, אסף, רדף

3. **Pe Alef** (abbreviated פ״א)
   Five verbs beginning with Alef differ from the Pe guttural pattern, but only in the Qal. Three are more common verbs: אבד ,אכל ,אמר. The other two are doubly weak, since they end in He: אבה, אפה.

4. **Ayin Guttural**
   Verbs with a guttural or Resh as their middle letter: בחר, שׁאל, בּרךְ

5. **Lamed Guttural**
   Verbs with certain gutturals (especially ח and ע) as their final letter: שָׁמַע, שָׁלַח

6. **Lamed Alef** (abbreviated ל״א)
   Verbs with quiescent Alef as their final letter: שָׂנֵא, מָלֵא, מָצָא

7. **Lamed He** (ל״ה)
   Verbs with the vowel letter He as their final letter: צִוָּה, בָּנָה, כָּלָה

8. **Pe Yod** (פ״י, originally פ״ו)
   Verbs originally with Vav as their initial letter. In the Qal, these verbs in biblical Hebrew have a Yod, although the Yod falls away in some forms. In other stems, a Vav (either as a consonant or as a vowel letter) appears in many forms: יָרַד, יָסַף, יָשַׁב

9. **Pe Yod** (פ״י, originally פ״י)
   Verbs originally with a Yod as their initial letter. In most stems, the Yod always remains (either as a consonant or as a vowel letter). Only in the Nifal and Hofal does the Yod appear as a Vav: יָצַב, יָטַב

10. **Pe Nun** (פ״נ)
    Verbs with Nun as their initial letter: נָגַד, נָגַשׁ, נָפַל

11. **Ayin Vav** (ע״ו) -- Hollow Verbs
    Actually not weak but biconsonantal, these verbs are still classified according to the same scheme. In their lexicon form, they exhibit the vowel letter Vav as their middle letter: בּוֹא, קוּם, שׁוּב

12. **Ayin Yod** (ע״י) -- Hollow Verbs
    Similarly, verbs that have the vowel letter Yod as their middle letter in their lexicon form: בִּין, שִׂים

13. **Ayin Ayin** (ע״ע)
    Also biconsonantal, these verbs reduplicate their second letter in the lexicon form, although only one of the doubled letters appears in many forms: הָלַל, רָעַע, סָבַב

Some verbs are doubly weak; i.e., they have more than one weak letter. Although they merely exhibit features of the classes already listed, some doubly weak verbs are so common that it is helpful to have charts for them. Some common classifications of doubly weak verbs appear on the next page:

14. **Pe Guttural, ל״ה**

    Verbs with a guttural as their initial letter and a He as their final letter:
    חנה ,עשׂה ,ענה

15. **ל״ה, פ״נ**

    Verbs with an initial Nun and a final He: נכה ,נטה

16. **ל״א, פ״נ**

    Verbs with an initial Nun and a final Alef: נשׂא ,נבא

17. **ל״ה, פ״י**

    Verbs with an original initial Vav (now a Yod) and a final He: ירה

18. **ל״א, פ״י**

    Verbs with an original initial Vav (now a Yod) and a final Alef: יצא

ANALYZING HEBREW VERB FORMS

The student should now be equipped to parse practically all Hebrew verb forms by using three reference tools:

1. The **clue pointing** as given in the synopsis in Chart 72 should be sufficient to identify many forms.

2. The **lexicon** includes many common forms, along with unusual or irregular forms.

3. The **verb paradigms** in the following charts help to confirm the parsing of a particular verb and to give the total picture of the verb.

After the verb has been accurately parsed, the lexicon must be consulted regularly to determine the translations that would be possible in a particular context.

Scan the following charts to see their format. Notice that each chart covers two pages. All the forms are given for each model verb, but some charts include the Qal of verbs in special categories within the class. Skip to p. 164 to begin the reading of Joshua 24. In that reading we will learn to use the verb paradigms.

VERB PARADIGMS

Classification	Model Verb	Other Verbs (Qal only)	Chart
The Strong Verb	קטל	כבד, קטן	130
The Weak Verbs			
פ Guttural and פ״א	עמד	חזק, אכל	132
ע Guttural	גאל		134
ל Guttural	שלח		136
ל״א	מצא	מלא	138
ל״ה	גלה	היה	140
פ״י (original פ״ו)	ישב	ירא, הלך	142
פ״י (original פ״י)	יטב		144
פ״ן	נגש	נפל, נתן, לקח	146
ע״ו Hollow Verb	קום	מות, בוש	148
ע״י Hollow Verb	שׂים		150
ל״ה Qal with suffixes	גלה		151
ע״ע	סבב		152
The Doubly Weak Verbs			
פ Guttural, ל״ה	עשׂה		154
ל״ה, פ״ן	נכה		156
ל״א, פ״ן	נשׂא		158
ל״ה, פ״י (original פ״ו)	ידה		160
ל״א, פ״י (original פ״ו)	יצא		162

7

Model Verb: קטל -- "to kill"

	Qal	Nifal	Piel	Pual
Perfect				
3ms	קָטַל	נִקְטַל	קִטֵּל	קֻטַּל
3fs	קָטְלָה	נִקְטְלָה	קִטְּלָה	קֻטְּלָה
2ms	קָטַ֫לְתָּ	נִקְטַ֫לְתָּ	קִטַּ֫לְתָּ	קֻטַּ֫לְתָּ
2fs	קָטַלְתְּ	נִקְטַלְתְּ	קִטַּלְתְּ	קֻטַּלְתְּ
1cs	קָטַ֫לְתִּי	נִקְטַ֫לְתִּי	קִטַּ֫לְתִּי	קֻטַּ֫לְתִּי
3cp	קָטְלוּ	נִקְטְלוּ	קִטְּלוּ	קֻטְּלוּ
2mp	קְטַלְתֶּם	נִקְטַלְתֶּם	קִטַּלְתֶּם	קֻטַּלְתֶּם
2fp	קְטַלְתֶּן	נִקְטַלְתֶּן	קִטַּלְתֶּן	קֻטַּלְתֶּן
1cp	קָטַ֫לְנוּ	נִקְטַ֫לְנוּ	קִטַּ֫לְנוּ	קֻטַּ֫לְנוּ
Imperfect				
3ms	יִקְטֹל	יִקָּטֵל	יְקַטֵּל	יְקֻטַּל
3fs	תִּקְטֹל	תִּקָּטֵל	תְּקַטֵּל	תְּקֻטַּל
2ms	תִּקְטֹל	תִּקָּטֵל	תְּקַטֵּל	תְּקֻטַּל
2fs	תִּקְטְלִי	תִּקָּטְלִי	תְּקַטְּלִי	תְּקֻטְּלִי
1cs	אֶקְטֹל	אֶקָּטֵל	אֲקַטֵּל	אֲקֻטַּל
3mp	יִקְטְלוּ	יִקָּטְלוּ	יְקַטְּלוּ	יְקֻטְּלוּ
3fp	תִּקְטֹ֫לְנָה	תִּקָּטַ֫לְנָה	תְּקַטֵּ֫לְנָה	תְּקֻטַּ֫לְנָה
2mp	תִּקְטְלוּ	תִּקָּטְלוּ	תְּקַטְּלוּ	תְּקֻטְּלוּ
2fp	תִּקְטֹ֫לְנָה	תִּקָּטַ֫לְנָה	תְּקַטֵּ֫לְנָה	תְּקֻטַּ֫לְנָה
1cp	נִקְטֹל	נִקָּטֵל	נְקַטֵּל	נְקֻטַּל
Imperative				
2ms	קְטֹל	הִקָּטֵל	קַטֵּל	
2fs	קִטְלִי	הִקָּטְלִי	קַטְּלִי	
2mp	קִטְלוּ	הִקָּטְלוּ	קַטְּלוּ	
2fs	קְטֹ֫לְנָה	הִקָּטַ֫לְנָה	קַטֵּ֫לְנָה	
Infinitive				
absolute	קָטוֹל	הִקָּטֹל נִקְטֹל	קַטֹּל	קֻטֹּל
construct	קְטֹל	הִקָּטֵל	קַטֵּל	קֻטַּל
Participle				
active ms	קֹטֵל		מְקַטֵּל	
passive ms	קָטוּל	נִקְטָל		מְקֻטָּל
Imperfect				
consec. 3ms	וַיִּקְטֹל	וַיִּקָּטֵל	וַיְקַטֵּל	וַיְקֻטַּל
Jussive				
3ms	יִקְטֹל	יִקָּטֵל	יְקַטֵּל	יְקֻטַּל
Cohortative				
1cs	אֶקְטְלָה	אֶקָּטְלָה	אֲקַטְּלָה	

7

קְטַל (קָטֹן, כָּבֵד)

	Stative Qal (קטן)	Stative Qal (כבד)	Hofal	Hifil	Hitpael
Perfect					
3ms	קָטֹן	כָּבֵד	הָקְטַל	הִקְטִיל	הִתְקַטֵּל
3fs	קָטְנָה	כָּבְדָה	הָקְטְלָה	הִקְטִילָה	הִתְקַטְּלָה
2ms	קָטֹנְתָּ	כָּבַדְתָּ	הָקְטַלְתָּ	הִקְטַלְתָּ	הִתְקַטַּלְתָּ
2fs	קָטֹנְתְּ	כָּבַדְתְּ	הָקְטַלְתְּ	הִקְטַלְתְּ	הִתְקַטַּלְתְּ
1cs	קָטֹנְתִּי	כָּבַדְתִּי	הָקְטַלְתִּי	הִקְטַלְתִּי	הִתְקַטַּלְתִּי
3cp	קָטְנוּ	כָּבְדוּ	הָקְטְלוּ	הִקְטִילוּ	הִתְקַטְּלוּ
2mp	קְטָנְתֶּם	כְּבַדְתֶּם	הָקְטַלְתֶּם	הִקְטַלְתֶּם	הִתְקַטַּלְתֶּם
2fp	קְטָנְתֶּן	כְּבַדְתֶּן	הָקְטַלְתֶּן	הִקְטַלְתֶּן	הִתְקַטַּלְתֶּן
1cp	קָטֹנּוּ	כָּבַדְנוּ	הָקְטַלְנוּ	הִקְטַלְנוּ	הִתְקַטַּלְנוּ
Imperfect					
3ms	יִקְטַן	יִכְבַּד	יָקְטַל	יַקְטִיל	יִתְקַטֵּל
3fs	תִּקְטַן	תִּכְבַּד	תָּקְטַל	תַּקְטִיל	תִּתְקַטֵּל
2ms	תִּקְטַן	תִּכְבַּד	תָּקְטַל	תַּקְטִיל	תִּתְקַטֵּל
2fs	תִּקְטְנִי	תִּכְבְּדִי	תָּקְטְלִי	תַּקְטִילִי	תִּתְקַטְּלִי
1cs	אֶקְטַן	אֶכְבַּד	אָקְטַל	אַקְטִיל	אֶתְקַטֵּל
3mp	יִקְטְנוּ	יִכְבְּדוּ	יָקְטְלוּ	יַקְטִילוּ	יִתְקַטְּלוּ
3fp	תִּקְטַנָּה	תִּכְבַּדְנָה	תָּקְטַלְנָה	תַּקְטֵלְנָה	תִּתְקַטֵּלְנָה
2mp	תִּקְטְנוּ	תִּכְבְּדוּ	תָּקְטְלוּ	תַּקְטִילוּ	תִּתְקַטְּלוּ
2fp	תִּקְטַנָּה	תִּכְבַּדְנָה	תָּקְטַלְנָה	תַּקְטֵלְנָה	תִּתְקַטֵּלְנָה
1cp	נִקְטַן	נִכְבַּד	נָקְטַל	נַקְטִיל	נִתְקַטֵּל
Imperative					
2ms	קְטַן	כְּבַד		הַקְטֵל	הִתְקַטֵּל
2fs	קְטְנִי	כִּבְדִי		הַקְטִילִי	הִתְקַטְּלִי
2mp	קְטְנוּ	כִּבְדוּ		הַקְטִילוּ	הִתְקַטְּלוּ
2fp	קְטַנָּה	כְּבַדְנָה		הַקְטֵלְנָה	הִתְקַטֵּלְנָה
Infinitive					
absolute	קָטוֹן	כָּבוֹד	הָקְטֵל	הַקְטֵל	הִתְקַטֹּל
construct	קְטֹן	כְּבֹד	הָקְטֵל	הַקְטִיל	הִתְקַטֵּל
Participle					
active ms	קָטֹן	כָּבֵד		מַקְטִיל	מִתְקַטֵּל
passive ms			מָקְטָל		
Imperfect					
consec. 3ms	וַיִּקְטַן	וַיִּכְבַּד	וַיָּקְטַל	וַיַּקְטֵל	וַיִּתְקַטֵּל
Jussive					
3ms	יִקְטַן	יִכְבַּד	יָקְטַל	יַקְטֵל	יִתְקַטֵּל
Cohortative					
1cs	אֶקְטְנָה	אֶכְבְּדָה		אַקְטִילָה	אֶתְקַטְּלָה

7

Chart 132: פ Guttural Verb

Model Verb: עמד -- "to stand"

	Qal	Nifal	Piel	Pual
Perfect				
3ms	עָמַד ·	נֶעֱמַד	עִמֵּד	עֻמַּד
3fs	עָמְדָה	נֶעֶמְדָה	עִמְּדָה	עֻמְּדָה
2ms	עָמַדְתָּ	נֶעֱמַדְתָּ	עִמַּדְתָּ	עֻמַּדְתָּ
2fs	עָמַדְתְּ	נֶעֱמַדְתְּ	עִמַּדְתְּ	עֻמַּדְתְּ
1cs	עָמַדְתִּי	נֶעֱמַדְתִּי	עִמַּדְתִּי	עֻמַּדְתִּי
3cp	עָמְדוּ	נֶעֶמְדוּ	עִמְּדוּ	עֻמְּדוּ
2mp	עֲמַדְתֶּם	נֶעֱמַדְתֶּם	עִמַּדְתֶּם	עֻמַּדְתֶּם
2fp	עֲמַדְתֶּן	נֶעֱמַדְתֶּן	עִמַּדְתֶּן	עֻמַּדְתֶּן
1cp	עָמַדְנוּ	נֶעֱמַדְנוּ	עִמַּדְנוּ	עֻמַּדְנוּ
Imperfect				
3ms	יַעֲמֹד	יֵעָמֵד	יְעַמֵּד	יְעֻמַּד
3fs	תַּעֲמֹד	תֵּעָמֵד	תְּעַמֵּד	תְּעֻמַּד
2ms	תַּעֲמֹד	תֵּעָמֵד	תְּעַמֵּד	תְּעֻמַּד
2fs	תַּעַמְדִי	תֵּעָמְדִי	תְּעַמְּדִי	תְּעֻמְּדִי
1cs	אֶעֱמֹד	אֵעָמֵד	אֲעַמֵּד	אֲעֻמַּד
3mp	יַעַמְדוּ	יֵעָמְדוּ	יְעַמְּדוּ	יְעֻמְּדוּ
3fp	תַּעֲמֹדְנָה	תֵּעָמַדְנָה	תְּעַמֵּדְנָה	תְּעֻמַּדְנָה
2mp	תַּעַמְדוּ	תֵּעָמְדוּ	תְּעַמְּדוּ	תְּעֻמְּדוּ
2fp	תַּעֲמֹדְנָה	תֵּעָמַדְנָה	תְּעַמֵּדְנָה	תְּעֻמַּדְנָה
1cp	נַעֲמֹד	נֵעָמֵד	נְעַמֵּד	נְעֻמַּד
Imperative				
2ms	עֲמֹד	הֵעָמֵד	עַמֵּד	
2fs	עִמְדִי	הֵעָמְדִי	עַמְּדִי	
2mp	עִמְדוּ	הֵעָמְדוּ	עַמְּדוּ	
2fs	עֲמֹדְנָה	הֵעָמַדְנָה	עַמֵּדְנָה	
Infinitive				
absolute	עָמוֹד	נַעֲמֹד	עַמֹּד	עֻמֹּד
construct	עֲמֹד	הֵעָמֵד	עַמֵּד	עֻמַּד
Participle				
active ms	עֹמֵד		מְעַמֵּד	
passive ms	עָמוּד	נֶעֱמָד		מְעֻמָּד
Imperfect				
consec. 3ms	וַיַּעֲמֹד	וַיֵּעָמֵד	וַיְעַמֵּד	וַיְעֻמַּד
Jussive				
3ms	יַעֲמֹד	יֵעָמֵד	יְעַמֵּד	יְעֻמַּד
Cohortative				
1cs	אֶעֶמְדָה	אֵעָמְדָה	אֲעַמְּדָה	

עמד (אכל, חזק)

Hitpael	Hifil	Hofal	Stative	Qal אכל	
					Perfect
הִתְעַמֵּד	הֶעֱמִיד	הָעֳמַד	חָזַק	אָכַל	3ms
הִתְעַמְּדָה	הֶעֱמִידָה	הָעֳמְדָה	חָזְקָה	אָכְלָה	3fs
הִתְעַמַּֽדְתָּ	הֶעֱמַֽדְתָּ	הָעֳמַֽדְתָּ	חָזַֽקְתָּ	אָכַֽלְתָּ	2ms
הִתְעַמַּדְתְּ	הֶעֱמַדְתְּ	הָעֳמַדְתְּ	חָזַקְתְּ	אָכַלְתְּ	2fs
הִתְעַמַּֽדְתִּי	הֶעֱמַֽדְתִּי	הָעֳמַֽדְתִּי	חָזַֽקְתִּי	אָכַֽלְתִּי	1cs
הִתְעַמְּדוּ	הֶעֱמִידוּ	הָעֳמְדוּ	חָזְקוּ	אָכְלוּ	3cp
הִתְעַמַּדְתֶּם	הֶעֱמַדְתֶּם	הָעֳמַדְתֶּם	חֲזַקְתֶּם	אֲכַלְתֶּם	2mp
הִתְעַמַּדְתֶּן	הֶעֱמַדְתֶּן	הָעֳמַדְתֶּן	חֲזַקְתֶּן	אֲכַלְתֶּן	2fp
הִתְעַמַּֽדְנוּ	הֶעֱמַֽדְנוּ	הָעֳמַֽדְנוּ	חָזַֽקְנוּ	אָכַֽלְנוּ	1cp
					Imperfect
יִתְעַמֵּד	יַעֲמִיד	יָעֳמַד	יֶחֱזַק	יֹאכַל	3ms
תִּתְעַמֵּד	תַּעֲמִיד	תָּעֳמַד	תֶּחֱזַק	תֹּאכַל	3fs
תִּתְעַמֵּד	תַּעֲמִיד	תָּעֳמַד	תֶּחֱזַק	תֹּאכַל	2ms
תִּתְעַמְּדִי	תַּעֲמִֽידִי	תָּעֳמְדִי	תֶּחֶזְקִי	תֹּאכְלִי	2fs
אֶתְעַמֵּד	אַעֲמִיד	אָעֳמַד	אֶחֱזַק	אֹכַל	1cs
יִתְעַמְּדוּ	יַעֲמִֽידוּ	יָעֳמְדוּ	יֶחֶזְקוּ	יֹאכְלוּ	3mp
תִּתְעַמֵּֽדְנָה	תַּעֲמֵֽדְנָה	תָּעֳמַֽדְנָה	תֶּחֱזַֽקְנָה	תֹּאכַֽלְנָה	3fp
תִּתְעַמְּדוּ	תַּעֲמִֽידוּ	תָּעֳמְדוּ	תֶּחֶזְקוּ	תֹּאכְלוּ	2mp
תִּתְעַמֵּֽדְנָה	תַּעֲמֵֽדְנָה	תָּעֳמַֽדְנָה	תֶּחֱזַֽקְנָה	תֹּאכַֽלְנָה	2fp
נִתְעַמֵּד	נַעֲמִיד	נָעֳמַד	נֶחֱזַק	נֹאכַל	1cp
					Imperative
הִתְעַמֵּד	הַעֲמֵד		חֲזַק	אֱכֹל	2ms
הִתְעַמְּדִי	הַעֲמִֽידִי		חִזְקִי	אִכְלִי	2fs
הִתְעַמְּדוּ	הַעֲמִֽידוּ		חִזְקוּ	אִכְלוּ	2mp
הִתְעַמֵּֽדְנָה	הַעֲמֵֽדְנָה		חֲזַֽקְנָה	אֱכֹֽלְנָה	2fp
					Infinitive
הִתְעַמֵּד	הַעֲמֵד	הָעֳמֵד	חָזוֹק	אָכוֹל	absolute
הִתְעַמֵּד	הַעֲמִיד	הָעֳמַד	חֲזֹק	אֱכֹל	construct
					Participle
מִתְעַמֵּד	מַעֲמִיד		חָזֵק	אֹכֵל	active ms
		מָעֳמָד		אָכוּל	passive ms
					Imperfect
וַיִּתְעַמֵּד	וַיַּעֲמֵד	וַיָּעֳמַד	וַיֶּחֱזַק	וַיֹּאכַל	consec. 3ms
					Jussive
יִתְעַמֵּד	יַעֲמֵד	יָעֳמַד	יֶחֱזַק	יֹאכַל	3ms
					Cohortative
אֶתְעַמְּדָה	אַעֲמִֽידָה		אֶחֱזְקָה	אֹכְלָה	1cs

7

Chart 134: ע Guttural Verb

Model Verb: גָּאַל -- "to redeem"

	Qal	Nifal	Piel	Pual
Perfect				
3ms	גָּאַל	נִגְאַל	גֵּאַל	גֹּאַל
3fs	גָּאֲלָה	נִגְאֲלָה	גֵּאֲלָה	גֹּאֲלָה
2ms	גָּאַלְתָּ	נִגְאַלְתָּ	גֵּאַלְתָּ	גֹּאַלְתָּ
2fs	גָּאַלְתְּ	נִגְאַלְתְּ	גֵּאַלְתְּ	גֹּאַלְתְּ
1cs	גָּאַלְתִּי	נִגְאַלְתִּי	גֵּאַלְתִּי	גֹּאַלְתִּי
3cp	גָּאֲלוּ	נִגְאֲלוּ	גֵּאֲלוּ	גֹּאֲלוּ
2mp	גְּאַלְתֶּם	נִגְאַלְתֶּם	גֵּאַלְתֶּם	גֹּאַלְתֶּם
2fp	גְּאַלְתֶּן	נִגְאַלְתֶּן	גֵּאַלְתֶּן	גֹּאַלְתֶּן
1cp	גָּאַלְנוּ	נִגְאַלְנוּ	גֵּאַלְנוּ	גֹּאַלְנוּ
Imperfect				
3ms	יִגְאַל	יִגָּאֵל	יְגָאֵל	יְגֹאַל
3fs	תִּגְאַל	תִּגָּאֵל	תְּגָאֵל	תְּגֹאַל
2ms	תִּגְאַל	תִּגָּאֵל	תְּגָאֵל	תְּגֹאַל
2fs	תִּגְאֲלִי	תִּגָּאֲלִי	תְּגָאֲלִי	תְּגֹאֲלִי
1cs	אֶגְאַל	אֶגָּאֵל	אֲגָאֵל	אֲגֹאַל
3mp	יִגְאֲלוּ	יִגָּאֲלוּ	יְגָאֲלוּ	יְגֹאֲלוּ
3fp	תִּגְאַלְנָה	תִּגָּאַלְנָה	תְּגָאַלְנָה	תְּגֹאַלְנָה
2mp	תִּגְאֲלוּ	תִּגָּאֲלוּ	תְּגָאֲלוּ	תְּגֹאֲלוּ
2fp	תִּגְאַלְנָה	תִּגָּאַלְנָה	תְּגָאַלְנָה	תְּגֹאַלְנָה
1cp	נִגְאַל	נִגָּאֵל	נְגָאֵל	נְגֹאַל
Imperative				
2ms	גְּאַל	הִגָּאֵל	גֵּאַל	
2fs	גַּאֲלִי	הִגָּאֲלִי	גָּאֲלִי	
2mp	גַּאֲלוּ	הִגָּאֲלוּ	גָּאֲלוּ	
2fp	גְּאַלְנָה	הִגָּאַלְנָה	גָּאַלְנָה	
Infinitive				
absolute	גָּאוֹל	נִגְאֹל	גֵּאַל	גֹּאַל
construct	גְּאֹל	הִגָּאֵל	גֵּאַל	גֹּאַל
Participle				
active ms	גֹּאֵל		מְגָאֵל	
passive ms	גָּאוּל	נִגְאָל		מְגֹאָל
Imperfect				
consec. 3ms	וַיִּגְאַל	וַיִּגָּאֵל	וַיְגָאֵל	וַיְגֹאַל
Jussive				
3ms	יִגְאַל	יִגָּאֵל	יְגָאֵל	יְגֹאַל
Cohortative				
1cs	אֶגְאֲלָה	אֶגָּאֲלָה	אֲגָאֲלָה	

גאל

Hitpael	Hifil	Hofal	
			Perfect
הִתְגָּאֵל	הִגְאִיל	הָגְאַל	3ms
הִתְגָּאֲלָה	הִגְאִילָה	הָגְאֲלָה	3fs
הִתְגָּאַלְתָּ	הִגְאַלְתָּ	הָגְאַלְתָּ	2ms
הִתְגָּאַלְתְּ	הִגְאַלְתְּ	הָגְאַלְתְּ	2fs
הִתְגָּאַלְתִּי	הִגְאַלְתִּי	הָגְאַלְתִּי	1cs
הִתְגָּאֲלוּ	הִגְאִילוּ	הָגְאֲלוּ	3cp
הִתְגָּאַלְתֶּם	הִגְאַלְתֶּם	הָגְאַלְתֶּם	2mp
הִתְגָּאַלְתֶּן	הִגְאַלְתֶּן	הָגְאַלְתֶּן	2fp
הִתְגָּאַלְנוּ	הִגְאַלְנוּ	הָגְאַלְנוּ	1cp
			Imperfect
יִתְגָּאֵל	יַגְאִיל	יָגְאַל	3ms
תִּתְגָּאֵל	תַּגְאִיל	תָּגְאַל	3fs
תִּתְגָּאֵל	תַּגְאִיל	תָּגְאַל	2ms
תִּתְגָּאֲלִי	תַּגְאִילִי	תָּגְאֲלִי	2fs
אֶתְגָּאֵל	אַגְאִיל	אָגְאַל	1cs
יִתְגָּאֲלוּ	יַגְאִילוּ	יָגְאֲלוּ	3mp
תִּתְגָּאֵלְנָה	תַּגְאֵלְנָה	תָּגְאַלְנָה	3fp
תִּתְגָּאֲלוּ	תַּגְאִילוּ	תָּגְאֲלוּ	2mp
תִּתְגָּאֵלְנָה	תַּגְאֵלְנָה	תָּגְאַלְנָה	2fp
נִתְגָּאֵל	נַגְאִיל	נָגְאַל	1cp
			Imperative
הִתְגָּאֵל	הַגְאֵל		2ms
הִתְגָּאֲלִי	הַגְאִילִי		2fs
הִתְגָּאֲלוּ	הַגְאִילוּ		2mp
הִתְגָּאֵלְנָה	הַגְאֵלְנָה		2fp
			Infinitive
הִתְגָּאֵל	הַגְאֵל	הָגְאֵל	absolute
הִתְגָּאֵל	הַגְאִיל	הָגְאֵל	construct
			Participle
מִתְגָּאֵל	מַגְאִיל		active ms
		מָגְאָל	passive ms
			Imperfect
וַיִּתְגָּאֵל	וַיַּגְאֵל	וַיָּגְאַל	consec. 3ms
			Jussive
יִתְגָּאֵל	יַגְאֵל	יָגְאַל	3ms
			Cohortative
אֶתְגָּאֲלָה	אַגְאִילָה		1cs

7

Chart 136: ל Guttural Verb

Model Verb: שָׁלַח -- "to send"

	Qal	Nifal	Piel	Pual
Perfect				
3ms	שָׁלַח	נִשְׁלַח	שִׁלַּח	שֻׁלַּח
3fs	שָׁלְחָה	נִשְׁלְחָה	שִׁלְּחָה	שֻׁלְּחָה
2ms	שָׁלַחְתָּ	נִשְׁלַחְתָּ	שִׁלַּחְתָּ	שֻׁלַּחְתָּ
2fs	שָׁלַחַתְּ	נִשְׁלַחַתְּ	שִׁלַּחַתְּ	שֻׁלַּחַתְּ
1cs	שָׁלַחְתִּי	נִשְׁלַחְתִּי	שִׁלַּחְתִּי	שֻׁלַּחְתִּי
3cp	שָׁלְחוּ	נִשְׁלְחוּ	שִׁלְּחוּ	שֻׁלְּחוּ
2mp	שְׁלַחְתֶּם	נִשְׁלַחְתֶּם	שִׁלַּחְתֶּם	שֻׁלַּחְתֶּם
2fp	שְׁלַחְתֶּן	נִשְׁלַחְתֶּן	שִׁלַּחְתֶּן	שֻׁלַּחְתֶּן
1cp	שָׁלַחְנוּ	נִשְׁלַחְנוּ	שִׁלַּחְנוּ	שֻׁלַּחְנוּ
Imperfect				
3ms	יִשְׁלַח	יִשָּׁלַח	יְשַׁלַּח	יְשֻׁלַּח
3fs	תִּשְׁלַח	תִּשָּׁלַח	תְּשַׁלַּח	תְּשֻׁלַּח
2ms	תִּשְׁלַח	תִּשָּׁלַח	תְּשַׁלַּח	תְּשֻׁלַּח
2fs	תִּשְׁלְחִי	תִּשָּׁלְחִי	תְּשַׁלְּחִי	תְּשֻׁלְּחִי
1cs	אֶשְׁלַח	אֶשָּׁלַח	אֲשַׁלַּח	אֲשֻׁלַּח
3mp	יִשְׁלְחוּ	יִשָּׁלְחוּ	יְשַׁלְּחוּ	יְשֻׁלְּחוּ
3fp	תִּשְׁלַחְנָה	תִּשָּׁלַחְנָה	תְּשַׁלַּחְנָה	תְּשֻׁלַּחְנָה
2mp	תִּשְׁלְחוּ	תִּשָּׁלְחוּ	תְּשַׁלְּחוּ	תְּשֻׁלְּחוּ
2fp	תִּשְׁלַחְנָה	תִּשָּׁלַחְנָה	תְּשַׁלַּחְנָה	תְּשֻׁלַּחְנָה
1cp	נִשְׁלַח	נִשָּׁלַח	נְשַׁלַּח	נְשֻׁלַּח
Imperative				
2ms	שְׁלַח	הִשָּׁלַח	שַׁלַּח	
2fs	שִׁלְחִי	הִשָּׁלְחִי	שַׁלְּחִי	
2mp	שִׁלְחוּ	הִשָּׁלְחוּ	שַׁלְּחוּ	
2fp	שְׁלַחְנָה	הִשָּׁלַחְנָה	שַׁלַּחְנָה	
Infinitive				
absolute	שָׁלוֹחַ	נִשְׁלוֹחַ	שַׁלֵּחַ	שֻׁלַּח
construct	שְׁלֹחַ	הִשָּׁלַח	שַׁלַּח	שֻׁלַּח
Participle				
active ms	שֹׁלֵחַ		מְשַׁלֵּחַ	
passive ms	שָׁלוּחַ	נִשְׁלָח		מְשֻׁלָּח
Imperfect				
consec. 3ms	וַיִּשְׁלַח	וַיִּשָּׁלַח	וַיְשַׁלַּח	וַיְשֻׁלַּח
Jussive				
3ms	יִשְׁלַח	יִשָּׁלַח	יְשַׁלַּח	יְשֻׁלַּח
Cohortative				
1cs	אֶשְׁלְחָה	אֶשָּׁלְחָה	אֲשַׁלְּחָה	

7

שָׁלַח

Hitpael	Hifil	Hofal	
			Perfect
הִשְׁתַּלַּח	הִשְׁלִיחַ	הָשְׁלַח	3ms
הִשְׁתַּלְּחָה	הִשְׁלִיחָה	הָשְׁלְחָה	3fs
הִשְׁתַּלַּ֫חְתָּ	הִשְׁלַ֫חְתָּ	הָשְׁלַ֫חְתָּ	2ms
הִשְׁתַּלַּ֫חַתְּ	הִשְׁלַ֫חַתְּ	הָשְׁלַ֫חַתְּ	2fs
הִשְׁתַּלַּ֫חְתִּי	הִשְׁלַ֫חְתִּי	הָשְׁלַ֫חְתִּי	1cs
הִשְׁתַּלְּחוּ	הִשְׁלִיחוּ	הָשְׁלְחוּ	3cp
הִשְׁתַּלַּחְתֶּם	הִשְׁלַחְתֶּם	הָשְׁלַחְתֶּם	2mp
הִשְׁתַּלַּחְתֶּן	הִשְׁלַחְתֶּן	הָשְׁלַחְתֶּן	2fp
הִשְׁתַּלַּ֫חְנוּ	הִשְׁלַ֫חְנוּ	הָשְׁלַ֫חְנוּ	1cp
			Imperfect
יִשְׁתַּלַּח	יַשְׁלִיחַ	יָשְׁלַח	3ms
תִּשְׁתַּלַּח	תַּשְׁלִיחַ	תָּשְׁלַח	3fs
תִּשְׁתַּלַּח	תַּשְׁלִיחַ	תָּשְׁלַח	2ms
תִּשְׁתַּלְּחִי	תַּשְׁלִ֫יחִי	תָּשְׁלְחִי	2fs
אֶשְׁתַּלַּח	אַשְׁלִיחַ	אָשְׁלַח	1cs
יִשְׁתַּלְּחוּ	יַשְׁלִ֫יחוּ	יָשְׁלְחוּ	3mp
תִּשְׁתַּלַּ֫חְנָה	תַּשְׁלַ֫חְנָה	תָּשְׁלַ֫חְנָה	3fp
תִּשְׁתַּלְּחוּ	תַּשְׁלִ֫יחוּ	תָּשְׁלְחוּ	2mp
תִּשְׁתַּלַּ֫חְנָה	תַּשְׁלַ֫חְנָה	תָּשְׁלַ֫חְנָה	2fp
נִשְׁתַּלַּח	נַשְׁלִיחַ	נָשְׁלַח	1cp
			Imperative
הִשְׁתַּלַּח	הַשְׁלַח		2ms
הִשְׁתַּלְּחִי	הַשְׁלִ֫יחִי		2fs
הִשְׁתַּלְּחוּ	הַשְׁלִ֫יחוּ		2mp
הִשְׁתַּלַּ֫חְנָה	הַשְׁלַ֫חְנָה		2fp
			Infinitive
הִשְׁתַּלֵּחַ	הַשְׁלֵחַ	הָשְׁלֵחַ	absolute
הִשְׁתַּלַּח	הַשְׁלִיחַ	הָשְׁלַח	construct
			Participle
מִשְׁתַּלֵּחַ	מַשְׁלִיחַ		active ms
		מָשְׁלָח	passive ms
			Imperfect
וַיִּשְׁתַּלַּח	וַיַּשְׁלַח	וַיָּשְׁלַח	consec. 3ms
			Jussive
יִשְׁתַּלַּח	יַשְׁלַח	יָשְׁלַח	3ms
			Cohortative
אֶשְׁתַּלְּחָה	אַשְׁלִ֫יחָה		1cs

Chart 138: ל"א Verb

Model Verb: מצא -- "to find"

	Qal	Nifal	Piel	Pual
Perfect				
3ms	מָצָא	נִמְצָא	מִצֵּא	מֻצָּא
3fs	מָצְאָה	נִמְצְאָה	מִצְּאָה	מֻצְּאָה
2ms	מָצָאתָ	נִמְצֵאתָ	מִצֵּאתָ	מֻצֵּאתָ
2fs	מָצָאת	נִמְצֵאת	מִצֵּאת	מֻצֵּאת
1cs	מָצָאתִי	נִמְצֵאתִי	מִצֵּאתִי	מֻצֵּאתִי
3cp	מָצְאוּ	נִמְצְאוּ	מִצְּאוּ	מֻצְּאוּ
2mp	מְצָאתֶם	נִמְצֵאתֶם	מִצֵּאתֶם	מֻצֵּאתֶם
2fp	מְצָאתֶן	נִמְצֵאתֶן	מִצֵּאתֶן	מֻצֵּאתֶן
1cp	מָצָאנוּ	נִמְצֵאנוּ	מִצֵּאנוּ	מֻצֵּאנוּ
Imperfect				
3ms	יִמְצָא	יִמָּצֵא	יְמַצֵּא	יְמֻצָּא
3fs	תִּמְצָא	תִּמָּצֵא	תְּמַצֵּא	תְּמֻצָּא
2ms	תִּמְצָא	תִּמָּצֵא	תְּמַצֵּא	תְּמֻצָּא
2fs	תִּמְצְאִי	תִּמָּצְאִי	תְּמַצְּאִי	תְּמֻצְּאִי
1cs	אֶמְצָא	אֶמָּצֵא	אֲמַצֵּא	אֲמֻצָּא
3mp	יִמְצְאוּ	יִמָּצְאוּ	יְמַצְּאוּ	יְמֻצְּאוּ
3fp	תִּמְצֶאנָה	תִּמָּצֶאנָה	תְּמַצֶּאנָה	תְּמֻצֶּאנָה
2mp	תִּמְצְאוּ	תִּמָּצְאוּ	תְּמַצְּאוּ	תְּמֻצְּאוּ
2fp	תִּמְצֶאנָה	תִּמָּצֶאנָה	תְּמַצֶּאנָה	תְּמֻצֶּאנָה
1cp	נִמְצָא	נִמָּצֵא	נְמַצֵּא	נְמֻצָּא
Imperative				
2ms	מְצָא	הִמָּצֵא	מַצֵּא	
2fs	מִצְאִי	הִמָּצְאִי	מַצְּאִי	
2mp	מִצְאוּ	הִמָּצְאוּ	מַצְּאוּ	
2fp	מְצֶאנָה	הִמָּצֶאנָה	מַצֶּאנָה	
Infinitive				
absolute	מָצוֹא	נִמְצֹא	מַצֵּא	מֻצָּא
construct	מְצֹא	הִמָּצֵא	מַצֵּא	מֻצָּא
Participle				
active ms	מֹצֵא		מְמַצֵּא	
passive ms	מָצוּא	נִמְצָא		מְמֻצָּא
Imperfect				
consec. 3ms	וַיִּמְצָא	וַיִּמָּצֵא	וַיְמַצֵּא	וַיְמֻצָּא
Jussive				
3ms	יִמְצָא	יִמָּצֵא	יְמַצֵּא	יְמֻצָּא
Cohortative				
1cs	אֶמְצְאָה	אֶמָּצְאָה	אֲמַצְּאָה	

7

Hitpael	Hifil	Hofal	Stative Qal	
				Perfect
הִתְמַצֵּא	הִמְצִיא	הֻמְצָא	מָלֵא	3ms
הִתְמַצְּאָה	הִמְצִיאָה	הֻמְצְאָה	מָלְאָה	3fs
הִתְמַצֵּאתָ	הִמְצֵאתָ	הֻמְצֵאתָ	מָלֵאתָ	2ms
הִתְמַצֵּאת	הִמְצֵאת	הֻמְצֵאת	מָלֵאת	2fs
הִתְמַצֵּאתִי	הִמְצֵאתִי	הֻמְצֵאתִי	מָלֵאתִי	1cs
הִתְמַצְּאוּ	הִמְצִיאוּ	הֻמְצְאוּ	מָלְאוּ	3cp
הִתְמַצֵּאתֶם	הִמְצֵאתֶם	הֻמְצֵאתֶם	מְלֵאתֶם	2mp
הִתְמַצֵּאתֶן	הִמְצֵאתֶן	הֻמְצֵאתֶן	מְלֵאתֶן	2fp
הִתְמַצֵּאנוּ	הִמְצֵאנוּ	הֻמְצֵאנוּ	מָלֵאנוּ	1cp
				Imperfect
יִתְמַצֵּא	יַמְצִיא	יֻמְצָא	יִמְלָא	3ms
תִּתְמַצֵּא	תַּמְצִיא	תֻּמְצָא	תִּמְלָא	3fs
תִּתְמַצֵּא	תַּמְצִיא	תֻּמְצָא	תִּמְלָא	2ms
תִּתְמַצְּאִי	תַּמְצִיאִי	תֻּמְצְאִי	תִּמְלְאִי	2fs
אֶתְמַצֵּא	אַמְצִיא	אֻמְצָא	אֶמְלָא	1cs
יִתְמַצְּאוּ	יַמְצִיאוּ	יֻמְצְאוּ	יִמְלְאוּ	3mp
תִּתְמַצֶּאנָה	תַּמְצֶאנָה	תֻּמְצֶאנָה	תִּמְלֶאנָה	3fp
תִּתְמַצְּאוּ	תַּמְצִיאוּ	תֻּמְצְאוּ	תִּמְלְאוּ	2mp
תִּתְמַצֶּאנָה	תַּמְצֶאנָה	תֻּמְצֶאנָה	תִּמְלֶאנָה	2fp
נִתְמַצֵּא	נַמְצִיא	נֻמְצָא	נִמְלָא	1cp
				Imperative
הִתְמַצֵּא	הַמְצֵא		מְלָא	2ms
הִתְמַצְּאִי	הַמְצִיאִי		מִלְאִי	2fs
הִתְמַצְּאוּ	הַמְצִיאוּ		מִלְאוּ	2mp
הִתְמַצֶּאנָה	הַמְצֶאנָה		מְלֶאנָה	2fp
				Infinitive
הִתְמַצֵּא	הַמְצֵא	הֻמְצֵא	מָלוֹא	absolute
הִתְמַצֵּא	הַמְצִיא	הֻמְצָא	מְלֹא	construct
				Participle
מִתְמַצֵּא	מַמְצִיא		מָלֵא	active ms
		מֻמְצָא		passive ms
				Imperfect
וַיִּתְמַצֵּא	וַיַּמְצֵא	וַיֻּמְצָא	וַיִּמְלָא	consec. 3ms
				Jussive
יִתְמַצֵּא	יַמְצֵא	יֻמְצָא	יִמְלָא	3ms
				Cohortative
אֶתְמַצְּאָה	אַמְצִיאָה		אֶמְלְאָה	1cs

7

Chart 140: ל״ה Verb

Model Verb: גָּלָה -- "to uncover, reveal, go into exile"

	Qal	Nifal	Piel	Pual
Perfect				
3ms	גָּלָה	נִגְלָה	גִּלָּה	גֻּלָּה
3fs	גָּלְתָה	נִגְלְתָה	גִּלְּתָה	גֻּלְּתָה
2ms	גָּלִיתָ	נִגְלֵיתָ	גִּלִּיתָ	גֻּלֵּיתָ
2fs	גָּלִית	נִגְלֵית	גִּלִּית	גֻּלֵּית
1cs	גָּלִיתִי	נִגְלֵיתִי	גִּלִּיתִי	גֻּלֵּיתִי
3cp	גָּלוּ	נִגְלוּ	גִּלּוּ	גֻּלּוּ
2mp	גְּלִיתֶם	נִגְלֵיתֶם	גִּלִּיתֶם	גֻּלֵּיתֶם
2fp	גְּלִיתֶן	נִגְלֵיתֶן	גִּלִּיתֶן	גֻּלֵּיתֶן
1cp	גָּלִינוּ	נִגְלֵינוּ	גִּלִּינוּ	גֻּלֵּינוּ
Imperfect				
3ms	יִגְלֶה	יִגָּלֶה	יְגַלֶּה	יְגֻלֶּה
3fs	תִּגְלֶה	תִּגָּלֶה	תְּגַלֶּה	תְּגֻלֶּה
2ms	תִּגְלֶה	תִּגָּלֶה	תְּגַלֶּה	תְּגֻלֶּה
2fs	תִּגְלִי	תִּגָּלִי	תְּגַלִּי	תְּגֻלִּי
1cs	אֶגְלֶה	אֶגָּלֶה	אֲגַלֶּה	אֲגֻלֶּה
3mp	יִגְלוּ	יִגָּלוּ	יְגַלּוּ	יְגֻלּוּ
3fp	תִּגְלֶינָה	תִּגָּלֶינָה	תְּגַלֶּינָה	תְּגֻלֶּינָה
2mp	תִּגְלוּ	תִּגָּלוּ	תְּגַלּוּ	תְּגֻלּוּ
2fp	תִּגְלֶינָה	תִּגָּלֶינָה	תְּגַלֶּינָה	תְּגֻלֶּינָה
1cp	נִגְלֶה	נִגָּלֶה	נְגַלֶּה	נְגֻלֶּה
Imperative				
2ms	גְּלֵה	הִגָּלֵה	גַּלֵּה	
2fs	גְּלִי	הִגָּלִי	גַּלִּי	
2mp	גְּלוּ	הִגָּלוּ	גַּלּוּ	
2fp	גְּלֶינָה	הִגָּלֶינָה	גַּלֶּינָה	
Infinitive				
absolute	גָּלֹה	נִגְלֹה	גַּלֵּה	גֻּלֹּה
construct	גְּלוֹת	הִגָּלוֹת	גַּלּוֹת	גֻּלּוֹת
Participle				
active ms	גֹּלֶה		מְגַלֶּה	
passive ms	גָּלוּי	נִגְלֶה		מְגֻלֶּה
Imperfect				
consec. 3ms	וַיִּגֶל	וַיִּגָּל	וַיְגַל	וַיְגֻל
Jussive				
3ms	יִגֶל	יִגָּל	יְגַל	יְגֻל
Cohortative				
1cs	אֶגְלֶה	אֶגָּלֶה	אֲגַלֶּה	

גלה (היה)

Hitpael	Hifil	Hofal	Qal היה	
				Perfect
הִתְגַּלָה	הִגְלָה	הָגְלָה	הָיָה	3ms
הִתְגַּלְתָה	הִגְלְתָה	הָגְלְתָה	הָיְתָה	2fs
הִתְגַּלִּיתָ	הִגְלִיתָ	הָגְלֵיתָ	הָיִיתָ	2ms
הִתְגַּלִּית	הִגְלִית	הָגְלֵית	הָיִית	2fs
הִתְגַּלִּיתִי	הִגְלִיתִי	הָגְלֵיתִי	הָיִיתִי	1cs
הִתְגַּלוּ	הִגְלוּ	הָגְלוּ	הָיוּ	3cp
הִתְגַּלִּיתֶם	הִגְלִיתֶם	הָגְלֵיתֶם	הֱיִיתֶם	2mp
הִתְגַּלִּיתֶן	הִגְלִיתֶן	הָגְלֵיתֶן	הֱיִיתֶן	2fp
הִתְגַּלִּינוּ	הִגְלִינוּ	הָגְלֵינוּ	הָיִינוּ	1cp
				Imperfect
יִתְגַּלֶּה	יַגְלֶה	יָגְלֶה	יִהְיֶה	3ms
תִּתְגַּלֶּה	תַּגְלֶה	תָּגְלֶה	תִּהְיֶה	3fs
תִּתְגַּלֶּה	תַּגְלֶה	תָּגְלֶה	תִּהְיֶה	2ms
תִּתְגַּלִּי	תַּגְלִי	תָּגְלִי	תִּהְיִי	2fs
אֶתְגַּלֶּה	אַגְלֶה	אָגְלֶה	אֶהְיֶה	1cs
יִתְגַּלוּ	יַגְלוּ	יָגְלוּ	יִהְיוּ	3mp
תִּתְגַּלֶּינָה	תַּגְלֶינָה	תָּגְלֶינָה	תִּהְיֶינָה	3fp
תִּתְגַּלוּ	תַּגְלוּ	תָּגְלוּ	תִּהְיוּ	2mp
תִּתְגַּלֶּינָה	תַּגְלֶינָה	תָּגְלֶינָה	תִּהְיֶינָה	2fp
נִתְגַּלֶּה	נַגְלֶה	נָגְלֶה	נִהְיֶה	1cp
				Imperative
הִתְגַּלֵּה	הַגְלֵה		הֱיֵה	2ms
הִתְגַּלִּי	הַגְלִי		הֲיִי	2fs
הִתְגַּלּוּ	הַגְלוּ		הֱיוּ	2mp
הִתְגַּלֶּינָה	הַגְלֶינָה		הֱיֶינָה	2fp
				Infinitive
הִתְגַּלֵּה	הַגְלֵה	הָגְלֵה	הָיֹה ,הָיוֹ	absolute
הִתְגַּלּוֹת	הַגְלוֹת	הָגְלוֹת	הֱיוֹת	construct
				Participle
מִתְגַּלֶּה	מַגְלֶה		הֹוֶה	active ms
		מָגְלֶה		passive ms
				Imperfect
וַיִּתְגַּל	וַיֶּגֶל		וַיְהִי	consec. 3ms
				Jussive
יִתְגַּל	יֶגֶל		יְהִי	3ms
				Cohortative
אֶתְגַּלֶּה	אַגְלֶה		אֶהְיֶה	1cs

7

Chart 142: פ״י Verb (Original פ״ו)

Model Verb: יָשַׁב -- "to sit, dwell, remain"

	Qal	Nifal	Piel	Pual
Perfect				
3ms	יָשַׁב	נוֹשַׁב	יִשֵּׁב	יֻשַּׁב
3fs	יָשְׁבָה	נוֹשְׁבָה	יִשְּׁבָה	יֻשְּׁבָה
2ms	יָשַׁבְתָּ	נוֹשַׁבְתָּ	יִשַּׁבְתָּ	יֻשַּׁבְתָּ
2fs	יָשַׁבְתְּ	נוֹשַׁבְתְּ	יִשַּׁבְתְּ	יֻשַּׁבְתְּ
1cs	יָשַׁבְתִּי	נוֹשַׁבְתִּי	יִשַּׁבְתִּי	יֻשַּׁבְתִּי
3cp	יָשְׁבוּ	נוֹשְׁבוּ	יִשְּׁבוּ	יֻשְּׁבוּ
2ms	יְשַׁבְתֶּם	נוֹשַׁבְתֶּם	יִשַּׁבְתֶּם	יֻשַּׁבְתֶּם
2fp	יְשַׁבְתֶּן	נוֹשַׁבְתֶּן	יִשַּׁבְתֶּן	יֻשַּׁבְתֶּן
1cp	יָשַׁבְנוּ	נוֹשַׁבְנוּ	יִשַּׁבְנוּ	יֻשַּׁבְנוּ
Imperfect				
3ms	יֵשֵׁב	יִוָּשֵׁב	יְיַשֵּׁב	יְיֻשַּׁב
3fs	תֵּשֵׁב	תִּוָּשֵׁב	תְּיַשֵּׁב	תְּיֻשַּׁב
2ms	תֵּשֵׁב	תִּוָּשֵׁב	תְּיַשֵּׁב	תְּיֻשַּׁב
2fs	תֵּשְׁבִי	תִּוָּשְׁבִי	תְּיַשְּׁבִי	תְּיֻשְּׁבִי
1cs	אֵשֵׁב	אִוָּשֵׁב	אֲיַשֵּׁב	אֲיֻשַּׁב
3mp	יֵשְׁבוּ	יִוָּשְׁבוּ	יְיַשְּׁבוּ	יְיֻשְּׁבוּ
3fp	תֵּשַׁבְנָה	תִּוָּשַׁבְנָה	תְּיַשֵּׁבְנָה	תְּיֻשַּׁבְנָה
2mp	תֵּשְׁבוּ	תִּוָּשְׁבוּ	תְּיַשְּׁבוּ	תְּיֻשְּׁבוּ
2fp	תֵּשַׁבְנָה	תִּוָּשַׁבְנָה	תְּיַשֵּׁבְנָה	תְּיֻשַּׁבְנָה
1cp	נֵשֵׁב	נִוָּשֵׁב	נְיַשֵּׁב	נְיֻשַּׁב
Imperative				
2ms	שֵׁב	הִוָּשֵׁב	יַשֵּׁב	
2fs	שְׁבִי	הִוָּשְׁבִי	יַשְּׁבִי	
2mp	שְׁבוּ	הִוָּשְׁבוּ	יַשְּׁבוּ	
2fp	שֵׁבְנָה	הִוָּשַׁבְנָה	יַשֵּׁבְנָה	
Infinitive				
absolute	יָשׁוֹב	הִוָּשֵׁב	יַשֵּׁב	יֻשַּׁב
construct	שֶׁבֶת	הִוָּשֵׁב	יַשֵּׁב	יֻשַּׁב
Participle				
active ms	יֹשֵׁב		מְיַשֵּׁב	
passive ms	יָשׁוּב	נוֹשָׁב		מְיֻשָּׁב
Imperfect				
consec. 3ms	וַיֵּשֶׁב	וַיִּוָּשֵׁב	וַיְיַשֵּׁב	וַיְיֻשַּׁב
Jussive				
3ms	יֵשֵׁב	יִוָּשֵׁב	יְיַשֵּׁב	יְיֻשַּׁב
Cohortative				
1cs	אֵשְׁבָה	אִוָּשְׁבָה	אֲיַשְּׁבָה	

7

יָשַׁב (הָלַךְ, יָרֵא)

Hitpael	Hifil	Hofal	Stative Qal	Qal הלך	
					Perfect
הִתְוַשֵׁב	הוֹשִׁיב	הוּשַׁב	יָרֵא	הָלַךְ	3ms
הִתְוַשְׁבָה	הוֹשִׁיבָה	הוּשְׁבָה	יָרְאָה	הָלְכָה	3fs
הִתְוַשַּׁבְתָּ	הוֹשַׁבְתָּ	הוּשַׁבְתָּ	יָרֵאתָ	הָלַכְתָּ	2ms
הִתְוַשַׁבְתְּ	הוֹשַׁבְתְּ	הוּשַׁבְתְּ	יָרֵאת	הָלַכְתְּ	2fs
הִתְוַשַּׁבְתִּי	הוֹשַׁבְתִּי	הוּשַׁבְתִּי	יָרֵאתִי	הָלַכְתִּי	1cs
הִתְוַשְׁבוּ	הוֹשִׁיבוּ	הוּשְׁבוּ	יָרְאוּ	הָלְכוּ	3cp
הִתְוַשַׁבְתֶּם	הוֹשַׁבְתֶּם	הוּשַׁבְתֶּם	יְרֵאתֶם	הֲלַכְתֶּם	2mp
הִתְוַשַׁבְתֶּן	הוֹשַׁבְתֶּן	הוּשַׁבְתֶּן	יְרֵאתֶן	הֲלַכְתֶּן	2fp
הִתְוַשַּׁבְנוּ	הוֹשַׁבְנוּ	הוּשַׁבְנוּ	יָרֵאנוּ	הָלַכְנוּ	1cp
					Imperfect
יִתְוַשֵׁב	יוֹשִׁיב	יוּשַׁב	יִירָא	יֵלֵךְ	3ms
תִּתְוַשֵׁב	תּוֹשִׁיב	תּוּשַׁב	תִּירָא	תֵּלֵךְ	3fs
תִּתְוַשֵׁב	תּוֹשִׁיב	תּוּשַׁב	תִּירָא	תֵּלֵךְ	2ms
תִּתְוַשְׁבִי	תּוֹשִׁיבִי	תּוּשְׁבִי	תִּירְאִי	תֵּלְכִי	2fs
אֶתְוַשֵׁב	אוֹשִׁיב	אוּשַׁב	אִירָא	אֵלֵךְ	1cs
יִתְוַשְׁבוּ	יוֹשִׁיבוּ	יוּשְׁבוּ	יִירְאוּ	יֵלְכוּ	3mp
תִּתְוַשֵּׁבְנָה	תּוֹשֵׁבְנָה	תּוּשַׁבְנָה	תִּירֶאנָה	תֵּלַכְנָה	3fp
תִּתְוַשְׁבוּ	תּוֹשִׁיבוּ	תּוּשְׁבוּ	תִּירְאוּ	תֵּלְכוּ	2mp
תִּתְוַשֵּׁבְנָה	תּוֹשֵׁבְנָה	תּוּשַׁבְנָה	תִּירֶאנָה	תֵּלַכְנָה	2fp
נִתְוַשֵׁב	נוֹשִׁיב	נוּשַׁב	נִירָא	נֵלֵךְ	1cp
					Imperative
הִתְוַשֵׁב	הוֹשֵׁב		יְרָא	לֵךְ	2ms
הִתְוַשְּׁבִי	הוֹשִׁיבִי		יִרְאִי	לְכִי	2fs
הִתְוַשְּׁבוּ	הוֹשִׁיבוּ		יִרְאוּ	לְכוּ	2mp
הִתְוַשֵּׁבְנָה	הוֹשֵׁבְנָה		יְרֶאנָה	לֵכְנָה	2fp
					Infinitive
הִתְוַשֵּׁב	הוֹשֵׁב	הוּשֵׁב	יָרוֹא	הָלוֹךְ	absolute
הִתְוַשֵּׁב	הוֹשֵׁב	הוּשַׁב	יְרֹא	לֶכֶת	construct
					Participle
מִתְוַשֵּׁב	מוֹשִׁיב		יָרֵא	הֹלֵךְ	active ms
		מוּשָׁב		הָלוּךְ	passive ms
					Imperfect
וַיִּתְוַשֵּׁב	וַיּוֹשֵׁב	וַיּוּשַׁב	וַיִּירָא	וַיֵּלֶךְ	consec. 3ms
					Jussive
יִתְוַשֵּׁב	יוֹשֵׁב	יוּשַׁב	יִירָא	יֵלֵךְ	3ms
					Cohortative
אֶתְוַשְּׁבָה	אוֹשִׁיבָה		אִירְאָה	אֵלְכָה	1cs

7

Chart 144: פ״י Verb (Original פ״י)

Model Verb: יטב -- "to be good"

	Qal	Nifal	Piel	Pual
Perfect				
3ms	יָטַב	נוֹטַב	יִטַּב	יֻטַּב
3fs	יָטְבָה	נוֹטְבָה	יִטְּבָה	יֻטְּבָה
2ms	יָטַבְתָּ	נוֹטַבְתָּ	יִטַּבְתָּ	יֻטַּבְתָּ
2fs	יָטַבְתְּ	נוֹטַבְתְּ	יִטַּבְתְּ	יֻטַּבְתְּ
1cs	יָטַבְתִּי	נוֹטַבְתִּי	יִטַּבְתִּי	יֻטַּבְתִּי
3cp	יָטְבוּ	נוֹטְבוּ	יִטְּבוּ	יֻטְּבוּ
2mp	יְטַבְתֶּם	נוֹטַבְתֶּם	יִטַּבְתֶּם	יֻטַּבְתֶּם
2fp	יְטַבְתֶּן	נוֹטַבְתֶּן	יִטַּבְתֶּן	יֻטַּבְתֶּן
1cp	יָטַבְנוּ	נוֹטַבְנוּ	יִטַּבְנוּ	יֻטַּבְנוּ
Imperfect				
3ms	יִיטַב	יִוָּטֵב	יְיַטֵּב	יְיֻטַּב
3fs	תִּיטַב	תִּוָּטֵב	תְּיַטֵּב	תְּיֻטַּב
2ms	תִּיטַב	תִּוָּטֵב	תְּיַטֵּב	תְּיֻטַּב
2fs	תִּיטְבִי	תִּוָּטְבִי	תְּיַטְּבִי	תְּיֻטְּבִי
1cs	אִיטַב	אִוָּטֵב	אֲיַטֵּב	אֲיֻטַּב
3mp	יִיטְבוּ	יִוָּטְבוּ	יְיַטְּבוּ	יְיֻטְּבוּ
3fp	תִּיטַבְנָה	תִּוָּטַבְנָה	תְּיַטֵּבְנָה	תְּיֻטַּבְנָה
2mp	תִּיטְבוּ	תִּוָּטְבוּ	תְּיַטְּבוּ	תְּיֻטְּבוּ
2fp	תִּיטַבְנָה	תִּוָּטַבְנָה	תְּיַטֵּבְנָה	תְּיֻטַּבְנָה
1cp	נִיטַב	נִוָּטֵב	נְיַטֵּב	נְיֻטַּב
Imperative				
2ms	יְטַב	הִוָּטֵב	יַטֵּב	
2fs	יִטְבִי	הִוָּטְבִי	יַטְּבִי	
2mp	יִטְבוּ	הִוָּטְבוּ	יַטְּבוּ	
2fp	יְטַבְנָה	הִוָּטַבְנָה	יַטֵּבְנָה	
Infinitive				
absolute	יָטוֹב	הִוָּטֹב	יַטֵּב	יֻטֹּב
construct	יְטֹב	הִוָּטֵב	יַטֵּב	יֻטַּב
Participle				
active ms	יֹטֵב		מְיַטֵּב	
passive ms	יָטוּב	נוֹטָב		מְיֻטָּב
Imperfect				
consec. 3ms	וַיִּיטַב	וַיִּוָּטֵב	וַיְיַטֵּב	וַיְיֻטַּב
Jussive				
3ms	יִיטַב	יִוָּטֵב	יְיַטֵּב	יְיֻטַּב
Cohortative				
1cs	אִיטְבָה	אִוָּטְבָה	אֲיַטְּבָה	

7

יטב

Hitpael	Hifil	Hofal		
			Perfect	
הִתְיַטֵּב	הֵיטִיב	הוּטַב	3ms	
הִתְיַטְּבָה	הֵיטִיבָה	הוּטְבָה	3fs	
הִתְיַטַּבְתָּ	הֵיטַבְתָּ	הוּטַבְתָּ	2ms	
הִתְיַטַּבְתְּ	הֵיטַבְתְּ	הוּטַבְתְּ	2fs	
הִתְיַטַּבְתִּי	הֵיטַבְתִּי	הוּטַבְתִּי	1cs	
הִתְיַטְּבוּ	הֵיטִיבוּ	הוּטְבוּ	3cp	
הִתְיַטַּבְתֶּם	הֵיטַבְתֶּם	הוּטַבְתֶּם	2mp	
הִתְיַטַּבְתֶּן	הֵיטַבְתֶּן	הוּטַבְתֶּן	2fp	
הִתְיַטַּבְנוּ	הֵיטַבְנוּ	הוּטַבְנוּ	1cp	
			Imperfect	
יִתְיַטֵּב	יֵיטִיב	יוּטַב	3ms	
תִּתְיַטֵּב	תֵּיטִיב	תּוּטַב	3fs	
תִּתְיַטֵּב	תֵּיטִיב	תּוּטַב	2ms	
תִּתְיַטְּבִי	תֵּיטִיבִי	תּוּטְבִי	2fs	
אֶתְיַטֵּב	אֵיטִיב	אוּטַב	1cs	
יִתְיַטְּבוּ	יֵיטִיבוּ	יוּטְבוּ	3mp	
תִּתְיַטֵּבְנָה	תֵּיטֵבְנָה	תּוּטַבְנָה	3fp	
תִּתְיַטְּבוּ	תֵּיטִיבוּ	תּוּטְבוּ	2mp	
תִּתְיַטֵּבְנָה	תֵּיטֵבְנָה	תּוּטַבְנָה	2fp	
נִתְיַטֵּב	נֵיטִיב	נוּטַב	1cp	
			Imperative	
הִתְיַטֵּב	הֵיטֵב		2ms	
הִתְיַטְּבִי	הֵיטִיבִי		2fs	
הִתְיַטְּבוּ	הֵיטִיבוּ		2mp	
הִתְיַטֵּבְנָה	הֵיטֵבְנָה		2fp	
			Infinitive	
הִתְיַטֵּב	הֵיטֵב	הוּטַב	absolute	
הִתְיַטֵּב	הֵיטִיב	הוּטַב	construct	
			Participle	
מִתְיַטֵּב	מֵיטִיב		active ms	
		מוּטָב	passive ms	
			Imperfect	
וַיִּתְיַטֵּב	וַיֵּיטֶב	וַיּוּטַב	consec. 3ms	
			Jussive	
יִתְיַטֵּב	יֵיטֶב	יוּטַב	3ms	
			Cohortative	
אֶתְיַטְּבָה	אֵיטִיבָה		1cs	

7

Chart 146: פ״ן Verb

Model Verb: נגשׁ -- "to draw near, approach"   (Qal: נפל)

	Qal		Nifal	Piel	Pual
Perfect					
3ms	נָגַשׁ	נָפַל	נִגַּשׁ	נִגֵּשׁ	נֻגַּשׁ
3fs	נָגְשָׁה	נָפְלָה	נִגְּשָׁה	נִגְּשָׁה	נֻגְּשָׁה
2ms	נָגַשְׁתָּ	נָפַלְתָּ	נִגַּשְׁתָּ	נִגַּשְׁתָּ	נֻגַּשְׁתָּ
2fs	נָגַשְׁתְּ	נָפַלְתְּ	נִגַּשְׁתְּ	נִגַּשְׁתְּ	נֻגַּשְׁתְּ
1cs	נָגַשְׁתִּי	נָפַלְתִּי	נִגַּשְׁתִּי	נִגַּשְׁתִּי	נֻגַּשְׁתִּי
3cp	נָגְשׁוּ	נָפְלוּ	נִגְּשׁוּ	נִגְּשׁוּ	נֻגְּשׁוּ
2mp	נְגַשְׁתֶּם	נְפַלְתֶּם	נִגַּשְׁתֶּם	נִגַּשְׁתֶּם	נֻגַּשְׁתֶּם
2fp	נְגַשְׁתֶּן	נְפַלְתֶּן	נִגַּשְׁתֶּן	נִגַּשְׁתֶּן	נֻגַּשְׁתֶּן
1cp	נָגַשְׁנוּ	נָפַלְנוּ	נִגַּשְׁנוּ	נִגַּשְׁנוּ	נֻגַּשְׁנוּ
Imperfect					
3ms	יִגַּשׁ	יִפֹּל	יִנָּגֵשׁ	יְנַגֵּשׁ	יְנֻגַּשׁ
3fs	תִּגַּשׁ	תִּפֹּל	תִּנָּגֵשׁ	תְּנַגֵּשׁ	תְּנֻגַּשׁ
2ms	תִּגַּשׁ	תִּפֹּל	תִּנָּגֵשׁ	תְּנַגֵּשׁ	תְּנֻגַּשׁ
2fs	תִּגְּשִׁי	תִּפְּלִי	תִּנָּגְשִׁי	תְּנַגְּשִׁי	תְּנֻגְּשִׁי
1cs	אֶגַּשׁ	אֶפֹּל	אֶנָּגֵשׁ	אֲנַגֵּשׁ	אֲנֻגַּשׁ
3mp	יִגְּשׁוּ	יִפְּלוּ	יִנָּגְשׁוּ	יְנַגְּשׁוּ	יְנֻגְּשׁוּ
3fp	תִּגַּשְׁנָה	תִּפֹּלְנָה	תִּנָּגַשְׁנָה	תְּנַגֵּשְׁנָה	תְּנֻגַּשְׁנָה
2mp	תִּגְּשׁוּ	תִּפְּלוּ	תִּנָּגְשׁוּ	תְּנַגְּשׁוּ	תְּנֻגְּשׁוּ
2fp	תִּגַּשְׁנָה	תִּפֹּלְנָה	תִּנָּגַשְׁנָה	תְּנַגֵּשְׁנָה	תְּנֻגַּשְׁנָה
1cp	נִגַּשׁ	נִפֹּל	נִנָּגֵשׁ	נְנַגֵּשׁ	נְנֻגַּשׁ
Imperative					
2ms	גַּשׁ	נְפֹל	הִנָּגֵשׁ	נַגֵּשׁ	
2fs	גְּשִׁי	נִפְלִי	הִנָּגְשִׁי	נַגְּשִׁי	
2mp	גְּשׁוּ	נִפְלוּ	הִנָּגְשׁוּ	נַגְּשׁוּ	
2fp	גַּשְׁנָה	נְפֹלְנָה	הִנָּגַשְׁנָה	נַגֵּשְׁנָה	
Infinitive					
absolute	נָגוֹשׁ	נָפוֹל	הִנָּגֵשׁ	נַגֵּשׁ	נֻגַּשׁ
construct	גֶּשֶׁת	נְפֹל	הִנָּגֵשׁ	נַגֵּשׁ	נֻגַּשׁ
Participle					
active ms	נֹגֵשׁ	נֹפֵל		מְנַגֵּשׁ	
passive ms	נָגוּשׁ	נָפוּל	נִגָּשׁ		מְנֻגָּשׁ
Imperfect					
consec. 3ms	וַיִּגַּשׁ	וַיִּפֹּל	וַיִּנָּגֵשׁ	וַיְנַגֵּשׁ	וַיְנֻגַּשׁ
Jussive					
3ms	יִגַּשׁ	יִפֹּל	יִנָּגֵשׁ	יְנַגֵּשׁ	יְנֻגַּשׁ
Cohortative					
1cs	אֶגְּשָׁה	אֶפְּלָה	אֶנָּגְשָׁה	אֲנַגְּשָׁה	

נגשׁ (לקח, נתן)

	Qal לקח	Qal נתן	Hofal	Hifil	Hitpael
Perfect					
3ms	לָקַח	נָתַן	הֻגַּשׁ	הִגִּישׁ	הִתְנַגֵּשׁ
3fs	לָקְחָה	נָתְנָה	הֻגְּשָׁה	הִגִּישָׁה	הִתְנַגְּשָׁה
2ms	לָקַחְתָּ	נָתַתָּה	הֻגַּשְׁתָּ	הִגַּשְׁתָּ	הִתְנַגַּשְׁתָּ
2fs	לָקַחַתְּ	נָתַתְּ	הֻגַּשְׁתְּ	הִגַּשְׁתְּ	הִתְנַגַּשְׁתְּ
1cs	לָקַחְתִּי	נָתַתִּי	הֻגַּשְׁתִּי	הִגַּשְׁתִּי	הִתְנַגַּשְׁתִּי
3cp	לָקְחוּ	נָתְנוּ	הֻגְּשׁוּ	הִגִּישׁוּ	הִתְנַגְּשׁוּ
2mp	לְקַחְתֶּם	נְתַתֶּם	הֻגַּשְׁתֶּם	הִגַּשְׁתֶּם	הִתְנַגַּשְׁתֶּם
2fp	לְקַחְתֶּן	נְתַתֶּן	הֻגַּשְׁתֶּן	הִגַּשְׁתֶּן	הִתְנַגַּשְׁתֶּן
1cp	לָקַחְנוּ	נָתַנּוּ	הֻגַּשְׁנוּ	הִגַּשְׁנוּ	הִתְנַגַּשְׁנוּ
Imperfect					
3ms	יִקַּח	יִתֵּן	יֻגַּשׁ	יַגִּישׁ	יִתְנַגֵּשׁ
3fs	תִּקַּח	תִּתֵּן	תֻּגַּשׁ	תַּגִּישׁ	תִּתְנַגֵּשׁ
2ms	תִּקַּח	תִּתֵּן	תֻּגַּשׁ	תַּגִּישׁ	תִּתְנַגֵּשׁ
2fs	תִּקְחִי	תִּתְּנִי	תֻּגְּשִׁי	תַּגִּישִׁי	תִּתְנַגְּשִׁי
1cs	אֶקַּח	אֶתֵּן	אֻגַּשׁ	אַגִּישׁ	אֶתְנַגֵּשׁ
3mp	יִקְחוּ	יִתְּנוּ	יֻגְּשׁוּ	יַגִּישׁוּ	יִתְנַגְּשׁוּ
3fp	תִּקַּחְנָה	תִּתֵּנָּה	תֻּגַּשְׁנָה	תַּגֵּשְׁנָה	תִּתְנַגֵּשְׁנָה
2mp	תִּקְחוּ	תִּתְּנוּ	תֻּגְּשׁוּ	תַּגִּישׁוּ	תִּתְנַגְּשׁוּ
2fp	תִּקַּחְנָה	תִּתֵּנָּה	תֻּגַּשְׁנָה	תַּגֵּשְׁנָה	תִּתְנַגֵּשְׁנָה
1cp	נִקַּח	נִתֵּן	נֻגַּשׁ	נַגִּישׁ	נִתְנַגֵּשׁ
Imperative					
2ms	קַח	תֵּן		הַגֵּשׁ	הִתְנַגֵּשׁ
2fs	קְחִי	תְּנִי		הַגִּישִׁי	הִתְנַגְּשִׁי
2mp	קְחוּ	תְּנִי		הַגִּישׁוּ	הִתְנַגְּשׁוּ
2fp	קַחְנָה	תֵּנָּה		הַגֵּשְׁנָה	הִתְנַגֵּשְׁנָה
Infinitive					
absolute	לָקוֹחַ	נָתוֹן	הֻגֵּשׁ	הַגֵּשׁ	הִתְנַגֵּשׁ
construct	קַחַת	תֵּת	הֻגֵּשׁ	הַגִּישׁ	הִתְנַגֵּשׁ
Participle					
active ms	לֹקֵחַ	נֹתֵן		מַגִּישׁ	מִתְנַגֵּשׁ
passive ms	לָקוּחַ	נָתוּן	מֻגָּשׁ		
Imperfect					
consec. 3ms	וַיִּקַּח	וַיִּתֵּן	וַיֻּגַּשׁ	וַיַּגֵּשׁ	וַיִּתְנַגֵּשׁ
Jussive					
3ms	יִקַּח	יִתֵּן	יֻגַּשׁ	יַגֵּשׁ	יִתְנַגֵּשׁ
Cohortative					
1cs	אֶקְחָה	אֶתְּנָה		אַגִּישָׁה	אֶתְנַגְּשָׁה

7

Chart 148: ע״ו Hollow Verb

Model Verb: קוּם -- "to arise, rise up, stand up"

	Qal	Nifal	Polel	Polal
Perfect				
3ms	קָם	נָקוֹם	קוֹמֵם	קוֹמַם
3fs	קָ֫מָה	נָק֫וֹמָה	קוֹמְמָה	קוֹמְמָה
2ms	קַ֫מְתָּ	נְקוּמ֫וֹתָ	קוֹמַ֫מְתָּ	קוֹמַ֫מְתָּ
2fs	קַמְתְּ	נְקוּמוֹת	קוֹמַמְתְּ	קוֹמַמְתְּ
1cs	קַ֫מְתִּי	נְקוּמ֫וֹתִי	קוֹמַ֫מְתִּי	קוֹמַ֫מְתִּי
3cp	קָ֫מוּ	נָק֫וֹמוּ	קוֹמְמוּ	קוֹמְמוּ
2mp	קַמְתֶּם	נְקוּמוֹתֶם	קוֹמַמְתֶּם	קוֹמַמְתֶּם
2fp	קַמְתֶּן	נְקוּמוֹתֶן	קוֹמַמְתֶּן	קוֹמַמְתֶּן
1cp	קַ֫מְנוּ	נְקוּמ֫וֹנוּ	קוֹמַ֫מְנוּ	קוֹמַ֫מְנוּ
Imperfect				
3ms	יָקוּם	יִקּוֹם	יְקוֹמֵם	יְקוֹמַם
3fs	תָּקוּם	תִּקּוֹם	תְּקוֹמֵם	תְּקוֹמַם
2ms	תָּקוּם	תִּקּוֹם	תְּקוֹמֵם	תְּקוֹמַם
2fs	תָּק֫וּמִי	תִּקּ֫וֹמִי	תְּקוֹמְמִי	תְּקוֹמְמִי
1cs	אָקוּם	אֶקּוֹם	אֲקוֹמֵם	אֲקוֹמַם
3mp	יָק֫וּמוּ	יִקּ֫וֹמוּ	יְקוֹמְמוּ	יְקוֹמְמוּ
3fp	תְּקוּמֶ֫ינָה	תִּקּוֹמְנָה	תְּקוֹמֵ֫מְנָה	תְּקוֹמַ֫מְנָה
2mp	תָּק֫וּמוּ	תִּקּ֫וֹמוּ	תְּקוֹמְמוּ	תְּקוֹמְמוּ
2fp	תְּקוּמֶ֫ינָה	תִּקּוֹמְנָה	תְּקוֹמֵ֫מְנָה	תְּקוֹמַ֫מְנָה
1cp	נָקוּם	נִקּוֹם	נְקוֹמֵם	נְקוֹמַם
Imperative				
2ms	קוּם	הִקּוֹם	קוֹמֵם	
2fs	ק֫וּמִי	הִקּ֫וֹמִי	קוֹמְמִי	
2mp	ק֫וּמוּ	הִקּ֫וֹמוּ	קוֹמְמוּ	
2fp	קֹ֫מְנָה	הִקּוֹמְנָה	קוֹמֵ֫מְנָה	
Infinitive				
absolute	קוֹם	הִקּוֹם	קוֹמֵם	קוֹמַם
construct	קוּם	הִקּוֹם	קוֹמֵם	קוֹמַם
Participle				
active ms	קָם		מְקוֹמֵם	
passive ms	קוּם	נָקוֹם		מְקוֹמָם
Imperfect				
consec. 3ms	וַיָּ֫קָם	וַיִּקּוֹם	וַיְקוֹמֵם	וַיְקוֹמַם
Jussive				
3ms	יָקֹם	יִקּוֹם	יְקוֹמֵם	יְקוֹמַם
Cohortative				
1cs	אָק֫וּמָה	אֶקּ֫וֹמָה	אֲקוֹמְמָה	

7

קוּם   (בּוֹשׁ, מוּת)

	Qal	Stative Qal	Hofal	Hifil	Hitpolel
Perfect					
3ms	בּוֹשׁ	מֵת	הוּקַם	הֵקִים	הִתְקוֹמֵם
3fs	בּוֹשָׁה	מֵ֫תָה	הוּקְמָה	הֵקִ֫ימָה	הִתְקוֹמְמָה
2ms	בֹּ֫שְׁתָּ	מַ֫תָּה	הוּקַמְתָּ	הֲקִימֹ֫תָ	הִתְקוֹמַ֫מְתָּ
2fs	בֹּשְׁתְּ	מַתְּ	הוּקַמְתְּ	הֲקִימֹת	הִתְקוֹמַמְתְּ
1cs	בֹּ֫שְׁתִּי	מַ֫תִּי	הוּקַמְתִּי	הֲקִימֹ֫תִי	הִתְקוֹמַ֫מְתִּי
3cp	בֹּ֫שׁוּ	מֵ֫תוּ	הוּקְמוּ	הֵקִ֫ימוּ	הִתְקוֹמְמוּ
2mp	בָּשְׁתֶּם	מַתֶּם	הוּקַמְתֶּם	הֲקִימוֹתֶם	הִתְקוֹמַמְתֶּם
2fp	בָּשְׁתֶּן	מַתֶּן	הוּקַמְתֶּן	הֲקִימוֹתֶן	הִתְקוֹמַמְתֶּן
1cp	בֹּ֫שְׁנוּ	קַ֫תְנוּ	הוּקַמְנוּ	הֲקִימֹ֫ונוּ	הִתְקוֹמַ֫מְנוּ
Imperfect					
3ms	יֵבוֹשׁ	יָמוּת	יוּקַם	יָקִים	יִתְקוֹמֵם
3fs	תֵּבוֹשׁ	תָּמוּת	תּוּקַם	תָּקִים	תִּתְקוֹמֵם
2ms	תֵּבוֹשׁ	תָּמוּת	תּוּקַם	תָּקִים	תִּתְקוֹמֵם
2fs	תֵּבוֹשִׁי	תָּמוּתִי	תּוּקְמִי	תָּקִ֫ימִי	תִּתְקוֹמְמִי
1cs	אֵבוֹשׁ	אָמוּת	אוּקַם	אָקִים	אֶתְקוֹמֵם
3mp	יֵבוֹשׁוּ	יָמֻ֫תוּ	יוּקְמוּ	יָקִ֫ימוּ	יִתְקוֹמְמוּ
3fp	תֵּבֹ֫שְׁנָה	תְּמוּתֶ֫ינָה	תּוּקַמְנָה	תָּקֵ֫מְנָה	תִּתְקוֹמֵ֫מְנָה
2mp	תֵּבֹ֫שׁוּ	תָּמֻ֫תוּ	תּוּקְמוּ	תָּקִ֫ימוּ	תִּתְקוֹמְמוּ
2fp	תֵּבֹ֫שְׁנָה	תְּמוּתֶ֫ינָה	תּוּקַמְנָה	תָּקֵ֫מְנָה	תִּתְקוֹמֵ֫מְנָה
1cp	נֵבוֹשׁ	נָמוּת	נוּקַם	נָקִים	נִתְקוֹמֵם
Imperative					
2ms	בּוֹשׁ	מוּת		הָקֵם	הִתְקוֹמֵם
2fs	בּ֫וֹשִׁי	מ֫וּתִי		הָקִ֫ימִי	הִתְקוֹמְמִי
2mp	בּ֫וֹשׁוּ	מ֫וּתוּ		הָקִ֫ימוּ	הִתְקוֹמְמוּ
2fp	בֹּ֫שְׁנָה	מֹ֫תְנָה		הָקֵ֫מְנָה	הִתְקוֹמֵ֫מְנָה
Infinitive					
absolute	בּוֹשׁ	מוֹת	הוּקֵם	הָקֵם	הִתְקוֹמֵם
construct	בּוֹשׁ	מוּת	הוּקַם	הָקִים	הִתְקוֹמֵם
Participle					
active ms	בּוֹשׁ	מֵת		מֵקִים	מִתְקוֹמֵם
passive ms			מוּקָם		
Imperfect					
consec. 3ms	וַיֵּ֫בֹשׁ	וַיָּ֫מֶת	וַיּוּקַם	וַיָּ֫קֶם	וַיִּתְקוֹמֵם
Jussive					
3ms	יֵבֹשׁ	יָמֹת	יוּקַם	יָקֵם	יִתְקוֹמֵם
Cohortative					
1cs	אֵב֫וֹשָׁה	אָמ֫וּתָה		אָקִ֫ימָה	אֶתְקוֹמְמָה

7

Chart 150: ע"י Hollow Verb

Model Verb: שִׂים -- "to put, set, place"

Qal

Perfect	
3ms	שָׂם
3fs	שָׂמָה
2ms	שַׂמְתָּ
2fs	שַׂמְתְּ
1cs	שַׂמְתִּי
3cp	שָׂמוּ
2mp	שַׂמְתֶּם
2fp	שַׂמְתֶּן
1cp	שַׂמְנוּ
Imperfect	
3ms	יָשִׂים
3fs	תָּשִׂים
2ms	תָּשִׂים
2fs	תָּשִׂימִי
1cs	אָשִׂים
3mp	יָשִׂימוּ
3fp	תְּשִׂימֶינָה
2mp	תָּשִׂימוּ
2fp	תְּשִׂימֶינָה
1cp	נָשִׂים
Imperative	
2ms	שִׂים
2fs	שִׂימִי
2mp	שִׂימוּ
2fp	שִׂמְנָה
Infinitive	
absolute	שׂוֹם
construct	שִׂים
Participle	
active ms	שָׂם
passive ms	שִׂים
Imperfect	
consec. 3ms	וַיָּשֶׂם
Jussive	
3ms	יָשֵׂם
Cohortative	
1cs	אָשִׂימָה

ע"י and ע"ו verbs differ only in the Qal. The rest of this paradigm is the same as the ע"ו verb in Chart 148.

7

Model Verb: גלה

Qal Perfect 3ms (גָּלָה) with Suffixes:

3ms sf.	גָּלָֽהוּ	3mp sf.	גָּלָם
3fs sf.	גָּלָהּ	3fp sf.	גָּלָן
2ms sf.	גָּלְךָ	2mp sf.	גָּלְכֶם
2fs sf.	גָּלָךְ	2fp sf.	גָּלְכֶן
1cs sf.	גָּלַֽנִי	1cp sf.	גָּלָֽנוּ

Qal Imperfect 3ms (יִגְלֶה) with Suffixes:

3ms sf.	יִגְלֵֽהוּ	3mp sf.	יִגְלֵם
3fs sf.	יִגְלֶֽהָ	3fp sf.	יִגְלֵן
2ms sf.	יִגְלְךָ	2mp sf.	יִגְלְכֶם
2fs sf.	יִגְלֵךְ	2fp sf.	יִגְלֶכֶן
1cs sf.	יִגְלֵֽנִי	1cp sf.	יִגְלֵֽנוּ

Qal Imperative 2ms (גְּלֵה) with Suffixes:

3ms sf.	גְּלֵֽהוּ	3mp sf.	גְּלֵם
3fs sf.	גְּלֵהָ	3fp sf.	גְּלֵן
2ms sf.	גְּלֵךְ	2mp sf.	גְּלֵכֶם
2fs sf.	גְּלֵךְ	2fp sf.	גְּלֵכֶן
1cs sf.	גְּלֵֽנִי	1cp sf.	גְּלֵֽנוּ

7

Qal Infinitive Construct (גְּלוֹת) with Suffixes:

3ms sf.	גְּלוֹתוֹ	3mp sf.	גְּלוֹתָם
3fs sf.	גְּלוֹתָהּ	3fp sf.	גְּלוֹתָן
2ms sf.	גְּלוֹתְךָ	2mp sf.	גְּלוֹתְכֶם
2fs sf.	גְּלוֹתֵךְ	2fp sf.	גְּלוֹתְכֶן
1cs sf.	גְּלוֹתִי	1cp sf.	גְּלוֹתֵֽנוּ

Chart 152: ע"ע Verb

Model Verb: סבב -- "to go around, turn, surround"

	Qal		Nifal	Polel	Polal
Perfect					
3ms	סַב		נָסַב	סוֹבֵב	סוֹבַב
3fs	סַבָּה		נָסַבָּה	סוֹבְבָה	סוֹבְבָה
2ms	סַבּוֹתָ		נְסַבּוֹתָ	סוֹבַבְתָּ	סוֹבַבְתָּ
2fs	סַבּוֹת		נְסַבּוֹת	סוֹבַבְתְּ	סוֹבַבְתְּ
1cs	סַבּוֹתִי		נְסַבּוֹתִי	סוֹבַבְתִּי	סוֹבַבְתִּי
3cp	סַבּוּ		נָסַבּוּ	סוֹבְבוּ	סוֹבְבוּ
2mp	סַבּוֹתֶם		נְסַבּוֹתֶם	סוֹבַבְתֶּם	סוֹבַבְתֶּם
2fp	סַבּוֹתֶן		נְסַבּוֹתֶן	סוֹבַבְתֶּן	סוֹבַבְתֶּן
1cp	סַבּוֹנוּ		נְסַבּוֹנוּ	סוֹבַבְנוּ	סוֹבַבְנוּ
Imperfect					
3ms	יָסֹב	יִסֹּב	יִסַּב	יְסוֹבֵב	יְסוֹבַב
3fs	תָּסֹב	תִּסֹּב	תִּסַּב	תְּסוֹבֵב	תְּסוֹבַב
2ms	תָּסֹב	תִּסֹּב	תִּסַּב	תְּסוֹבֵב	תְּסוֹבַב
2fs	תָּסֹבִּי	תִּסֹּבִּי	תִּסַּבִּי	תְּסוֹבְבִי	תְּסוֹבְבִי
1cs	אָסֹב	אֶסֹּב	אֶסַּב	אֲסוֹבֵב	אֲסוֹבַב
3mp	יָסֹבּוּ	יִסֹּבּוּ	יִסַּבּוּ	יְסוֹבְבוּ	יְסוֹבְבוּ
3fp	תְּסֻבֶּינָה	תִּסֹּבְנָה	תְּסֻבֶּינָה	תְּסוֹבֵבְנָה	תְּסוֹבַבְנָה
2mp	תָּסֹבּוּ	תִּסֹּבּוּ	תִּסַּבּוּ	תְּסוֹבְבוּ	תְּסוֹבְבוּ
2fp	תְּסֻבֶּינָה	תִּסֹּבְנָה	תְּסֻבֶּינָה	תְּסוֹבֵבְנָה	תְּסוֹבַבְנָה
1cp	נָסֹב	נִסֹּב	נִסַּב	נְסוֹבֵב	נְסוֹבַב
Imperative					
2ms	סֹב		הִסַּב	סוֹבֵב	
2fs	סֹבִּי		הִסַּבִּי	סוֹבְבִי	
2mp	סֹבּוּ		הִסַּבּוּ	סוֹבְבוּ	
2fp	סֻבֶּינָה		הִסַּבֶּינָה	סוֹבֵבְנָה	
Infinitive					
absolute	סָבוֹב		הִסֹּב	סוֹבֵב	סוֹבַב
construct	סֹב		הִסַּב	סוֹבֵב	סוֹבַב
Participle					
active ms	סוֹבֵב			מְסוֹבֵב	
passive ms	סָבוּב		נָסָב		מְסוֹבָב
Imperfect					
consec. 3ms	וַיָּסָב	וַיִּסֹּב	וַיִּסַּב	וַיְסוֹבֵב	וַיְסוֹבַב
Jussive					
3ms	יָסֹב	יִסֹּב	יִסַּב	יְסוֹבֵב	יְסוֹבַב
Cohortative					
1cs	אָסֹבָּה	אֶסֹּבָּה	אֶסַּבָּה	אֲסוֹבְבָה	

7

סבב

Hitpolel	Hifil	Hofal		
			Perfect	
הִסְתּוֹבֵב	הֵסֵב	הוּסַב	3ms	
הִסְתּוֹבְבָה	הֵסֵׁבָּה	הוּסַׁבָּה	3fs	
הִסְתּוֹבַׁבְתָּ	הֲסִבּׁוֹתָ	הוּסַבּׁוֹתָ	2ms	
הִסְתּוֹבַׁבְתְּ	הֲסִבּוֹת	הוּסַבּוֹת	2fs	
הִסְתּוֹבַׁבְתִּי	הֲסִבּׁוֹתִי	הוּסַבּׁוֹתִי	1cs	
הִסְתּוֹבְבוּ	הֵסֵׁבּוּ	הוּסַׁבּוּ	3cp	
הִסְתּוֹבַבְתֶּם	הֲסִבּוֹתֶם	הוּסַבּוֹתֶם	2mp	
הִסְתּוֹבַבְתֶּן	הֲסִבּוֹתֶן	הוּסַבּוֹתֶן	2fp	
הִסְתּוֹבַׁבְנוּ	הֲסִבּׁוֹנוּ	הוּסַבּׁוֹנוּ	1cp	
			Imperfect	
יִסְתּוֹבֵב	יָסֵב	יוּסַב	3ms	
תִּסְתּוֹבֵב	תָּסֵב	תּוּסַב	3fs	
תִּסְתּוֹבֵב	תָּסֵב	תּוּסַב	2ms	
תִּסְתּוֹבְבִי	תָּסֵׁבִּי	תּוּסַׁבִּי	2fs	
אֶסְתּוֹבֵב	אָסֵב	אוּסַב	1cs	
יִסְתּוֹבְבוּ	יָסֵׁבּוּ	יוּסַׁבּוּ	3mp	
תִּסְתּוֹבֵׁבְנָה	תְּסֻבֶּׁינָה	תּוּסַבֶּׁינָה	3fp	
תִּסְתּוֹבְבוּ	תָּסֵׁבּוּ	תּוּסַׁבּוּ	2mp	
תִּסְתּוֹבֵׁבְנָה	תְּסֻבֶּׁינָה	תּוּסַבֶּׁינָה	2fp	
נִסְתּוֹבֵב	נָסֵב	נוּסַב	1cp	
			Imperative	
הִסְתּוֹבֵב	הָסֵב		2ms	
הִסְתּוֹבְבִי	הָסֵׁבִּי		2fs	
הִסְתּוֹבְבוּ	הָסֵׁבּוּ		2mp	
הִסְתּוֹבֵׁבְנָה	הֲסֻבֶּׁינָה		2fp	
			Infinitive	
הִסְתּוֹבֵב	הָסֵב	הוּסֵב	absolute	
הִסְתּוֹבֵב	הָסֵב	הוּסַב	construct	
			Participle	
מִסְתּוֹבֵב	מֵסֵב		active ms	
		מוּסָב	passive ms	
			Imperfect	
וַיִּסְתּוֹבֵב	וַיָּׁסָב	וַיּוּסַב	consec. 3ms	
			Jussive	
יִסְתּוֹבֵב	יָסֵב	יוּסַב	3ms	
			Cohortative	
אֶסְתּוֹבְבָה	אָסֵׁבָּה		1cs	

7

Chart 154: פ Guttural, ל״ה Verb

Model Verb: עשׂה -- "to do, make"

	Qal	Nifal	Piel	Pual
Perfect				
3ms	עָשָׂה	נַעֲשָׂה	עִשָּׂה	עֻשָּׂה
3fs	עָשְׂתָה	נֶעֶשְׂתָה	עִשְּׂתָה	עֻשְּׂתָה
2ms	עָשִׂיתָ	נַעֲשֵׂיתָ	עִשִּׂיתָ	עֻשֵּׂיתָ
2fs	עָשִׂית	נַעֲשֵׂית	עִשִּׂית	עֻשֵּׂית
1cs	עָשִׂיתִי	נַעֲשֵׂיתִי	עִשִּׂיתִי	עֻשֵּׂיתִי
3cp	עָשׂוּ	נַעֲשׂוּ	עִשּׂוּ	עֻשּׂוּ
2mp	עֲשִׂיתֶם	נַעֲשֵׂיתֶם	עִשִּׂיתֶם	עֻשֵּׂיתֶם
2fp	עֲשִׂיתֶן	נַעֲשֵׂיתֶן	עִשִּׂיתֶן	עֻשֵּׂיתֶן
1cp	עָשִׂינוּ	נַעֲשֵׂינוּ	עִשִּׂינוּ	עֻשֵּׂינוּ
Imperfect				
3ms	יַעֲשֶׂה	יֵעָשֶׂה	יְעַשֶּׂה	יְעֻשֶּׂה
3fs	תַּעֲשֶׂה	תֵּעָשֶׂה	תְּעַשֶּׂה	תְּעֻשֶּׂה
2ms	תַּעֲשֶׂה	תֵּעָשֶׂה	תְּעַשֶּׂה	תְּעֻשֶּׂה
2fs	תַּעֲשִׂי	תֵּעָשִׂי	תְּעַשִּׂי	תְּעֻשִּׂי
1cs	אֶעֱשֶׂה	אֵעָשֶׂה	אֲעַשֶּׂה	אֲעֻשֶּׂה
3mp	יַעֲשׂוּ	יֵעָשׂוּ	יְעַשּׂוּ	יְעֻשּׂוּ
3fp	תַּעֲשֶׂינָה	תֵּעָשֶׂינָה	תְּעַשֶּׂינָה	תְּעֻשֶּׂינָה
2mp	תַּעֲשׂוּ	תֵּעָשׂוּ	תְּעַשּׂוּ	תְּעֻשּׂוּ
2fp	תַּעֲשֶׂינָה	תֵּעָשֶׂינָה	תְּעַשֶּׂינָה	תְּעֻשֶּׂינָה
1cp	נַעֲשֶׂה	נֵעָשֶׂה	נְעַשֶּׂה	נְעֻשֶּׂה
Imperative				
2ms	עֲשֵׂה	הֵעָשֶׂה	עַשֵּׂה	
2fs	עֲשִׂי	הֵעָשִׂי	עַשִּׂי	
2mp	עֲשׂוּ	הֵעָשׂוּ	עַשּׂוּ	
2fp	עֲשֶׂינָה	הֵעָשֶׂינָה	עַשֶּׂינָה	
Infinitive				
absolute	עָשֹׂה	הֵעָשֹׂה	עַשֹּׂה	עֻשֹּׂה
construct	עֲשׂוֹת	הֵעָשׂוֹת	עַשּׂוֹת	עֻשּׂוֹת
Participle				
active ms	עֹשֶׂה		מְעַשֶּׂה	
passive ms	עָשׂוּי	נַעֲשֶׂה		מְעֻשֶּׂה
Imperfect				
consec. 3ms	וַיַּעַשׂ	וַיֵּעָשׂ	וַיְעַשׂ	וַיְעֻשׂ
Jussive				
3ms	יַּעַשׂ	יֵעָשׂ	יְעַשׂ	יְעֻשׂ
Cohortative				
1cs	אֶעֱשֶׂה	אֵעָשֶׂה	אֲעַשֶּׂה	

7

עֹשֶׂה

Hitpael	Hifil	Hofal	
			Perfect
הִתְעַשָּׂה	הֶעֱשָׂה	הָעֳשָׂה	3ms
הִתְעַשְּׂתָה	הֶעֶשְׂתָה	הָעֳשְׂתָה	3fs
הִתְעַשִּׂיתָ	הֶעֱשִׂיתָ	הָעֳשִׂיתָ	2ms
הִתְעַשִּׂית	הֶעֱשִׂית	הָעֳשִׂית	2fs
הִתְעַשִּׂיתִי	הֶעֱשִׂיתִי	הָעֳשִׂיתִי	1cs
הִתְעַשּׂוּ	הֶעֱשׂוּ	הָעֳשׂוּ	3cp
הִתְעַשִּׂיתֶם	הֶעֱשִׂיתֶם	הָעֳשִׂיתֶם	2mp
הִתְעַשִּׂיתֶן	הֶעֱשִׂיתֶן	הָעֳשִׂיתֶן	2fp
הִתְעַשִּׂינוּ	הֶעֱשִׂינוּ	הָעֳשִׂינוּ	1cp
			Imperfect
יִתְעַשֶּׂה	יַעֲשֶׂה	יָעֳשֶׂה	3ms
תִּתְעַשֶּׂה	תַּעֲשֶׂה	תָּעֳשֶׂה	3fs
תִּתְעַשֶּׂה	תַּעֲשֶׂה	תָּעֳשֶׂה	2ms
תִּתְעַשִּׂי	תַּעֲשִׂי	תָּעֳשִׂי	2fs
אֶתְעַשֶּׂה	אַעֲשֶׂה	אָעֳשֶׂה	1cs
יִתְעַשּׂוּ	יַעֲשׂוּ	יָעֳשׂוּ	3mp
תִּתְעַשֶּׂינָה	תַּעֲשֶׂינָה	תָּעֳשֶׂינָה	3fp
תִּתְעַשּׂוּ	תַּעֲשׂוּ	תָּעֳשׂוּ	2mp
תִּתְעַשֶּׂינָה	תַּעֲשֶׂינָה	תָּעֳשֶׂינָה	2fp
נִתְעַשֶּׂה	נַעֲשֶׂה	נָעֳשֶׂה	1cp
			Imperative
הִתְעַשֵּׂה	הַעֲשֵׂה		2ms
הִתְעַשִּׂי	הַעֲשִׂי		2fs
הִתְעַשּׂוּ	הַעֲשׂוּ		2mp
הִתְעַשֶּׂינָה	הַעֲשֶׂינָה		2fp
			Infinitive
הִתְעַשֵּׂה	הַעֲשֵׂה	הָעֲשֵׂה	absolute
הִתְעַשּׂוֹת	הַעֲשׂוֹת	הָעֲשׂוֹת	construct
			Participle
מִתְעַשֶּׂה	מַעֲשֶׂה		active ms
		מָעֳשֶׂה	passive ms
			Imperfect
וַיִּתְעַשׂ	וַיַּעַשׂ		consec. 3ms
			Jussive
יִתְעַשׂ	יַעַשׂ		3ms
			Cohortative
אֶתְעַשֶּׂה	אַעֲשֶׂה		1cs

7

Chart 156: Verb ל״ה, פ״ן

Model Verb: נכה -- "to strike, smite, hit" (Hif.)

	Qal	Nifal	Piel	Pual
Perfect				
3ms	נָכָה	נִכָּה	נִכָּה	נֻכָּה
3fs	נָכְתָה	נִכְּתָה	נִכְּתָה	נֻכְּתָה
2ms	נָכִֵיתָ	נִכֵּיתָ	נִכֵּיתָ	נֻכֵּיתָ
2fs	נָכִית	נִכֵּית	נִכֵּית	נֻכֵּית
1cs	נָכִֵיתִי	נִכֵּיתִי	נִכֵּיתִי	נֻכֵּיתִי
3cp	נָכוּ	נִכּוּ	נִכּוּ	נֻכּוּ
2mp	נְכִיתֶם	נִכֵּיתֶם	נִכֵּיתֶם	נֻכֵּיתֶם
2fp	נְכִיתֶן	נִכֵּיתֶן	נִכֵּיתֶן	נֻכֵּיתֶן
1cp	נָכִֵינוּ	נִכֵּינוּ	נִכֵּינוּ	נֻכֵּינוּ
Imperfect				
3ms	יִכֶּה	יִנָּכֶה	יְנַכֶּה	יְנֻכֶּה
3fs	תִּכֶּה	תִּנָּכֶה	תְּנַכֶּה	תְּנֻכֶּה
2ms	תִּכֶּה	תִּנָּכֶה	תְּנַכֶּה	תְּנֻכֶּה
2fs	תִּכִּי	תִּנָּכִי	תְּנַכִּי	תְּנֻכִּי
1cs	אֶכֶּה	אֶנָּכֶה	אֲנַכֶּה	אֲנֻכֶּה
3mp	יִכּוּ	יִנָּכוּ	יְנַכּוּ	יְנֻכּוּ
3fp	תִּכֶּֽינָה	תִּנָּכֶֽינָה	תְּנַכֶּֽינָה	תְּנֻכֶּֽינָה
2mp	תִּכּוּ	תִּנָּכוּ	תְּנַכּוּ	תְּנֻכּוּ
2fp	תִּכֶּֽינָה	תִּנָּכֶֽינָה	תְּנַכֶּֽינָה	תְּנֻכֶּֽינָה
1cp	נִכֶּה	נִנָּכֶה	נְנַכֶּה	נְנֻכֶּה
Imperative				
2ms	נְכֵה	הִנָּכֵה	נַכֵּה	
2fs	נְכִי	הִנָּכִי	נַכִּי	
2mp	נְכוּ	הִנָּכוּ	נַכּוּ	
2fp	נְכֶֽינָה	הִנָּכֶֽינָה	נַכֶּֽינָה	
Infinitive				
absolute	נָכֹה	הִנָּכֹה	נַכֹּה	נֻכֹּה
construct	נְכוֹת	הִנָּכוֹת	נַכּוֹת	נֻכּוֹת
Participle				
active ms	נֹכֶה		מְנַכֶּה	
passive ms	נָכוּי	נִכֶּה		מְנֻכֶּה
Imperfect				
consec. 3ms	וַיֵּךְ	וַיִּנָּךְ	וַיְנַךְ	וַיְנֻךְ
Jussive				
3ms	יֵךְ	יִנָּךְ	יְנַךְ	יְנֻךְ
Cohortative				
1cs	אֶכֶּה	אֶנָּכֶה	אֲנַכֶּה	

Hitpael	Hifil	Hofal	
			Perfect
הִתְנַכָּה	הִכָּה	הֻכָּה	3ms
הִתְנַכְּתָה	הִכְּתָה	הֻכְּתָה	3fs
הִתְנַכִּיתָ	הִכִּיתָ	הֻכֵּיתָ	2ms
הִתְנַכִּית	הִכִּית	הֻכֵּית	2fs
הִתְנַכִּיתִי	הִכִּיתִי	הֻכֵּיתִי	1cs
הִתְנַכּוּ	הִכּוּ	הֻכּוּ	3cp
הִתְנַכִּיתֶם	הִכִּיתֶם	הֻכֵּיתֶם	2mp
הִתְנַכִּיתֶן	הִכִּיתֶן	הֻכֵּיתֶן	2fp
הִתְנַכִּינוּ	הִכִּינוּ	הֻכֵּינוּ	1cp
			Imperfect
יִתְנַכֶּה	יַכֶּה	יֻכֶּה	3ms
תִּתְנַכֶּה	תַּכֶּה	תֻּכֶּה	3fs
תִּתְנַכֶּה	תַּכֶּה	תֻּכֶּה	2ms
תִּתְנַכִּי	תַּכִּי	תֻּכִּי	2fs
אֶתְנַכֶּה	אַכֶּה	אֻכֶּה	1cs
יִתְנַכּוּ	יַכּוּ	יֻכּוּ	3mp
תִּתְנַכֶּינָה	תַּכֶּינָה	תֻּכֶּינָה	3fp
תִּתְנַכּוּ	תַּכּוּ	תֻּכּוּ	2mp
תִּתְנַכֶּינָה	תַּכֶּינָה	תֻּכֶּינָה	2fp
נִתְנַכֶּה	נַכֶּה	נֻכֶּה	1cp
			Imperative
הִתְנַכֵּה	הַכֵּה		2ms
הִתְנַכִּי	הַכִּי		2fs
הִתְנַכּוּ	הַכּוּ		2mp
הִתְנַכֶּינָה	הַכֶּינָה		2fp
			Infinitive
הִתְנַכֹּה	הַכֵּה	הֻכֵּה	absolute
הִתְנַכּוֹת	הַכּוֹת	הֻכּוֹת	construct
			Participle
מִתְנַכֶּה	מַכֶּה		active ms
		מֻכֶּה	passive ms
			Imperfect
וַיִּתְנַךְ	וַיַּךְ		consec. 3ms
			Jussive
יִתְנַךְ	יַךְ		3ms
			Cohortative
אֶתְנַכֶּה	אַכֶּה		1cs

7

Chart 158: ל"א, פ"ן **Verb**

Model Verb: נשׂא -- "to raise, lift up, bear, carry"

	Qal	Nifal	Piel	Pual
Perfect				
3ms	נָשָׂא	נִשָּׂא	נִשֵּׂא	נֻשָּׂא
3fs	נָשְׂאָה	נִשְּׂאָה	נִשְּׂאָה	נֻשְּׂאָה
2ms	נָשֵׂאתָ	נִשֵּׂאתָ	נִשֵּׂאתָ	נֻשֵּׂאתָ
2fs	נָשֵׂאת	נִשֵּׂאת	נִשֵּׂאת	נֻשֵּׂאת
1cs	נָשֵׂאתִי	נִשֵּׂאתִי	נִשֵּׂאתִי	נֻשֵּׂאתִי
3cp	נָשְׂאוּ	נִשְּׂאוּ	נִשְּׂאוּ	נֻשְּׂאוּ
2mp	נְשָׂאתֶם	נִשֵּׂאתֶם	נִשֵּׂאתֶם	נֻשֵּׂאתֶם
2fp	נְשָׂאתֶן	נִשֵּׂאתֶן	נִשֵּׂאתֶן	נֻשֵּׂאתֶן
1cs	נָשֵׂאנוּ	נִשֵּׂאנוּ	נִשֵּׂאנוּ	נֻשֵּׂאנוּ
Imperfect				
3ms	יִשָּׂא	יִנָּשֵׂא	יְנַשֵּׂא	יְנֻשָּׂא
3fs	תִּשָּׂא	תִּנָּשֵׂא	תְּנַשֵּׂא	תְּנֻשָּׂא
2ms	תִּשָּׂא	תִּנָּשֵׂא	תְּנַשֵּׂא	תְּנֻשָּׂא
2fs	תִּשְׂאִי	תִּנָּשְׂאִי	תְּנַשְּׂאִי	תְּנֻשְּׂאִי
1cs	אֶשָּׂא	אֶנָּשֵׂא	אֲנַשֵּׂא	אֲנֻשָּׂא
3mp	יִשְׂאוּ	יִנָּשְׂאוּ	יְנַשְּׂאוּ	יְנֻשְּׂאוּ
3fp	תִּשֶּׂאנָה	תִּנָּשֶׂאנָה	תְּנַשֶּׂאנָה	תְּנֻשֶּׂאנָה
2mp	תִּשְׂאוּ	תִּנָּשְׂאוּ	תְּנַשְּׂאוּ	תְּנֻשְּׂאוּ
2fp	תִּשֶּׂאנָה	תִּנָּשֶׂאנָה	תְּנַשֶּׂאנָה	תְּנֻשֶּׂאנָה
1cp	נִשָּׂא	נִנָּשֵׂא	נְנַשֵּׂא	נְנֻשָּׂא
Imperative				
2ms	שָׂא	הִנָּשֵׂא	נַשֵּׂא	
2fs	שְׂאִי	הִנָּשְׂאִי	נַשְּׂאִי	
2mp	שְׂאוּ	הִנָּשְׂאוּ	נַשְּׂאוּ	
2fp	שֶּׂאנָה	הִנָּשֶׂאנָה	נַשֶּׂאנָה	
Infinitive				
absolute	נָשׂוֹא	הִנָּשֵׂא	נַשֵּׂא	נֻשָּׂא
construct	שְׂאת	הִנָּשֵׂא	נַשֵּׂא	נֻשָּׂא
Participle				
active ms	נֹשֵׂא		מְנַשֵּׂא	
passive ms	נָשׂוּא	נִשָּׂא		מְנֻשָּׂא
Imperfect				
consec. 3ms	וַיִּשָּׂא	וַיִּנָּשֵׂא	וַיְנַשֵּׂא	וַיְנֻשָּׂא
Jussive				
3ms	יִשָּׂא	יִנָּשֵׂא	יְנַשֵּׂא	יְנֻשָּׂא
Cohortative				
1cs	אֶשְּׂאָה	אֶנָּשְׂאָה	אֲנַשְּׂאָה	

7

נ שֹׂא

Hitpael	Hifil	Hofal	
			Perfect
הִתְנַשֵּׂא	הִשִּׂיא	הֻשָּׂא	3ms
הִתְנַשְּׂאָה	הִשִּׂיאָה	הֻשְּׂאָה	3fs
הִתְנַשֵּׂאתָ	הִשֵּׂאתָ	הֻשֵּׂאתָ	2ms
הִתְנַשֵּׂאת	הִשֵּׂאת	הֻשֵּׂאת	2fs
הִתְנַשֵּׂאתִי	הִשֵּׂאתִי	הֻשֵּׂאתִי	1cs
הִתְנַשְּׂאוּ	הִשִּׂיאוּ	הֻשְּׂאוּ	3cp
הִתְנַשֵּׂאתֶם	הִשֵּׂאתֶם	הֻשֵּׂאתֶם	2mp
הִתְנַשֵּׂאתֶן	הִשֵּׂאתֶן	הֻשֵּׂאתֶן	2fp
הִתְנַשֵּׂאנוּ	הִשֵּׂאנוּ	הֻשֵּׂאנוּ	1cp
			Imperfect
יִתְנַשֵּׂא	יַשִּׂיא	יֻשָּׂא	3ms
תִּתְנַשֵּׂא	תַּשִּׂיא	תֻּשָּׂא	3fs
תִּתְנַשֵּׂא	תַּשִּׂיא	תֻּשָּׂא	2ms
תִּתְנַשְּׂאִי	תַּשִּׂיאִי	תֻּשְּׂאִי	2fs
אֶתְנַשֵּׂא	אַשִּׂיא	אֻשָּׂא	1cs
יִתְנַשְּׂאוּ	יַשִּׂיאוּ	יֻשְּׂאוּ	3mp
תִּתְנַשֵּׂאנָה	תַּשֵּׂאנָה	תֻּשֵּׂאנָה	3fp
תִּתְנַשְּׂאוּ	תַּשִּׂיאוּ	תֻּשְּׂאוּ	2mp
תִּתְנַשֵּׂאנָה	תַּשֵּׂאנָה	תֻּשֵּׂאנָה	2fp
נִתְנַשֵּׂא	נַשִּׂיא	נֻשָּׂא	1cp
			Imperative
הִתְנַשֵּׂא	הַשֵּׂא		2ms
הִתְנַשְּׂאִי	הַשִּׂיאִי		2fs
הִתְנַשְּׂאוּ	הַשִּׂיאוּ		2mp
הִתְנַשֵּׂאנָה	הַשֵּׂאנָה		2fp
			Infinitive
הִתְנַשֵּׂא	הַשֵּׂא	הֻשֵּׂא	absolute
הִתְנַשֵּׂא	הַשִּׂיא	הֻשָּׂא	construct
			Participle
מִתְנַשֵּׂא	מַשִּׂיא		active ms
		מֻשָּׂא	passive ms
			Imperfect
וַיִּתְנַשֵּׂא	וַיַּשֵּׂא	וַיֻּשָּׂא	consec. 3ms
			Jussive
יִתְנַשֵּׂא	יַשֵּׂא	יֻשָּׂא	3ms
			Cohortative
אֶתְנַשְּׂאָה	אַשִּׂיאָה		1cs

7

Chart 160: ‫(פ״ו‬ Verb (Original ‫ל״ה, פ״י‬

Model Verb: ‫ידה‬ -- "to thank, praise, confess" (Hif.)

	Qal	Nifal	Piel	Pual
Perfect				
3ms	יָדָה	נוֹדָה	יִדָּה	יֻדָּה
3fs	יָדְתָה	נוֹדְתָה	יִדְּתָה	יֻדְּתָה
2ms	יָדִיתָ	נוֹדֵיתָ	יִדִּיתָ	יֻדֵּיתָ
2fs	יָדִית	נוֹדֵית	יִדִּית	יֻדֵּית
1cs	יָדִיתִי	נוֹדֵיתִי	יִדִּיתִי	יֻדֵּיתִי
3cp	יָדוּ	נוֹדוּ	יִדּוּ	יֻדּוּ
2mp	יְדִיתֶם	נוֹדֵיתֶם	יִדִּיתֶם	יֻדֵּיתֶם
2fp	יְדִיתֶן	נוֹדֵיתֶן	יִדִּיתֶן	יֻדֵּיתֶן
1cp	יָדִינוּ	נוֹדֵינוּ	יִדִּינוּ	יֻדֵּינוּ
Imperfect				
3ms	יֵדֶה	יִוָּדֶה	יְוַדֶּה	יְוֻדֶּה
3fs	תֵּדֶה	תִּוָּדֶה	תְּוַדֶּה	תְּוֻדֶּה
2ms	תֵּדֶה	תִּוָּדֶה	תְּוַדֶּה	תְּוֻדֶּה
2fs	תֵּדִי	תִּוָּדִי	תְּוַדִּי	תְּוֻדִּי
1cs	אֵדֶה	אֶוָּדֶה	אֲוַדֶּה	אֲוֻדֶּה
3mp	יֵדוּ	יִוָּדוּ	יְוַדּוּ	יְוֻדּוּ
3fp	תֵּדֶינָה	תִּוָּדֶינָה	תְּוַדֶּינָה	תְּוֻדֶּינָה
2mp	תֵּדוּ	תִּוָּדוּ	תְּוַדּוּ	תְּוֻדּוּ
2fp	תֵּדֶינָה	תִּוָּדֶינָה	תְּוַדֶּינָה	תְּוֻדֶּינָה
1cp	נֵדֶה	נִוָּדֶה	נְוַדֶּה	נְוֻדֶּה
Imperative				
2ms	דֵּה	הִוָּדֵה	וַדֵּה	
2fs	דִּי	הִוָּדִי	וַדִּי	
2mp	דּוּ	הִוָּדוּ	וַדּוּ	
2fp	דֶּינָה	הִוָּדֶינָה	וַדֶּינָה	
Infinitive				
absolute	יָדֹה	הִוָּדֹה	וַדֹּה	יֻדֹּה
construct	דֵּית	הִוָּדוֹת	וַדּוֹת	יֻדּוֹת
Participle				
active ms	יֹדֶה		מְוַדֶּה	
passive ms	יָדוּי	נוֹדֶה		מְוֻדֶּה
Imperfect				
consec. 3ms	וַיֵּדְ	וַיִּוָּדְ	וַיְוַדְ	וַיְוֻדְ
Jussive				
3ms	יֵדְ	יִוָּדְ	יְוַדְ	יְוֻדְ
Cohortative				
1cs	אֵדֶה	אֶוָּדֶה	אֲוַדֶּה	

7

ידה

Hitpael	Hifil	Hofal		
			Perfect	
הִתְוַדָּה	הוֹדָה	הוּדָה	3ms	
הִתְוַדֵּתָ	הוֹדֵתָ	הוּדֵתָ	3fs	
הִתְוַדֵּיתָ	הוֹדֵיתָ	הוּדֵיתָ	2ms	
הִתְוַדֵּית	הוֹדֵית	הוּדֵית	2fs	
הִתְוַדֵּיתִי	הוֹדֵיתִי	הוּדֵיתִי	1cs	
הִתְוַדּוּ	הוֹדוּ	הוּדוּ	3cp	
הִתְוַדֵּיתֶם	הוֹדֵיתֶם	הוּדֵיתֶם	2mp	
הִתְוַדִּיתֶן	הוֹדִיתֶן	הוּדֵיתֶן	2fp	
הִתְוַדֵּינוּ	הוֹדֵינוּ	הוּדֵינוּ	1cp	
			Imperfect	
יִתְוַדֶּה	יוֹדֶה	יוּדֶה	3ms	
תִּתְוַדֶּה	תּוֹדֶה	תּוּדֶה	3fs	
תִּתְוַדֶּה	תּוֹדֶה	תּוּדֶה	2ms	
תִּתְוַדִּי	תּוֹדִי	תּוּדִי	2fs	
אֶתְוַדֶּה	אוֹדֶה	אוּדֶה	1cs	
יִתְוַדּוּ	יוֹדוּ	יוּדוּ	3mp	
תִּתְוַדֶּינָה	תּוֹדֶינָה	תּוּדֶינָה	3fp	
תִּתְוַדּוּ	תּוֹדוּ	תּוּדוּ	2mp	
תִּתְוַדֶּינָה	תּוֹדֶינָה	תּוּדֶינָה	2fp	
נִתְוַדֶּה	נוֹדֶה	נוּדֶה	1cp	
			Imperative	
הִתְוַדֵּה	הוֹדֵה		2ms	
הִתְוַדִּי	הוֹדִי		2fs	
הִתְוַדּוּ	הוֹדוּ		2mp	
הִתְוַדֶּינָה	הוֹדֵינָה		2fp	
			Infinitive	
הִתְוַדֹּה	הוֹדֵה	הוּדֵה	absolute	
הִתְוַדּוֹת	הוֹדוֹת	הוּדוֹת	construct	
			Participle	
מִתְוַדֶּה	מוֹדֶה		active ms	
		מוּדֶה	passive ms	
			Imperfect	
וַיִּתְוַד	וַיּוֹד		consec. 3ms	
			Jussive	
יִתְוַד	יוֹד		3ms	
			Cohortative	
אֶתְוַדֶּה	אוֹדֶה		1cs	

7

Chart 162: ל״א פ״י Verb (Original פ״ו)

Model Verb: יצא -- "to go out"

	Qal	Nifal	Piel	Pual
Perfect				
3ms	יָצָא	נוֹצָא	יִצֵּא	יֻצָּא
3fs	יָצְאָה	נוֹצְאָה	יִצְּאָה	יֻצְּאָה
2ms	יָצֹאתָ	נוֹצֵאתָ	יִצֵּאתָ	יֻצֵּאתָ
2fs	יָצָאת	נוֹצֵאת	יִצֵּאת	יֻצֵּאת
1cs	יָצֹאתִי	נוֹצֵאתִי	יִצֵּאתִי	יֻצֵּאתִי
3cp	יָצְאוּ	נוֹצְאוּ	יִצְּאוּ	יֻצְּאוּ
2mp	יְצָאתֶם	נוֹצֵאתֶם	יִצֵּאתֶם	יֻצֵּאתֶם
2fp	יְצָאתֶן	נוֹצֵאתֶן	יִצֵּאתֶן	יֻצֵּאתֶן
1cp	יָצֹאנוּ	נוֹצֵאנוּ	יִצֵּאנוּ	יֻצֵּאנוּ
Imperfect				
3ms	יֵצֵא	יִוָּצֵא	יְוַצֵּא	יְוֻצָּא
3fs	תֵּצֵא	תִּוָּצֵא	תְּוַצֵּא	תְּוֻצָּא
2ms	תֵּצֵא	תִּוָּצֵא	תְּוַצֵּא	תְּוֻצָּא
2fs	תֵּצְאִי	תִּוָּצְאִי	תְּוַצְּאִי	תְּוֻצְּאִי
1cs	אֵצֵא	אִוָּצֵא	אֲוַצֵּא	אֲוֻצָּא
3mp	יֵצְאוּ	יִוָּצְאוּ	יְוַצְּאוּ	יְוֻצְּאוּ
3fp	תֵּצֶּאנָה	תִּוָּצֶאנָה	תְּוַצֶּאנָה	תְּוֻצֶּאנָה
2mp	תֵּצְאוּ	תִּוָּצְאוּ	תְּוַצְּאוּ	תְּוֻצְּאוּ
2fp	תֵּצֶּאנָה	תִּוָּצֶאנָה	תְּוַצֶּאנָה	תְּוֻצֶּאנָה
1cp	נֵצֵא	נִוָּצֵא	נְוַצֵּא	נְוֻצָּא
Imperative				
2ms	צֵא	הִוָּצֵא	וַצֵּא	
2fs	צְאִי	הִוָּצְאִי	וַצְּאִי	
2mp	צְאוּ	הִוָּצְאוּ	וַצְּאוּ	
2fp	צֶּאנָה	הִוָּצֶאנָה	וַצֶּאנָה	
Infinitive				
absolute	יָצוֹא	הִוָּצֹא	וַצֵּא	יֻצָּא
construct	צֵאת	הִוָּצֵא	וַצֵּא	יֻצָּא
Participle				
active ms	יֹצֵא		מְוַצֵּא	
passive ms	יָצוּא	נוֹצָא		מְוֻצָּא
Imperfect				
consec. 3ms	וַיֵּצֵא	וַיִּוָּצֵא	וַיְוַצֵּא	וַיְוֻצָּא
Jussive				
3ms	יֵצֵא	יִוָּצֵא	יְוַצֵּא	יְוֻצָּא
Cohortative				
1cs	אֵצְאָה	אִוָּצְאָה	אֲוַצְּאָה	

7

רצא

Hitpael	Hifil	Hofal	
			Perfect
הִתְוַצֵּא	הוֹצִיא	הוּצָא	3ms
הִתְוַצְּאָה	הוֹצִיאָה	הוּצְאָה	3fs
הִתְוַצֵּאתָ	הוֹצֵאתָ	הוּצֵאתָ	2ms
הִתְוַצֵּאת	הוֹצֵאת	הוּצֵאת	2fs
הִתְוַצֵּאתִי	הוֹצֵאתִי	הוּצֵאתִי	1cs
הִתְוַצְּאוּ	הוֹצִיאוּ	הוּצְאוּ	3cp
הִתְוַצֵּאתֶם	הוֹצֵאתֶם	הוּצֵאתֶם	2mp
הִתְוַצֵּאתֶן	הוֹצֵאתֶן	הוּצֵאתֶן	2fp
הִתְוַצֵּאנוּ	הוֹצֵאנוּ	הוּצֵאנוּ	1cp
			Imperfect
יִתְוַצֵּא	יוֹצִיא	יוּצָא	3ms
תִּתְוַצֵּא	תּוֹצִיא	תּוּצָא	3fs
תִּתְוַצֵּא	תּוֹצִיא	תּוּצָא	2ms
תִּתְוַצְּאִי	תּוֹצִיאִי	תּוּצְאִי	2fs
אֶתְוַצֵּא	אוֹצִיא	אוּצָא	1cs
יִתְוַצְּאוּ	יוֹצִיאוּ	יוּצְאוּ	3mp
תִּתְוַצֵּאנָה	תּוֹצֵאנָה	תּוּצֶאנָה	3fp
תִּתְוַצְּאוּ	תּוֹצִיאוּ	תּוּצְאוּ	2mp
תִּתְוַצֵּאנָה	תּוֹצֵאנָה	תּוּצֶאנָה	2fp
נִתְוַצֵּא	נוֹצִיא	נוּצָא	1cp
			Imperative
הִתְוַצֵּא	הוֹצֵא		2ms
הִתְוַצְּאִי	הוֹצִיאִי		2fs
הִתְוַצְּאוּ	הוֹצִיאוּ		2mp
הִתְוַצֵּאנָה	הוֹצֵאנָה		2fp
			Infinitive
הִתְוַצֹּא	הוֹצֵא	הוּצֵא	absolute
הִתְוַצֵּא	הוֹצִיא	הוּצָא	construct
			Participle
מִתְוַצֵּא	מוֹצִיא		active ms
		מוּצָא	passive ms
			Imperfect
וַיִּתְוַצֵּא	וַיּוֹצֵא	וַיּוּצָא	consec. 3ms
			Jussive
יִתְוַצֵּא	יוֹצֵא	יוּצָא	3ms
			Cohortative
אֶתְוַצְּאָה	אוֹצִיאָה		1cs

7

MORE ON USING THE WORKBOOK

The format of the material provided in this *Workbook* has progressed in three stages:

1. The first stage was the study of Genesis 22. For that chapter, everything was provided in the *Workbook*. The Hebrew text was printed in its entirety on p. 21 and portions were printed at the top of each page. All words were given with their translations as you proceeded through the chapter.

2. The second stage was the study of Genesis 12 and Deuteronomy 5. For those chapters, you began to use the Hebrew text in *Biblia Hebraica Stuttgartensia*. All of the words continued to be given, but you began to use a lexicon to find suitable translations.

3. Now we are ready to proceed to the third and final stage as we study Joshua 24 and subsequent readings. In these chapters, you will continue to use BHS for the Hebrew text.

   But now not all of the new words you will encounter will be given to you. Only new vocabulary words to be learned (those occurring more than 100 times in the Hebrew Bible) will be given. Other less frequent words will occur in the readings, but you are expected to be able to determine the lexicon form of such words and to look them up. Some helps are provided, however, to assist you when it is anticipated that a form might cause difficulty.

   The new vocabulary words in their lexicon form will be listed separately at the beginning of each reading. They continue to be numbered in the order they appear. No longer will the symbol + be given to indicate Holladay's reference to this passage. But the Roman numerals will still be provided to distinguish homonyms.

Three helps:

1. Look up the vocabulary words listed at the beginning of each reading only as you proceed through the study of the chapter. Do not try to look up all of the words first and then start to translate. The reason is that you will be able not only to scan the entry to determine basic meanings but also to select appropriate translations for the particular context.

2. Continue to develop your own glossary in **Appendix II**. Refer to this listing when you come upon a word that you think is a vocabulary word but you either have forgotten its meaning or want to check its lexicon form.

3. Remember that hollow verbs are pointed in the vocabulary listings in the *Workbook* but not in Holladay's lexicon. For example, the word סוּר appears as סור in the lexicon.

CHAPTER V: THE STUDY OF JOSHUA 24:1-28

VOCABULARY TO BE LEARNED

Verse:

(v. 1)	188.	אסף		(v. 13)	212.	עִיר I
	189.	יְהוֹשֻׁעַ			213.	אַתֶּם
	190.	שֵׁבֶט			214.	אכל
	191.	זָקֵן		(v. 14)	215.	אֱמֶת
	192.	רֹאשׁ I			216.	סוּר
	193.	שׁפט		(v. 15)	217.	אִם
(v. 2)	194.	עַם II			218.	רַע
	195.	נָהָר			219.	בחר I
	196.	עוֹלָם			220.	מִי
(v. 4)	197.	יַעֲקֹב		(v. 16)	221.	עזב I
(v. 5)	198.	אַהֲרוֹן		(v. 17)	222.	אוֹת I
	199.	קֶרֶב			223.	דֶּרֶךְ
(v. 6)	200.	רדף		(v. 18)	224.	גַּם
	201.	רֶכֶב		(v. 19)	225.	יכל
(v. 7)	202.	כסה			226.	קָדוֹשׁ
	203.	מִדְבָּר			227.	פֶּשַׁע
	204.	רַב			228.	חַטָּאת
(v. 8)	205.	יַרְדֵּן		(v. 20)	229.	רעע I
	206.	לחם I			230.	כלה I
(v. 9)	207.	מֶלֶךְ I		(v. 23)	231.	לֵבָב
	208.	מוֹאָב		(v. 26)	232.	סֵפֶר I
(v. 10)	209.	נצל			233.	תּוֹרָה
(v. 11)	210.	בַּעַל I		(v. 27)	234.	פֶּן־
(v. 12)	211.	חֶרֶב		(v. 28)	235.	נַחֲלָה I

166

LEARNING HELPS FOR JOSHUA 24:1-28

Verse:

(v. 1)

Note 166A: פ Guttural Verbs

Alef differs from the other gutturals in that it often prefers Segol rather than Patah. **REVIEW Note 51B.** Keeping this difference in mind, the form וַיֵּאָסֵף is analogous to וַיַּעֲמֹד or to the stative form וַיֶּחֱזַק (both Qal impf. consec. 3ms) of the פ Guttural verb in **Chart 132.** But unlike other manuscripts, Codex Leningradensis points the form וַיֵּאָסֵף, as the footnote (ª) in the critical apparatus indicates.

▸   שְׁכֶמָה   **REVIEW Note 83C** before referring to the lexicon.

▸   וּלְשֹׁפְטָיו   **REVIEW Note 107B.**

▸   וַיִּתְיַצְּבוּ   The root is a פ"י verb with an original Yod that remains in most forms. **REVIEW Note 121A** for the stem. See **Chart 144.** (Notice that each verb chart covers two pages.)

▸   לִפְנֵי   **REVIEW Note 111A.**

(v. 2)

Note 166B: פ"א Verbs

Five verbs, all beginning with Alef, differ from the פ Guttural verbs only in the Qal impf. and impf. consec. In these verbs the Alef is quiescent and the vowel of the prefix is Holem, as in וַיֹּאמֶר. The five verbs are: אמר, אכל, אבד, אפה, and אבה. See **Chart 132** for the Qal of אכל.

▸   יָשְׁבוּ   Is this form the Qal impf. 3mp of שׁוּב or the Qal pf. 3cp of יֹשֵׁב? Cf. **Chart 148** for the hollow verb and **Chart 142** for the פ"י verb.

Note 166C: The Meteg

In Chart 142 the form יָשְׁבוּ (Qal pf. 3cp) appears with a short vertical line to the left of the Qamets: יָשְׁבוּ. This marking is called a **Meteg** and has several functions. The Meteg should not be confused with a Silluq, which appears only on the last stressed syllable of each verse. Two uses of the Meteg are the following:

1. A Meteg is placed beside a Qamets that is followed by a Sheva to indicate that the vowel is the long Qamets and not the short Qamets

Hatuf and that the Sheva is vocal. It is this use of the Meteg that is consistently employed in the verb paradigms in the *Workbook* (see especially Qal pf. 3fs and 3cp forms). Codex Leningradensis, however, often omits the Meteg in such verb forms. Thus the form יָשְׁבוּ appears in the text of BHS but the form יָֽשְׁבוּ appears in Chart 142.

2. A Meteg is often placed on a long vowel two or more syllables before the main stress. It serves as a kind of secondary stress mark and helps in pronouncing longer words. Example: אֲבוֹתֵיכֶם מֵעוֹלָם. The Meteg with this function is not indicated in the *Workbook*.

▶ אֲבוֹתֵיכֶם See **Chart 102**.

▶ אֲבִי Is this the word אָב with the 1cs suffix or the sg. const. form? See **Chart 102**.

▶ וַיַּעַבְדוּ The Patah under the prefix might suggest the Hifil stem (Note 65C). But is this form Qal or Hifil? **REVIEW Note 84A** and see **Chart 132**.

(v. 3) | **Note 167A: Vav Consecutive with Alef Prefix**

The Vav consecutive is pointed with a Qamets before the 1cs prefix, since Alef rejects the Dagesh Forte. Example: וָאֶקַּח. **REVIEW Note 26A** for a similar compensatory lengthening.

▶ וָאוֹלֵךְ The root הלך follows the pattern of the פ״י (original פ״ו) verb outside the Qal. **REVIEW Note 112A** and see **Chart 142**.

▶ אוֹתוֹ The sign of the definite direct object with suffixes is often written fully. Example: אוֹתוֹ for אֹתוֹ.

Note 167B: Qere-Ketiv

The small circle or *circule* placed over a word was used by the Masoretes to call attention to a marginal note. The *circule* over the form וָאֶרֶב refers to the margin where the unpointed consonants וארבה appear over the letter ק. The Masoretes for various reasons (of tradition or grammar, or perhaps of varying textual evidence) preferred at times a reading other than that of the consonantal text. **REVIEW Note 53A**. In the case of the divine name, אֲדֹנָי was to be read instead of יהוה.

168

(Js 24:3-5)

Therefore, יהוה received the pointing of אֲדֹנָי. The word that is
<u>written</u> in the text is called the **Ketiv** (from the Aramaic כְּתִיב --
"written") and the word from the margin to be <u>read</u> is called the **Qere**
(from the Aramaic קְרִי -- "read"). The vowels that go with the Qere
are placed in the text with the consonants of the Ketiv. Because of the
frequency of the Qere-Ketiv associated with the Tetragrammaton, no
circule or marginal notation is ever provided. Such an instance is called
a Qere *perpetuum*. Another example of this "perpetual" Qere is the form
הוּא for הִיא. **REVIEW Note 94A**. Yet another Qere-Kethiv was
discussed without using the terms in **Note 115A**.

In the case of וָאֵרֶב, the recommended reading, the Qere, is וָאַרְבֶּה,
which consists of the consonants that appear in the margin and the
vowels that appear in the text. The letter ק (or sometimes קרי) in
the margin marks the presence of a Qere-Ketiv. Here the Ketiv
presupposes the apocopated impf. consec. 1cs form וָאֵרֶב (**REVIEW
Note 84B**), while the Qere is the unapocopated (perhaps cohortative)
form. The difference in meaning is slight. Holladay lists the forms of
the Qere-Ketiv for this passage under the Hifil of רבה.

(v. 4) לָרֶשֶׁת   **REVIEW Notes 83A, 81C**, and **83B**. See **Charts 142** and **146**
for the פ"י and פ"ן verbs.

▶ מִצְרָיְם   **REVIEW Note 95C.**

(v. 5) וָאֶשְׁלַח   If the model verb is pointed וַיִּקְטֹל, can you explain the
changes in pointing in this form? **REVIEW Note 167A** for
the pointing of the Vav. **REVIEW Note 78A** for the pointing
of the prefix. And **REVIEW Note 50B** for the pointing before
the guttural.

Note 168A: Assimilated Nun

Using the missing letter rules of Note 43A, it is clear that the form
וָאֶגֹּף has an assimilated Nun. A Nun assimilates to the next letter
causing a doubling of that letter whenever the Nun would appear with a
silent Sheva (syllable divider). On the analogy of the model verb
וַיִּקְטֹל, this form would be וָאֶנְגֹּף, but the Nun with the silent Sheva
assimilates to the Gimel, which then receives a Dagesh Forte instead of
a Dagesh Lene. Cf. **Charts 130** and **146**.

▶ עָשִׂ֫יתִי   **REVIEW Note 63A** and see **Chart 154**.

▶ אַחַר   Not always a preposition. Here it is an adverb.

▶ הוֹצֵ֫אתִי   **REVIEW Note 112A** and see **Chart 162**.

(v. 6)

** תּ___וּ   (prefix)   *you*   (2mp of the imperfect)
See this prefix in **Chart 23B**.

▶ הַיָּ֫מָּה   What is the initial He? What is the final He?

▶ מִצְרַ֫יִם   Sometimes the name of the country suffices for the people of the country: "Egyptians."

▶ אַחֲרֵי   Another way of writing the preposition אַחַר. See **Chart 125**.

(v. 7)   **Note 169A: Hollow Verbs**

There are two classes of hollow verbs: ע״י and ע״ו. The Qal and Hifil impf. (and impf. consec.) forms of the ע״י verbs are identical and distinguished only by context. But the Qal and the Hifil impf. of the ע״ו verb are distinguished by the vowel between the two root consonants. The Hifil, as expected, has a 2nd class vowel. See **Charts 148** and **150** and compare:

Class	Verb Root	Qal	Hifil
ע״י	שִׂים	וַיָּ֫שֶׂם	וַיָּ֫שֶׂם
ע״ו	קוּם	וַיָּ֫קָם	וַיָּ֫קֶם
ע״ו	בוֹא	וַיָּבֹא	וַיָּבֵא

▶ בֵּינֵיכֶם   See **Chart 125** for this preposition.

▶ עָלָיו   The sg. suffix here may suggest a *distributive* sense: "upon each one of them."

▶ וַיְכַסֵּ֫הוּ   The 3ms suffix with the pf., impf., and impv. of a ל״ה verb is הוּ____. See **Chart 151**. What stem is the verb here?

** תּ___נָה   (prefix)   *you, they*   (2 or 3fp of the imperfect)
See this prefix with its two uses in **Chart 23B**.

▶ וַתִּרְאֶ֫ינָה עֵינֵיכֶם   **REVIEW Note 42A** for the fem. form of the verb and see **Chart 140** for the ל״ה verb.

►   יָמִים   See **Chart 104** for this irregular noun.

(v. 8)   וָאָבִאה   The *circule* refers of the marginal note marked by the letter ק. **REVIEW Note 167B**. The Ketiv is the cohortative and the Qere is simply the impf. consec. **REVIEW Note 169A** for the stem.

►   הַיּוֹשֵׁב   Written fully for הַיֹּשֵׁב. **REVIEW Notes 85B** and **107B**. How is a definite participle usually translated? **REVIEW Note 79B**.

►   וַיִּלָּחֲמוּ   Most occurrences of this verb are in this stem. See **Chart 134** for the ע Guttural paradigm.

►   אֶתְכֶם   See **Chart 125** for the comparison of the suffix forms of the preposition אֶת־ and the sign of the definite direct object אֵת־.

►   וַתִּירְשׁוּ   This verb has a mixture of פ״י (original פ״י) and פ״י (original פ״ו) forms. The impf. and impf. consec. follow the original פ״י pattern. See **Chart 144**.

(v. 9)

**   ◻◻◻   (the pointing of the Piel infinitive construct) See **Chart 72**.

Note 170A: Piel Infinitive Construct

The pointing of the Piel inf. const. of the strong verb is קַטֵּל -- "to massacre." **REVIEW Note 116A**.

►   לְקַלֵּל   Although קלל is an ע״ע verb, it follows the pointing of the strong verb in the Piel.

(v. 10)   אָבִיתִי   A ל״ה verb.

**   ◻◻◻   (the pointing of the Qal infinitive construct) See **Chart 72**.

Note 170B: Qal Infinitive Construct

The Qal inf. const. of the strong verb is קְטֹל -- "to kill." Notice in

Chart 72 that the Qal inf. const. and the Qal impv. 2ms have the same pointing. These two forms are often identical in the various classes of verbs, especially outside the Qal. Compare several verb paradigms. Often the inf. const. will have a preposition, as in לִשְׁמֹעַ.

Note 171A: Consecutive Forms

The consecutive verb forms may differ from the perfect and imperfect by **a shift of the accent**. We have seen that the stress in an impf. consec. form may move toward the beginning of the word (**REVIEW Note 84B**):

impf. -- יְבָרֶךְ but impf. consec. -- וַיְבָרֶךְ.

Although there is no instance in our reading at this point, the converse also happens. The stress in a pf. consec. form may move to the otherwise unstressed affix:

pf. -- קָטַלְתָּ but pf. consec. -- וְקָטַלְתָּ.

**   ☐☐☐   (the pointing of the Piel infinitive absolute)
See **Chart 72**.

►   בָּרוֹךְ   On the basis of Note 87C, this form appears to be a Qal inf. abs. But it is actually a Piel inf. abs., which is pointed in the strong verb as קַטֹּל. The main clue is that the verb of the same root that precedes this form is Piel, and one expects the inf. abs. to be in the same stem. Also the pointing of בָּרוֹךְ can be explained from the regular pointing: ☐☐☐. The Dagesh Forte is rejected from the Resh with the resulting compensatory lengthening of the Patah to a Qamets under the Bet. Then the Holem is written fully as a Holem Vav. Thus the form בָּרוֹךְ is either the Qal inf. abs. or the Piel inf. abs. written fully. Context requires the latter. **REVIEW Note 63B** for the use of the inf. abs.

►   וָאַצִּל   What is the root? Notice the clues for the stem.

(v. 11)   בַּעֲלֵי־   Note the several definitions of I בַּעַל.

(v. 12)   וַתְּגָרֶשׁ   Why the Qamets under the Gimel instead of a Patah? What person, gender, and number and why?

►   שְׁנֵי   See **Chart 106** for the numerals.

172

(Js 24:13-14)

Note 172A: אֲשֶׁר Clauses

REVIEW Note 111C. אֲשֶׁר in its broader usage can be likened to all the words of English that begin with "wh": <u>who</u>, <u>whom</u>, <u>which</u>, <u>whose</u>, <u>when</u>, <u>whence</u>, and <u>whither</u>. Which of these meanings אֲשֶׁר may have depends on the context. Usually you must render the clause literally and then rephrase it to make good English sense. Compare the following examples:

(1) הַמָּקוֹם אֲשֶׁר יָשַׁב בּוֹ "the place which he dwelt in it"

Rephrased: "the place in which he dwelt"

(2) הַמָּקוֹם אֲשֶׁר יָשַׁב שָׁם "the place which he dwelt there"

Rephrased: "the place where he dwelt"

(3) הַמָּקוֹם אֲשֶׁר הָלַךְ שָׁמָּה "the place which he went toward there"

Rephrased: "the place toward which he went"

(4) הָאִישׁ אֲשֶׁר לָקַחְתִּי אֶת־סִפְרוֹ "the man who I took his book"

Rephrased: "the man whose book I took"

(5) אֶרֶץ אֲשֶׁר לֹא־יָגַעְתָּ בָּהּ

How would this phrase from our reading be rendered?

▸ עָרִים   See **Chart 105** for this irregular noun.

▸ בְּנִיתֶם   For the Sheva, **REVIEW Note 108A** and see **Chart 140**.

▸ בָּהֶם   The Atnah punctuates this verse.

▸ אַתֶּם אֹכְלִים See **Chart 123A** for the pronoun and **REVIEW Note 107C**.

Note 172B: ל״ה and ל״א Verbs

ל״ה and ל״א verbs are sometimes confused, as in the irregular form יְראוּ. The impv. 2mp of the model ל״ה verb is גְּלוּ (see **Chart 140**). The same form of the model ל״א verb is מִצְאוּ (see **Chart 138**). Thus the form יְראוּ is pointed like a ל״ה verb with the quiescent Alef remaining in the form. See **Chart 142** for the regular forms of ירא in the Qal.

▸ וְעִבְדוּ   See **Chart 132**.

▸ וְהָסִירוּ   See **Chart 148**.

▶ תַּעֲבֹדוּן֮   REVIEW Note 119B and see the following Note.

(v. 15)   ┌─────────────────────────────────┐
                │   **Note 173A: Pausal Forms**   │
                └─────────────────────────────────┘

We have seen that pausal forms occur with the two major accents Atnah
(▢) and Silluq (▢) and with the accent Zaqef Qaton (▢). **REVIEW
Notes 61C** and **119C**. Another accent that may produce pausal forms is
Segolta (▢). The Segolta appears as a first major accent when the first
half of the verse before the Atnah is especially long. It is not very
frequent. In the pausal form תַּעֲבֹדוּן֮, the Segolta causes a long vowel
to remain in the penultimate syllable (notice the Holem instead of a
Sheva as in the non-pausal form; see **Chart 132**).

▶ אִם...וְאִם   "whether...or"

▶ בַּעֵבֶר   Can you explain the Qere-Ketiv?

▶ אֲשֶׁר...בְּאַרְצָם   **REVIEW Note 172A.**

(v. 16) וַיַּעַן   REVIEW Note 113B and see **Chart 154** for the consec. forms
                     of this doubly weak verb.

▶ חָלִילָה לָּנוּ מֵעֲזֹב   See II חָלִיל in the lexicon and note its usage.

(v. 17) הַמַּעֲלֶה   REVIEW Note 79A and see **Chart 72** for the form. **REVIEW
                      Notes 107C** and **79B** for the usage.

▶ וַאֲשֶׁר עָשָׂה   Notice that this relative clause stands parallel to the previous
                   participial clause.

▶ הָאֹתוֹת   The noun אוֹת in the sg. and the sign of the definite direct
               object with suffixes may look alike, since both may be written
               defectively or fully (אֹת_ or אוֹת_). But here the noun is pl.
               and has the article, making it distinguishable.

▶ אֲשֶׁר הָלַכְנוּ בָהּ   **REVIEW Note 172A.**

**   נוּ___   (affix)   *we*   (1cp of the perfect)
                  See **Chart 23A**. Notice that the 1cp affix and suffix are the
                  same. Cf. **Chart 24A**.

174

(v. 18)   וַיְגָרֶשׁ   Can you explain the pointing of this form?

▸   יֹשֵׁב הָאָרֶץ   A construct chain.

(v. 19)

> ### Note 174A: Qal Imperfect of יכל

The unusual Qal imperfect of the verb יכל has retained the original Vav, even if only as a vowel letter, as in the form תּוּכְלוּ. The verb regularly follows this pattern in the imperfect and only appears in the Qal stem.

▸ אֱלֹהִים קְדֹשִׁים   Although the noun אֱלֹהִים is plural in form it is grammatically singular. **REVIEW Note 27A**. But if attributive adjectives are to agree with the noun they modify in number, why is קְדֹשִׁים plural? See the following Note.

> ### Note 174B: Attraction

Attributive adjectives agree in gender, number, and definiteness with the noun they modify. But in the phrase אֱלֹהִים קְדֹשִׁים the noun is not numerically plural but a plural of majesty. The adjective may be plural in form **by attraction** to the form of its noun, but it too may be numerically singular: "a holy God." Hebrew has no distinctive forms for the superlative, but sometimes the context suggests it. Here the phrase may be rendered "a most holy God" or perhaps "the most holy God."

▸   הוּא   The Atnah shows that הוּא goes with the previous phrase, since it ends the first verse half. For the word order in such nominal clauses with pronouns, **REVIEW Note 57C**.

    וּלְחַטֹּאותֵיכֶם   The pl. is usually pointed חַטָּאוֹת, but the pl. with suffixes is חַטֹּאות_. Notice that the Vav is a vowel letter in combination with the quiescent Alef and the Holem.

(v. 20)   כִּי   This could be the conditional use of the conjunction: "if." **REVIEW Note 56A**.

▸   אֱלֹהֵי נֵכָר   **REVIEW Note 120A**.

▶   וְשָׁב   See **Chart 148** for the ע״ו hollow verb. The form with the pointing ◻ְ◻ could be either the Qal pf. 3ms or the Qal active part. ms. Context must decide. Notice the sequence of verbs in this narrative context. **REVIEW** Note 117A. Here the imperfect תַעַזְבוּ is followed by several pf. consec. forms: וְשָׁב...וְהֵרַע...וְכִלָּה...

▶   וְהֵרַע   From the ע״ע verb רעע. It corresponds to הֵסֵב of the model verb סבב in **Chart 152**. Why the Patah under the Resh? What stem?

▶   וְכִלָּה   **REVIEW** Note 119A.

▶   אַחֲרֵי אֲשֶׁר   **REVIEW** Note 62B.

(v. 21)   לֹא כִּי   "No! But...." **REVIEW** Note 56A.

(v. 22)   כִּי   Not "because" but "that."

Note 175A: Expressed Pronoun Subject

When an independent personal pronoun is used as the expressed subject of a verb form that already has a pronominal subject indicator, such as an affix or prefix, emphasis is being placed on the subject. Example: אַתֶּם בְּחַרְתֶּם.

(v. 23)   הָסִירוּ   What stem and branch? See **Chart 148**.

▶   וְהַטּוּ   **REVIEW** Note 87A for the root. What stem? See **Chart 156**.

(v. 24)   וּבְקוֹלוֹ נִשְׁמָע   **REVIEW** Note 69A.

(v. 25)   וַיָּשֶׂם   **REVIEW** Note 169A.

(v. 26)   תּוֹרַת   What is the ת_ _ _ _ ending? **REVIEW** Note 67A.

▶   אֶבֶן גְּדוֹלָה   What gender is אֶבֶן?

176

▶ וַיְקִימֶהָ The consec. form without the suffix is וַיָּ֫קֶם. The pointing of the form with a suffix is close to the impf. 3ms form in this stem: יָקִים. For the reduction of the Qamets under the prefix to a Sheva, **REVIEW Note 108A**. Thus, the Sheva under the prefix is here not the sign of the Piel. What stem is this? **REVIEW Note 169A**.

(v. 27) לְעֵדָה See II עֵדָה in the lexicon.

▶ וְהָיְתָה **REVIEW Note 93C** and see **Chart 140** for the Qal paradigm of היה. In the Charts the pf. 3fs forms are written with a Meteg to indicate that the Qamets is long and the Sheva is vocal: הָֽיְתָה. **REVIEW Note 166C**. The Meteg is again omitted here in BHS.

▶ תְּכַחֲשׁוּן **REVIEW Note 119B**. What stem is this?

▶ בֵּאלֹהֵיכֶם **REVIEW Note 85C** for the pointing of the inseparable prepositions with אֱלֹהִים.

(v. 28)

> ### Note 176A: Distributive Use of אִישׁ

The noun אִישׁ is said to be used **distributively** when it means "each one, everyone."

CHAPTER VI: THE STUDY OF II SAMUEL 11:1-12:25

VOCABULARY TO BE LEARNED

Verse:

(11:1)	236.	דָּוִד		261.	נגשׁ
	237.	יוֹאָב		262.	חוֹמָה
	238.	שׁחת	(v. 21)	263.	שׁלך
	239.	עַמּוֹן	(v. 25)	264.	חזק
	240.	יְרוּשָׁלַ֫ם	(v. 27)	265.	ילד
(v. 2)	241.	עֶ֫רֶב II	(12:3)	266.	אַ֫יִן I
	242.	טוֹב I		267.	כֶּ֫בֶשׂ
(v. 3)	243.	דרשׁ	(v. 5)	268.	אַף II
	244.	הֲ		269.	מָ֫וֶת
(v. 4)	245.	שׁכב	(v. 6)	270.	שׁלם
(v. 7)	246.	שׁאל	(v. 7)	271.	משׁח
	247.	שָׁלוֹם		272.	שָׁאוּל
	248.	מִלְחָמָה	(v. 8)	273.	מְעַט
(v. 8)	249.	רֶ֫גֶל	(v. 11)	274.	שֶׁ֫מֶשׁ
(v. 9)	250.	פֶּ֫תַח	(v. 12)	275.	נֶ֫גֶד
	251.	אָדוֹן	(v. 13)	276.	חטא
(v. 11)	252.	אָרוֹן	(v. 16)	277.	בקשׁ
	253.	יְהוּדָה		278.	בַּעַד I
	254.	חנה I	(v. 17)	279.	לֶ֫חֶם
	255.	שׁתה II	(v. 19)	280.	בִּין
(v. 15)	256.	נכה	(v. 21)	281.	בכה
	257.	מות	(v. 22)	282.	עוֹד
(v. 16)	258.	חַ֫יִל	(v. 24)	283.	נחם
(v. 17)	259.	נפל		284.	שְׁלֹמֹה
(v. 20)	260.	חֵמָה	(v. 25)	285.	נָבִיא

177

LEARNING HELPS FOR II SAMUEL 11:1-12:25

Verse:

(11:1)

Note 178A: Nouns Beginning with תּ

We have seen nouns that are formed by adding Mem before a verb root. **REVIEW Note 91B**. Another smaller class of nouns is formed by adding Tav before a verb root. Such a noun is תְּשׁוּבָה. Compare:

תּוֹרָה ("teaching") from יָרה (Qal: "to throw"; Hifil: "to teach")

תְּפִלָּה ("prayer") from פלל (Hitpael: "to pray")

תְּבוּנָה ("understanding") from בִּין (Qal: "to understand")

תְּשׁוּבָה ("return") from שׁוּב (Qal: "to turn, return")

▸ לִתְשׁוּבַת   What is the תּ‗‗‗‗ ending?

▸ לְעֵת צֵאת...   There can be more than one construct before the absolute in a construct chain.

▸ צֵאת   **REVIEW Note 81C** and see **Chart 162**.

▸ הַמַּלְאָכִיםᵃ   Refer to the footnote in BHS and follow many manuscripts in reading הַמְּלָכִים. See **Chart 100**.

▸ בְּנֵי עַמּוֹן   This is the ordinary expression for "Ammonites." How would the phrase בְּנֵי יִשְׂרָאֵל be translated?

▸ וְדָוִד יוֹשֵׁב   **REVIEW Note 92A**. Since the series of consecutive verbs has been broken here by inverted word order and by the use of the participle, we are to understand that David was in Jerusalem during the preceding events.

(v. 2) וַיִּתְהַלֵּךְ   Notice how the use of this stem gives a vivid picture of the action of this verb.

Note 178B: Feminine Participles

Feminine participles in the sg. sometimes end in הָ‗‗, but more often end in תּ‗‗‗. The resultant feminine participial forms have a two syllable segolate ending with the stress on the first of the segolate syllables. Example: רֹחֶצֶת. Notice that the Qal fem. part. has the clue Holem between the first two root letters. **REVIEW Note 107A**.

(v. 3)

Note 179A: Questions

Questions in Hebrew can be recognized in three ways:

1. By an interrogative word, such as לָ֫מָה or ,מֶה ,מִי.

2. By adding the interrogative particle הֲ‌ـــــ to the beginning of the first word of the question. The הַ (somtimes הָ or הֶ) serves as a kind of question mark.

3. By context alone.

▶   הֲלוֹא   Written fully for הֲלֹא. A negatively formed question expects an affirmative answer.

▶   בַּת־שֶׁ֫בַע   Proper noun.

▶   אֵ֫שֶׁת   See **Chart 103**.

(v. 4)   מִתְקַדֶּ֫שֶׁת   **REVIEW Note 79A, Chart 72**, and **Note 178B**.

Note 179B: Changes in Hitpael Verbs

We have no occurrences in the readings of the *Workbook* of certain changes that take place within some Hitpael forms. The rules, however, are these:

1. Whenever שׂ, שׁ, or ס (the sibilants) follow the Hitpael stem sign הִת, the ת changes places with the sibilant. Example: הִשְׁתַּמֵּר from שׁמר. This transposition of letters is called **metathesis**.

2. Whenever צ follows הִת, the ת is modified to ט and changes places with the צ. Example: הִצְטַדֵּק from צדק.

3. Whenever ד, ט, or ת (the dentals) follows הִת, the ת is assimilated to the dental, which receives a Dagesh Forte. Example: הִטַּהֵר from טהר.

See the Hitpael of שׁלח in **Chart 136** to illustrate metathesis.

(v. 5)   הָרָה   See under הָרָה in the lexicon.

(v. 6)   שָׁלַח   **REVIEW Note 107A** and see **Chart 136**.

180

(II Sm 11:7-11)

(v. 7)

► לְשָׁלוֹם...הַמִּלְחָמָה What does שָׁלוֹם mean in this context?

(v. 8) רֵד The impf. 3ms form is יֵרֵד. **REVIEW Note 92B** and see **Chart 142**.

► וַתֵּצֵא The prefix could be 2ms or 3fs. Note the gender of the expressed subject.

(v. 9)

Note 180A: Plural of Majesty

The so-called "plural of majesty" that applies to the word אֱלֹהִים (**REVIEW Note 27A**) may also apply to human beings of prominence. Here אָדוֹן appears in a plural form when the reference is to David the king: אֲדֹנָיו. It is the same word אֲדֹנָי (literally, "my lords") that is used to substitute for the Tetragrammaton and is translated "LORD." **REVIEW Note 53A**.

(v. 10) הֲלוֹא **REVIEW Note 179A**.

► אַתָּה בָא What is the root of this verb? This form can be either the Qal pf. 3ms or the Qal active part. ms. See **Chart 148**. Since the subject אַתָּה is 2ms, what must the form בָא be? **REVIEW Note 107C**.

(v. 11)

► וַאֲנִי...אִשְׁתִּי **REVIEW Note 179A**.

Note 180B: Oath Formula

The noun חַי (construct חֵי) is part of the usual formula for swearing. See under I חַי in the lexicon. Example: חַי יהוה -- "as Yahweh lives." The formula חֵי נַפְשֶׁךָ may be the equivalent of saying "I swear."

► אִם A special use of אִם as an emphatic negative in oaths. See Holladay under אִם (4b).

(v. 12)   בָּזֶה   "in this (place)" or "here."

Note 181A: Energic Nun

As in the form אֲשַׁלְּחֶךָ, sg. and 1cp suffixes to the imperfect are occasionally strengthened by the addition of a Nun, called the **energic Nun**, which is usually assimilated to the suffix as a Dagesh Forte. It occurs chiefly in pausal forms. No difference in meaning is attached to such forms. See Gen 12:1, where an energic Nun (assimilated as a Dagesh Forte) occurred in the suffix of the form אַרְאֶךָּ, although it was not explained at that time. CAUTION: The 3ms and the 1cp suffixes with energic Nun both appear as נּוּ‎____. Cf. the preposition מִן with suffixes, which also has the same form in 3ms and 1cp (see **Chart 124**).

(v. 13)   וַיֹּאכַל   **REVIEW Note 166B** and see **Chart 132**.

▸   וַיֵּשְׁתְּ   Do not apply the missing letter rules, for this is an unusual form of a לַ״ה verb which seems to preserve some older form. The verb שׁתה regularly has this unusual pointing in its apocopated forms. **REVIEW Note 84B** and see the lexicon. (The Dagesh Lene indicates the hard pronunciation of the Tav.)

▸   וַיְשַׁכְּרֵהוּ   **REVIEW Note 119A** and see the lexicon.

(v. 15)   הָבוּ   See under I הַב in the lexicon. This uncommon verb (perhaps from a root יהב) occurs only in the Qal imperative.

Note 181B: Superlative Adjectives

Hebrew adjectives have no special forms for the superlative, but at times the context suggests it, as is probably the case with the adjective הַחֲזָקָה in this context. **REVIEW Note 174B** for another possible superlative adjective.

▸   ...וְשַׁבְתֶּם   **REVIEW Note 117A**.

▸   וְנִכָּה   What class of verbs is this? See **Chart 156**. Notice that the Nifal and Piel pf. 3ms of this class are identical in form. Which stem does this context require?

182

(II Sm 11:15-20)

▶   וְנִכָּה וָמֵת   The conjunction in both instances might be translated "so that" or "in order that." **REVIEW Note 93B**.

Note 182A: Hollow Verbs

The Qal pf. 3ms and the Qal active part. ms of a hollow verb are identical in form. See **Chart 148** and notice the Qal forms of the stative verb מוּת. Which form of מֵת is suggested by the context?

(v.16)

▶   בִּשְׁמוֹר יוֹאָב   **REVIEW Note 82A**. Notice the full writing of the inf. const.

▶   אֲשֶׁר...שָׁם   **REVIEW Note 172A**.

▶   אַנְשֵׁי   See **Chart 102** for this irregular noun.

(v. 17)

Note 182B: Partitive Use of מִן

The preposition מִן at times has a **partitive** usage and is translated "some from" or "some of." Such is the case in the phrase מֵעַבְדֵי, which serves as the subject of the sg. verb. The verb might also be thought of as impersonal: "and there fell...."

(v. 19)   וַיְצַו   See **Chart 140**.

▶   כְּכַלּוֹתְךָ   **REVIEW Notes 109A, 82A, and 119A**. See **Chart 140**.

▶   לְדַבֵּר   **REVIEW Note 111B**. The direct object of this inf. const. precedes it here but would be translated after it in English.

(v. 20)   וְהָיָה   Is the Vav conjunctive or consecutive?

▶   תַּעֲלֶה   2ms or 3fs?

▶   נִגַּשְׁתֶּם   The Nifal and Piel pf. forms of a פ״ן verb are identical. See **Chart 146** and consult the lexicon for the usual stem of this verb in the pf.

**   הַ◻◻◻   (the clue pointing of the Nifal infinitive construct) See **Chart 72**.

Note 183A: Nifal Imperative and Infinitives

The presence of a He before the root in the form לְהִלָּחֵם might suggest the Hifil. But the Dagesh Forte in the first of three root letters is always the assimilated Nun of the Nifal (**REVIEW Note 110B**). Some forms of the Nifal, in particular the imperative and infinitives, have the stem sign ‗‗‗ִהָ. See **Chart 134**.

▶ אֵת אֲשֶׁר   Here equivalent to כִּי after verbs of seeing, hearing, knowing, etc.

▶ יְרוּ   **REVIEW Note 112A**. What class verb is this? See I ירה in the lexicon and cf. **Chart 160**.

(v. 21) הֻכָּה   The initial He is the stem sign. What is the root? See **Chart 156**.

▶ מֵת   **REVIEW Note 182A**.

(v. 22) שְׁלָחוֹ   **REVIEW Note 108A**. The Qamets of the clue pointing ◻◻ָ◻ has been reduced to a Sheva.

(v. 23) כִּי   Notice that כִּי here introduces *direct* and not indirect discourse. **REVIEW Note 56A**.

(v. 24)

▶ וַיֹּראוּ הַמּוֹרִאים   **REVIEW Note 167B**. Can you explain the Qere-Ketiv? In the margin of BHS the Qere is וַיֹּרוּ הַמּוֹרִים. **REVIEW Note 172B**. See II ירא (and I ירה) in the lexicon.

▶ הַמּוֹרִאים   **REVIEW Note 79A**.

▶ עֲבָדֶךָ   Written defectively for עֲבָדֶיךָ. What would the pointing of the sg. be? See **Chart 100**.

▶ מֵעַבְדֵי   **REVIEW Note 182B**. This time the verb is pl.

(v. 25) יֵרַע   From I רעע. Can you derive יֵרַע by comparison with יֵטַב of the model verb? **REVIEW Note 51B** and see **Chart 152**. See the following Note.

Note 184A: Jussive

We have seen that the cohortative expresses wish or intention in 1st person verbs (**REVIEW Note 46A**). The **jussive** expresses wish or intention in the 2nd and 3rd persons. In the 2nd person, the jussive often accompanies אַל to express prohibition (**REVIEW Note 55A**). In the 3rd person, as in יֵרַע , the jussive is translated "let him (it)..." or "may he (it)..." and may have the negative particle אַל. The jussive is a somewhat shortened form of the impf. and is like the impf. consec. without the Vav. Sometimes the impf. and jussive are identical and can be distinguished only by context, as here with יֵרַע. See several verb charts and cf. the impf., impf. consec., and jussive forms.

Note 184B: אֶת־ as Sign of the Subject

In a few places אֶת־ introduces the subject (perhaps incorrectly) rather than the direct object of the verb. Here it introduces הַדָּבָר as the subject of יֵרַע.

▸ כָּזֹה וְכָזֶה This phrase occurs only three times in the Hebrew Bible. See under זֶה in the lexicon (meaning 16.b). It intends to show that killing in battle happens by chance, not by prearrangement or planning -- so says David! No translation is very satisfactory.

▸ הֶחֱרֵב What gender? The pausal form punctuates the verse.

** הַ□□□ (the clue pointing of the Hifil imperative 2ms)
    See **Chart 72**.

Note 184C: Hifil Imperative

The **Hifil imperative** 2ms of the strong verb is הַקְטֵל. See **Chart 132** for the pointing of הַחֲזֵק.

▸ וְהָרְסָהּ Qal impv. 2ms with a 3fs sf. from הרס.

▸ וְחַזְּקֵהוּ What is הוּ____? Without the sf. the form of the strong verb is קַטֵּל. **REVIEW Note 118B** and consult the lexicon for the meaning in this stem.

(v.27) וַיַּאַסְפָהּ See the lexicon for an analogous form. What stem is this?

▶   וַיֵּרַע   What root, stem, and branch?

(12:1)   אֶחָת   **REVIEW Note 119C**. This is a pausal form of אַחַת, the fem. of אֶחָד. See **Chart 106** for the numbers. The Zaqef Qaton also helps punctuate the sentence.

▶   אֶחָד עָשִׁיר ◀   **REVIEW Note 57C**.

▶   רָאשׁ   Also spelled רָשׁ, as in v. 3 below. See under רוּשׁ in the lexicon.

(v. 2)

**   הַ◻◻◻   (the clue pointing of the Hifil infinitive absolute) See **Chart 72**.

Note 185A: Hifil Infinitive Absolute

The **Hifil infinitive absolute** of the strong verb is הַקְטֵל. See **Chart 140** for the analogous form of הַרְבֵּה.

▶   הַרְבֵּה   **REVIEW Note 115B**. Here the inf. abs. of רבה is used adverbially, meaning "much, many."

Note 185B: The Quasi-verbs אַיִן and יֵשׁ

The nouns אַיִן ("non-existence") and יֵשׁ ("existence") function as quasi-verbs meaning "there is not" and "there is" respectively. אַיִן almost always appears as the const. אֵין.

▶   כִּי אִם   "except"

▶   קְטַנָּה   See I קָטָן in the lexicon.

▶   וַיְחַיֶּהָ   See **Chart 151** for the 3fs. sf. with impf. verbs. What stem is this form?

▶   וּמִכֹּסוֹ   The noun is I כּוֹס.

(v. 4)   הֵלֶךְ   Not a verb form but a noun.

186

▸ וַיַּחְמֹל   The verb חמל occurs here and in v. 6 below with slightly different meanings. The lexicon refers to both verses.

▸ לָקַחַת   **REVIEW Notes 83B** and **81C** and see **Chart 146**.

▸ לָאֹרֵחַ   A definite participle with a preposition.

▸ הַבָּא   The form בָּא by itself could be parsed in two ways. **REVIEW Note 182A**. But what must it be, since it has the article? **REVIEW Note 85B**.

(v. 5)   חַי־יהוה   **REVIEW Note 180B**.

▸ כִּי   **REVIEW Note 56A**. Remember the special usage of כִּי in oaths.

▸ בֶן־מָוֶת   An idiomatic usage of בֶּן. See under בֶּן in the lexicon (meaning 7).

(v. 6)   עֵקֶב אֲשֶׁר   **REVIEW Note 62B**.

(v. 8)   וָאֶתְּנָה   What form is this verb with a final Qamets He? **REVIEW Note 46A** and see the Qal of this verb in **Chart 146**.

▸ נְשֵׁי   נָשִׁים is the pl. of what irregular noun? See **Chart 103**.

▸ וְאֹסְפָה   Written fully it would be וְאוֹסִיפָה. What kind of Vav?

▸ כָּהֵנָּה וְכָהֵנָּה   "this and that" or "so and so" -- used when details need not be specified.

(v. 9)   בְּעֵינֻו   Can you explain the Qere-Ketiv? The Segolta helps punctuate this verse (**REVIEW Note 173A**).

(v. 10)   תָסוּר   Is the prefix 2ms or 3fs?

     בְזִתָנִי   A perfect verb form with a suffix. Cf. the form בָּזִיתָ in v. 9.

(v. 11)

▶   הִנְנִי מֵקִים   This is הִנֵּה with a suffix followed by a participle. **REVIEW Note 107C**. Here the suffix serves as the pronominal subject of the participle. What stem is the participle? See **Chart 148**.

Note 187A: Feminine Used for Abstract Ideas

The feminine is used in Hebrew for abstract ideas. רָעָה is the fem. form of the adjective רַע.

▶   וְלָקַחְתִּי   For the shift of the stress to the affix, **REVIEW Note 171A**.

Note 187B: The Verb נתן

The final Nun of נתן is usually assimilated to the affix in perfect forms, as in the form וְנָתַתִּי. See **Chart 146** for the Qal paradigm of נתן.

▶   לְרֵעֶיךָ   This is not a pl. form as the Yod would suggest, but the sg. pausal form רֵעֶךָ written fully.

(v. 13)   הֶעֱבִיר   See **Chart 132**.

(v. 14)

**   ☐◌̇☐◌̇   (the pointing of the Piel infinitive absolute) See **Chart 72**.

Note 187C: Piel Infinitive Absolute

The **Piel infinitive absolute** of the strong verb is קַטֹּל (sometimes קַטֵּל).

▶   נָאֵץ נִאַצְתָּ   The usual form of the Piel inf. abs. of an Ayin Guttural verb is גָּאֵל (see **Chart 134**), but the verb נאץ retains a Hireq under the first root letter throughout in the Piel. **REVIEW Note 63B** for the usage.

▶   מוֹת   See the paradigm of מות in **Chart 148**.

188

(II Sm 12:15-20)

(v. 15) וַיִּגֹּף What stem? **REVIEW Note 61A.**

(v. 16)

| Note 188A: Cognate Accusative |

When the direct object is derived from the same root as the verb, it is said to be a **cognate accusative**. Example: וַיָּ֫צָם דָּוִד צוֹם -- "and David fasted a fast." The cognate accusative is proper in Hebrew but is not good English.

▶ וּבָא וְלָן וְשָׁכַב Are the Vavs conjunctive or consecutive?

(v. 17) בְּרָא **REVIEW Note 172B.** See under IV ברא in the lexicon.

(v. 18)

| Note 188B: Meteg |

Besides the use of the Meteg to indicate a long Qamets before a vocal Sheva, such as in 3fs and 3cp pf. forms (**REVIEW Note 166C**), the Meteg is used in other situations to show that the syllable on which the Meteg falls is open and the Sheva following is vocal. Example: וַיִּֽרְאוּ. The Meteg indicates that this form is not וַיִּרְאוּ from ראה, but is written defectively for וַיִּֽירְאוּ from ירא. The Meteg is the only clue to distinguish these forms.

▶ אָמְרוּ Here the expected Meteg is included in BHS. **REVIEW Note 166C.**

▶ בִּהְיוֹת **REVIEW Note 82A.**

(v. 19) מִתְלַחֲשִׁים What stem and branch?

(v. 20) וַיָּ֫סֶךְ **REVIEW Note 169A.**

▶ שִׂמְלֹתָו Can you explain the Qere-Ketiv? Consult the lexicon for various forms of שִׂמְלָה and see **Chart 99** for the way the 3ms suffix appears with the sg. and pl. fem. noun.

▶ וַיִּשְׁתָּ֫חוּ **REVIEW Note 113D.** The form of this uniquely unusual verb, which may appear to be pl. because of the Shureq, is

actually the apocopated impf. consec. 3ms form וַיִּשְׁתָּֽחוּ.
The unapocopated impf. 3ms form is יִשְׁתַּחֲוֶה. Remember
that the stem of this verb is to be designated Eshtafal or
simply Shin Tav.

(v. 21)

> ## Note 189A: 2ms Affix

Occasionally the 2ms affix תָ֫___ is written fully with the vowel letter
as ___תָה. Example: עָשִׂיתָה.

▶ בַּעֲבוּר   This word occurred in Gn 12:13.

▶ וַתֵּבְךְ   Do not apply the missing letter rules. Cf. וַיֵּשְׁתְּ in II Sm
11:13 above. The final Kaf here has a Dagesh Lene to indicate
the hard pronunciation.

(v. 22) בְּעוֹד   עוֹד plus בְּ = "as long as."

▶ יוֹדֵעַ   Written fully for יֹדֵעַ. **REVIEW** Notes **107B** and **107C**.

▶ יְחָנַּ֫נִי   From the ע״ע verb חָנַן with a 1cs suffix. The Qere is the
Qal pf. consec. form: וְחַנַּ֫נִי. The Ketiv is the Qal impf. (or
jussive): יְחָנֵּ֫נִי. Without the suffix, the Qal impf. is יָחֹן.
Can you explain the reduction of the Qamets to a Sheva
under the prefix in the form יְחָנֵּ֫נִי? **REVIEW Note 108A**.
The word may be translated: "he may be gracious to me."

(v. 23) לָ֫מָּה זֶּה   **REVIEW Notes 96A** and **179A**. This interrogative word
occurs either as לָ֫מָּה or לָמָה.

> ## Note 189B: Interrogative Particle

The **interrogative particle** is regularly הֲ. **REVIEW Note 179A**. But
before a guttural or simple Sheva it is הַ. Example: הַאוּכַל. If the
guttural has a Qamets, the interrogative is הֶ.

▶ הַאוּכַל   **REVIEW Note 174A**.

190

(v. 24)   וַיְנַחֵם   What stem? According to the paradigm in **Chart 134**, we would expect a Qamets under the first root consonant as compensatory lengthening for the rejection of the Dagesh Forte in the middle guttural letter. But **REVIEW Note 45B** for the reason there is no compensatory lengthening in this form.

▶   אֲהֵבוֹ   What form of what verb?

(v. 25)   יְדִידְיָה   This proper noun is composed of the noun יָדִיד and a shortened form of the Tetragrammaton יָה that is often used in names with Yahweh as an element. This name means "beloved of Yahweh."

MORE ON USING THE WORKBOOK

In the last three readings from Gn 1, Jr 1, and Ps 51, fewer helps will be provided, for by now you have most of the tools to read and study on your own.

The new vocabulary words will be listed and a few learning helps will be supplied, but you are expected to know how to refer to the lexicon and to the charts and notes in the *Workbook* for added assistance.

CHAPTER VII: THE STUDY OF GENESIS 1:1-2:4a

VOCABULARY TO BE LEARNED

Verse:

(1:1)	286.	I בָּרָא	(v. 21)	292.	I חַיָּה	
				293.	כָּנָף	
(v. 2)	287.	רוּחַ	(v. 22)	294.	מלא	
(v. 3)	288.	אוֹר				
(v. 5)	289.	לַיְלָה	(v. 26)	295.	I אָדָם	
(v. 11)	290.	פְּרִי	(2:1)	296.	I צָבָא	
(v. 14)	291.	מוֹעֵד	(v. 2)	297.	שׁבת	

LEARNING HELPS FOR GENESIS 1:1-2:4a

(1:2) הָיְתָה **REVIEW** Note **93C**. This form is written with a Meteg in **Chart 140**.

► מְרַחֶפֶת **REVIEW** Notes **79A** and **178B**.

(v. 3)

Note 191A: Jussive of היה

REVIEW Note **184A**. The form of the **jussive** in the strong verb is the same as the impf. except in the Hifil. See **Chart 130**. But the form of the jussive in many weak verbs is apocopated if possible. Thus the Qal impf. 3ms of היה is יְהְיֶה ("he [it] will be") but the jussive is יְהִי ("let him [it] be"). See the paradigm of היה in **Chart 140**.

Note 191B: Meteg

The form וַיְהִי was at times pronounced with a vocal Sheva and is so indicated by the presence of a Meteg (either וַיְיהִי or וְיְהִי). **REVIEW** Note **188B**. For the lack of a Dagesh Forte in the prefix of this impf. consec. form, **REVIEW** Note **39B**.

(v. 5) וְלַחֹשֶׁךְ קָרָא **REVIEW** Note **92A**. The verb קָרָא followed by לְ means "to name."

	Note 192A: The Noun לַיְלָה	

The noun לַיְלָה is masc. and always has a stressed first syllable. Thus the Qamets He ending is not fem. in this case, for the fem. sg. noun/adjective ending is always part of a final stressed syllable.

(v. 6) וִיהִי The Vav conjunction with the jussive. **REVIEW Note 86A** for the pointing.

(v. 9) יִקָּווּ By context, this form is a jussive of this ל״ה verb. What stem?

▸ וְתֵרָאֶה A jussive with the Vav conjunction. It is unusual that this form is not apocopated. **REVIEW Note 61A** for the stem.

(v. 10)

	Note 192B: Construct Forms	

The construct ending of nouns that end in ֶה is ֵה. Examples: מְרֵה = const. of מִקְוֶה; מַרְאֵה = const. of מַרְאֶה.

▸ יַמִּים See **Chart 104**.

(v. 11) תַּדְשֵׁא Since the impf. form is תַּדְשִׁיא, what stem and branch must this be? See **Chart 138**. What person, gender, and number?

▸ מַזְרִיעַ **REVIEW Note 79A**.

	Note 192C: Collective Nouns	

Many nouns in this chapter and in Hebrew generally are singular in form but collective in meaning. In English we translate such nouns in the plural. Example: עֵץ -- "tree," but in this context "trees."

▸ אֲשֶׁר...בּוֹ **REVIEW Note 172A**.

(v. 14) מְאֹרֹת The lexicon form is written fully as מָאוֹר.

▸ וְהָיוּ How does the context suggest that this pf. consec. form should be translated?

▸ לְאֹתֹת See **Word 222**.

▸ וְשָׁנִים See **Word 100**.

(v. 16) הַגְּדֹל   **REVIEW Note 181B.** Here a comparative sense may be implied.

▶ לְמֶמְשֶׁלֶת   A noun and not a verb form.

(v. 20) חַיָּה   In the phrase נֶפֶשׁ חַיָּה, חַיָּה is an attributive adjective, the fem. sg. of II חַי. Why is it fem.?

Note 193A: Polel, Polal, and Hitpolel Stems

The stems of the hollow verb and the ע"ע verb that correspond to the Piel, Pual, and Hitpael stems in the strong verb are called the **Polel**, **Polal**, and **Hitpolel**. The form יְעוֹפֵף is the Polel impf. or juss. 3ms of the verb עוּף. Since these two types of verbs really have only two root consonants, the characteristic doubling in these stems is achieved by reduplicating the second consonant. A Holem Vav vowel appears between the first two consonants in all forms. See **Charts 148** and **152**.

(v. 21) הַחַיָּה   The phrase נֶפֶשׁ הַחַיָּה is a construct chain with חַיָּה as the absolute noun. See I חַיָּה in the lexicon. Notice that the adj. I חַי in the fem. sg. and the noun חַיָּה are the same in form.

▶ הָרֹמֶשֶׂת   This participle is used as an attributive adjective modifying הַחַיָּה.

(v. 22) פְּרוּ   By use of the verb charts, can you find the root, stem, and branch of this form through the process of elimination? The root must be either פ"י (original פ"ו), ע"ו, ל"ה, or פ"ן.

▶ יִרֶב   What form of what verb? See **Chart 140**.

(v. 24) וְחַיְתוֹ   A less frequent, alternative form of the sg. const. of חַיָּה, which would ordinarily be חַיַּת, as in v. 25.

(v. 26)

Note 193B: Cohortative of ל"ה Verbs

The **cohortative** is identical in form to the impf. in all ל"ה verbs. See **Charts 140, 154, 156,** and **160**. Context alone indicates that נַעֲשֶׂה is cohortative here.

194

(v. 27)   הָאָדָם   **REVIEW Note 192C.**   אָדָם = "human beings."

(v. 28)   וְכִבְשֻׁהָ   Written defectively for וְכִבְשׁוּהָ.   Note the affix.   What branch?

(v. 29)   נָתַתִּי   **REVIEW Note 187B.**

(v. 30)   נֶפֶשׁ חַיָּה   What is the meaning of נֶפֶשׁ in this phrase?

(2:1)

**   יְ□□□   (the pointing of the Pual imperfect) See **Chart 72.**

Note 194A: Pual Imperfect

The impf. 3ms of the **Pual** stem (the so-called "intensive" passive) of the strong verb is יְקֻטַּל -- "he will be massacred." Notice that, like the Piel, the Pual has a Sheva under the prefix and a Dagesh Forte in the middle root consonant. But the vowel under the first root consonant is not the Patah (**REVIEW Note 116A**) but the **Qibbuts.** For the analogous form of וַיְכֻלּוּ, see **Chart 140.**

(v. 4a)   תּוֹלְדוֹת   **REVIEW Note 178A.**   * תּוֹלְדוֹת is from ילד ("to bear, beget").

▶   בְּהִבָּרְאָם   **REVIEW Notes 183A and 82A.**

CHAPTER VIII: THE STUDY OF JEREMIAH 1 AND PSALM 51

VOCABULARY TO BE LEARNED FROM JEREMIAH 1:1-19

Verse:

(v. 1)	298.	יִרְמְיָהוּ		308.	אבד
	299.	כֹּהֵן	(v. 13)	309. I	צָפוֹן
	300.	בִּנְיָמִין	(v. 14)	310. I	פתח
(v. 2)	301.	שָׁלֹשׁ	(v. 15)	311.	כִּסֵּא
	302.	עָשָׂר, עֶשְׂרֵה		312.	סָבִיב
	303. I	מלך		313.	קטר
(v. 3)	304.	גלה		314.	מַעֲשֶׂה
	305. I	חֹדֶשׁ	(v. 18)	315.	עַמּוּד
(v. 9)	306.	פֶּה		316. I	נְחֹשֶׁת
(v. 10)	307.	מַמְלָכָה			

LEARNING HELPS FOR JEREMIAH 1:1-19

(v. 1)   יִרְמְיָהוּ   Besides יָה, another shortened form of the Tetragrammaton used as an element in names is יָהוּ.

(v. 2)   בִּימֵי   See **Chart 104** for the noun and **REVIEW Note 85C** for the pointing of the preposition.

Note 195A: Numerals 11-19

Numbers 11-19 are formed by combining Word 302 (עָשָׂר, עֶשְׂרֵה -- from the root meaning "ten") with the construct of the numbers 1-9. The numbers 11 and 12 have alternative forms. See **Chart 106** for the numerals and **REVIEW Note 81A**. From the number 11 upwards, the cardinals serve also as ordinals, as in the present context.

▶   לְמָלְכוֹ   An inf. const. with a suffix. See the lexicon to confirm the form.

(v. 3) עַשְׁתֵּי עֶשְׂרֵה   **REVIEW** Note **195A** and see **Chart 106**.

(v.5)   ## Note 196A: Imperfect as Past Time

We are accustomed to regarding the imperfect with the Vav consecutive as past time. But several other words often function like a Vav consecutive with the imperfect. An imperfect verb form following אָז ("then"), טֶרֶם ("not yet"), and בְּטֶרֶם ("before") is often past time.

▶   אֶצֽוֹּרְךָ   Notice the Qere-Ketiv. This is a פּ"י verb in which the Yod, by exception, is assimilated as a Dagesh Forte, making the form look deceptively like a פּ"ן verb. The Ketiv is merely written fully (אֶצֽוֹרְךָ) and the Qere defectively (אֶצָּרְךָ).

(v. 6) וָאֹמַר   **REVIEW** Note **35B**.

Note 196B: Another Substitute Word for יהוה

In the phrase אֲדֹנָי יֱהֹוִה, the word אֲדֹנָי has its usual sense "Lord" when referring to God. Since the word אֲדֹנָי occurs here before יהוה, the Qere for the Tetragrammaton cannot again be אֲדֹנָי. The pointing of יֱהֹוִה suggests that the Qere in this case is אֱלֹהִים. The phrase is to be translated "Lord GOD." Notice that the substitute word for the Tetragrammaton is in upper case letters.

▶   דַּבֵּר   What stem and branch?

(v. 7) אַל־תֹּאמַר   **REVIEW** Note **55A**.

(v. 9) פִּי   See **Chart 105** for this irregular noun.

(v. 10) לַהֲרוֹס   The verb root is הרס.

(v. 13) נָפֽוּחַ   **REVIEW** Note **118A**.

▶   צָפֽוֹנָה   Same as צָפוֹן. The Qamets He ending is here not the He directive, as it might be in other contexts.

(v. 15) אִישׁ   **REVIEW** Note **176A**.

▸   עָרֵי   See **Chart 105** for this irregular noun.

(v. 16)   וְדִבַּרְתִּי   **REVIEW Note 171A.** This form must be consecutive because of the shift of the stress.

▸   אוֹתָםᵃ   The footnote indicates that many manuscripts and editions have אֹתָם at this point. What is the difference?

▸   רָעָתָם   **REVIEW Note 82B** and see **Chart 99** for fem. nouns.

▸   וַיִּשְׁתַּחֲווּ   **REVIEW Note 113D.**

(v. 17)   וְקַמְתָּ וְדִבַּרְתָּ   **REVIEW Note 171A.**

▸   אֲצַוֶּךָ   **REVIEW Note 181A.**

▸   תֵּחַת...אֲחִתְּךָ   Both forms are from the same ע″ע root. Consult the lexicon for these two forms in different stems. **REVIEW Note 108A** for the composite Sheva under the prefix in the latter form.

(v. 18)   לְעִיר מִבְצָר   **REVIEW Note 120A.**

(v. 19)   יוּכְלוּ   **REVIEW Note 174A.**

▸   לָךְ   **REVIEW Note 119C.**

VOCABULARY TO BE LEARNED FROM PSALM 51

Verse:

(v. 3) 317. רֹב   (v. 8) 321. חָכְמָה

(v. 5) 318. תָּמִיד   (v. 10) 322. I עֶצֶם

(v. 6) 319. לְבַד   (v. 12) 323. לֵב

(v. 7) 320. I הֵן   324. כּוּן

(continued on the next page)

198

(Ps 51:1)

Verse:

(v. 13)	325.	קֹדֶשׁ	(v. 19)	330. I	שׁבר
(v. 16)	326.	דָּם	(v. 20)	331.	צִיּוֹן
	327.	לָשׁוֹן	(v. 21)	332.	צֶדֶק
	328.	צְדָקָה		333.	פַּר
(v. 18)	329. I	זֶבַח			

LEARNING HELPS FOR PSALM 51

Our readings up to now have been largely in a narrative setting. But for the last reading from Psalm 51, we will get a taste of a poetic passage. Hebrew poetry does not rely on rhyming the ends of lines nor on a strict pattern of rhythmic meter. Instead, there are usually two half-lines in each verse in which at least some of the elements of one half-line parallel the elements of the other half-line in form or meaning. This feature of Hebrew poetry is called *parallelismus membrorum*. Several features of Hebrew prose are not as evident in poetry, such as regular word order, the use of consecutive verb forms, and the presence of the sign of the definite direct object. In addition, the vocabulary is far more extensive, so that you will have to consult the lexicon very often. The superscription in vv. 1-2 was not a part of the original psalm. Most standard translations start counting verses at v. 3 in the MT.

(v. 1)

Note 198A: Piel and Pual Participles

Normally we would expect the Dagesh Forte of the definite article in the Mem in the form לַמְנַצֵּחַ. However, it is almost always omitted in the Mem of the Piel and Pual participles.

Note 198B: מִזְמוֹר לְדָוִד

Following the rule of definiteness in construct chains in **Note 33C**, the phrase מִזְמוֹר דָּוִד would be translated "**the** psalm of David." But a way of indicating an indefinite first element in the phrase is to use the preposition לְ. The phrase מִזְמוֹר לְדָוִד may be translated "**a** psalm **of** David," although the word לְדָוִד is subject to more than one interpretation.

(v. 2)

| Note 199A: Construct Chain |

By exception, a short prepositional phrase stands between the construct and the absolute in this construct chain: בְּבוֹא־אֵלָיו נָתָן.

(v. 3) חָנֵּנִי An imperative of an ע״ע verb with a suffix. See the lexicon to confirm the stem.

| Note 199B: Chiastic Parallelism |

When the elements of a second half-line reverse the order of the parallel elements in the first half-line, the parallelism is said to be **chiastic**. Chiasm is often employed in Hebrew poetry. Both vv. 3 and 4 exhibit chiastic features, since the order of the verb form (with its object) and the prepositional phrase is reversed in the second half-line.

(v. 4) הֶרְבֵּה The Qere is הֶרֶב, an apocopated form of הַרְבֵּה, the Hifil imperative. See the lexicon. The Ketiv is הַרְבֵּה, which could be either the Hifil imperative or infinitive absolute. If the latter, it would compare to the same adverbial usage of the same form in II Sm 12:2.

▶ טַהֲרֵנִי What stem? **REVIEW Notes 116A** and **45B**.

(v. 6) לְבַדְּךָ The word לְבַד is composed of the preposition לְ and the noun I בַּד ("separation, solitude"), but it always occurs idiomatically as לְבַד meaning "alone, only, by oneself."

▶ בְדָבְרֶךָ Is this a noun or verb form? Cf. **Chart 99** to see if it can be a noun form and consult the lexicon for the verb form.

(v. 7)

| Note 199C: Polal Stem |

The stem of a **hollow verb** corresponding to the Piel of the strong verb is called the **Polel**. **REVIEW Note 193A**. The stem of the hollow verb corresponding to the Pual of the strong verb is called the **Polal**. For the form חוֹלָלְתִּי, see **Chart 148**, remembering that this form is in pause, and consult the lexicon under the root I חִיל.

200

(Ps 51:7-9)

▶ יְרֶחֱמַתְנִי
The root of this verb form is יחם. See the lexicon. It is the Piel perfect 3fs with a 1cs suffix. To explain the form, we first must notice that the 3fs affix ה‎ָ___ has become ת before the suffix, as we might expect on the analogy of feminine nouns with suffixes (**REVIEW Note 82B**). The pointing that indicates the stem is difficult. The same form of the strong verb (without the suffix) is קִטְּלָה. Since Het is one of the gutturals that implies the Dagesh Forte and does not require compensatory lengthening before it (**REVIEW Note 45B**), the form of this Ayin Guttural verb should be יְחַמָה. However, this verb appears irregularly as יֶחֱמָה.

Note 200A: The Noun אֵם with Suffixes

The noun אֵם ("mother") has a Hireq under the Alef and a Dagesh Forte in the Mem in all forms with suffixes and in the plural. Examples: אִמִּי, אִמּוֹ, אִמּוֹת.

Note 200B: 2fs Perfect Verbs with Suffixes

One feature of verbs with suffixes that does not occur in the readings of the *Workbook* should be mentioned. When a suffix is added to a **2fs perfect** verb form, the ordinary 2fs affix תְּ___ appears as תִּי___. It cannot be distinguished from the 1cs form except by context. Compare:

שָׁמַרְתְּ -- "you kept" (2fs)

שְׁמַרְתִּיו -- "you kept him" (2fs) or
"I kept him" (1cs)

(v. 8) וּבְסָתֻם
REVIEW Note 118A and see the lexicon.

▶ תּוֹדִיעֵנִי
REVIEW Note 112A for the root and stem. The imperfect has the force of an imperative in many contexts.

(v. 9) וְאֶטְהָר
Notice the Vav conjunction. There are few consecutive forms in the psalms.

Note 201A: Comparatives with מִן

Context alone may suggest the comparative degree, as is the case also with the superlative degree (**REVIEW Note 181B**). Or the preposition מִן may be used to indicate the comparative. Example:

גָּדוֹל מִן־שָׁאוּל -- "greater than Saul"

In the phrase וּמִשֶּׁלֶג אַלְבִּין, the comparative sense is derived partly from the verb.

(v. 10) תִּגֵלְנָה

An ע״י verb in the Qal stem. Why the 3fp prefix? The form is jussive. **REVIEW Note 184A.** See **Chart 150** and observe the Tsere after the first root letter in the jussive and the Hireq Yod in the imperfect.

Note 201B: Omission of Understood Words

The ecomony of words required by poetry often results in the omission of some understood words. Here אֲשֶׁר is to be understood before דִּכִּיתָ.

(v. 12) נָכוֹן

Unlike the parallel word טָהוֹר earlier in the verse which was an adjective, נָכוֹן is a verb form, a participle, which is a verbal adjective. It is from a hollow verb and the Nun is the stem sign. See **Chart 148**.

(v. 13) מִלְפָנֶיךָ

See **Word 154** and **REVIEW Note 111A**. The form of פָּנִים with a combination of two prepositions is listed under פָּנֶה * in the lexicon, meaning 13.

Note 201C: Construct Chains

The translation of the construct chain רוּחַ קָדְשְׁךָ would appear to be "the spirit of your holiness." But we know that the absolute in a construct chain may at times convey an adjectival sense (**REVIEW Note 120A**). In some construct chains, a suffix or adjective after the absolute may actually modify the construct. This phrase may thus be translated "your holy spirit." Compare:

202

(Ps 51:13-15)

Construct chains in which the absolute may have an adjectival sense:

הַר־קֹדֶשׁ -- "a mountain of holiness" or "a holy mountain"

הַר־הַקֹּדֶשׁ -- "the mountain of holiness" or "the holy mountain"

הַר־קָדְשׁוֹ -- "the mountain of his holiness" or "his holy mountain"

Construct chains with adjectives modifying the construct or the absolute:

עַבְדֵי הַמֶּלֶךְ הַטּוֹב -- "the servants of the good king"

עַבְדֵי הַמֶּלֶךְ הַטּוֹבִים -- "the good servants of the king"

עֶבֶד הַמֶּלֶךְ הַטּוֹב -- either "the good servant of the king" or "the servant of the good king"

There may be some ambiguity in such construct chains. Whether the absolute has an adjectival sense or whether an adjective modifies the construct or the absolute will depend on the interpretation of specific contexts.

(v. 14) הָשִׁיבָה   The initial He is a stem sign and the final Qamets He is explained in the following Note. What verb root?

Note 202A: Emphatic Imperative

The ending הָ‍ָ‍‍‍ is added to the imperative 2ms to give it emphasis. Such a form is called the **emphatic imperative**. Compare:

זְכֹר -- "remember!" (2ms)

זָכְרָה -- "oh! remember!" (2ms)

The emphatic imperative 2ms of the strong verb can be distinguished from the perfect 3fs by the Meteg. **REVIEW Note 166C.** Compare:

זָכְרָה -- "she remembered" (pf. 3fs)

זָכְרָה -- "oh! remember!" (emph. impv. 2ms)

▶ שְׂשׂוֹן יִשְׁעֶךָ   Do you see more than one way to understand this phrase? **REVIEW Note 201C.**

(v. 15) אֲלַמְּדָה   What does the final Qamets He signify in this first person verb form? Notice the meaning of the verb in this stem.

(v. 16) מִדָּמִים   For the use of the plural of דָּם, see the lexicon.

▶ אֱלֹהֵי תְשׁוּעָתִי   **REVIEW Note 201C.**

(v. 18) וְאֶתֵּנָה   The context suggests that the cohortative may imply a conditional usage: "or else I would give it."

(v. 19) זִבְחֵי אֱלֹהִים   Presumably not "God's sacrifices" but "sacrifices of (i.e., pleasing to) God." But see the footnote for זִבְחֵי ͣ in BHS.

** נ͜קְטָׄל   (clue pointing of the Nifal participle)
See **Chart 72**.

Note 203A: Nifal Participle

Although we have seen Nifal participles before, the first in Gn 12:7, none has appeared in the strong verb to exhibit the clue pointing. The **Nifal participle** ms of the strong verb is נִקְטָל -- "killed." Notice the characteristic Qamets as the vowel of the second root letter, rather than the Patah of the perfect. In the present context, we have both a fem. sg. (נִשְׁבָּרָה) and a masc. sg. (נִשְׁבָּר) form of the Nifal participle. Also, we have a Nifal participle of a ל״ה verb (נִדְכֶּה). See **Charts 130** and **140** for the pointing that distinguishes these Nifal participles from the perfect.

▶ [תְבְזֶה:]   When a line of poetry is too long, the editors of BHS have placed the extra word(s) within a bracket at the end of the line above or below.

(v. 20) הֵיטִׄיבָה   **REVIEW Note 202A.**

(v. 21) יַעֲלוּ   **REVIEW Note 113B** and see **Chart 154**.

ADDITIONAL VOCABULARY LESSONS

During the course of the readings in the *Workbook,* some common Hebrew words were not encountered. The following three groupings will complete all the words that occur 100 times or more in the Hebrew Bible. You may look them up in the lexicon and record basic translations in Appendix II to complete your own glossary.

1. Additional words occurring more than 175 times

334.	אוֹ	350.	כַּף
335.	I אַמָּה	351.	לֵוִי
336.	אֶפְרַיִם	352.	לָכֵן
337.	אַרְבַּע	353.	I מֵאָה
338.	בָּבֶל	354.	מַחֲנֶה
339.	II בֶּגֶד	355.	מַטֶּה
340.	בָּשָׂר	356.	מִנְחָה
341.	גְּבוּל	357.	מצא
342.	הֵם, הֵמָּה	358.	עֶשְׂרִים
343.	זָהָב	359.	פְּלִשְׁתִּי
344.	חָצֵר	360.	צַדִּיק
345.	יוֹסֵף	361.	רִאשׁוֹן
346.	ישׁע	362.	רום
347.	כָּבוֹד	363.	רָשָׁע
348.	כְּלִי	364.	שֶׁמֶן
349.	כֶּסֶף		

2. Additional words occurring from 125 to 174 times

365.	אַךְ	386.	I מִסְפָּר	
366.	I אַף	387.	מִשְׁכָּן	
367.	אַרְבָּעִים	388.	נוּס	
368.	אֲרָם	389.	I נַחַל	
369.	אַשּׁוּר	390.	I נָשִׂיא	
370.	I בּוֹשׁ	391.	סבב	
371.	גִּבּוֹר	392.	I סוּס	
372.	II דּוֹר	393.	ספר	
373.	זבח	394.	עֲבֹדָה	
374.	חוּץ	395.	I עֵדָה	
375.	חִזְקִיָּ֫ח(וּ)	396.	פנה	
376.	חַיִּים (see I חַי)	397.	קבץ	
377.	חָכָם	398.	קבר	
378.	I חלל	399.	II קרא	
379.	חֲמִשִּׁים	400.	I רעה	
380.	טמא	401.	שׂמח	
381.	יָ֫יִן	402.	שֶׁ‑ ֶ ‑ ‑ ‑ (see שֶׁ)	
382.	I יָמִין	403.	שׁאר	
383.	יֵשׁ	404.	שׁכן	
384.	I כֹּחַ	405.	שְׁלֹשִׁים	
385.	מְנַשֶּׁה	406.	שְׁמוּאֵל	

3. Additional words occurring from 100 to 124 times

407.	אַבְשָׁלוֹם	426.		כפר
408.	אֱדוֹם	427.		לבשׁ
409.	I אמן	428		לכד
410.	I בטח	429.		מִגְרָשׁ
411.	בְּכוֹר	430.		נבא
412.	בִּלְתִּי	431.		עָפָר
413.	בָּמָה	432.	*	II פלל
414.	I גאל	433.		פַּעַם
415.	גִּלְעָד	434.		רוּץ
416.	* הֵיכָל	435.		I רֹחַב
417.	חֲצִי	436.		II רַק
418.	חֻקָּה	437.		שֹׂרף
419.	חשׁב	438.		שׁכח
420.	II ידה	439.		שְׁמֹנֶה
421.	יְהוֹנָתָן	440.		שֹׁמְרוֹן
422.	יָרָבְעָם	441.		שׁפךְ
423.	* יְשׁוּעָה	442.		שׁקר
424.	יָשָׁר	443.		תּוֹעֵבָה
425.	יתר	444.	*	תְּפִלָּה

* occurs fewer than 100 times.

APPENDIX I

HEBREW LANGUAGE RESOURCES FOR EXEGESIS AND FURTHER LANGUAGE STUDY

When you have finished this *Workbook*, you may desire to broaden and deepen your Hebrew language skills through continuing study along two intersecting lines. You may want to advance your understanding of the grammar and syntax of biblical Hebrew and you may want to develop further your ability to read and translate the Hebrew Bible. For these goals, the following resources are recommended.

1. Hebrew Grammars

Once you have become familiar with biblical Hebrew through an inductive method, you will find that a more deductive approach as a second stage will enhance your mastery of the grammar of the language. Here are several deductive textbooks that can be used with profit.

> Lambdin, Thomas O. *Introduction to Biblical Hebrew*. New York: Charles Scribner's Sons, 1971.
>
> Seow, C. L. *A Grammar for Biblical Hebrew*. Nashville: Abingdon, 1987.
>
> Weingreen, J. *A Practical Grammar for Classical Hebrew*. 2nd ed. Oxford: Clarendon, 1959.

Weingreen uses the more traditional grammatical terminology, but Lambdin and Seow both employ more modern descriptive terms. Seow's exercises are all biblical passages.

In addition to textbook grammars, two works on the syntax of biblical Hebrew can be recommended.

> Williams, Ronald J. *Hebrew Syntax: An Outline*. 2nd ed. Toronto/Buffalo: University of Toronto, 1976.
>
> Waltke, Bruce K. *Introduction to Biblical Syntax*. Winona Lake, IN: Eisenbrauns, 1987.

Finally, the classic and still standard reference work for Hebrew grammar and syntax stems from the work of W. Gesenius in the 19th century. The edition still in print is the English translation of the 28th revised and enlarged edition.

> Gesenius, W. *Gesenius' Hebrew Grammar*. Edited and enlarged by E. Kautzsch. 2nd English edition by A. E. Cowley. Oxford: Clarendon, 1910.

2. Reading Aids

Besides knowing the fundamentals of grammar, building your Hebrew vocabulary is essential for reading the Hebrew Bible without having to spend so much time looking up unfamiliar words.   Two collections of all words that occur ten or more times in the Hebrew Bible are the following. Each is organized into frequency sections.

> Landes, George M. *A Student's Vocabulary of Biblical Hebrew Listed According to Frequency and Cognate*. New York: Charles Scribner's Sons, 1961.

> Mitchel, Larry A. *A Student's Vocabulary for Biblical Hebrew and Aramaic*. Grand Rapids: Academie Books, Zondervan, 1984.

Two works that aim to assist in reading the Hebrew Bible are especially helpful. The first lists the Hebrew root of every word in every verse in biblical sequence along with a translation and a page reference to Brown-Driver-Briggs. The second assumes a Hebrew vocabulary down to a frequency of 50, but then lists for every verse all words of less frequency with a translation and page reference to Brown-Driver-Briggs.

> Einspahr, Bruce. *Index to Brown, Driver and Briggs Hebrew Lexicon*. 2nd ed. Chicago: Moody, 1977.

> Armstrong, Terry A.; Busby, Douglas L.; and Carr, Cyril F.   *A Reader's Hebrew-English Lexicon of the Old Testament*. 3 vols. Grand Rapids: Zondervan, 1980-86.

3. Using BHS

Two guides have recently been published to help understand the material presented in the margins and notes of *Biblia Hebraica Stuttgartensia*.

> Wonneberger, Reinhard. *Understanding BHS: A Manual for the Users of Biblia Hebraica Stuttgartensia*. Trans. Dwight R. Daniels. Subsidia Biblica 8. Rome: Biblical Institute, 1984.

> Scott, William R. *A Simplified Guide to BHS*. Berkeley: BIBAL, 1987. Bound in this book and also available separately is H. P. Rüger's leaflet *An English Key to the Latin Words and Abbreviations and the Symbols of Biblia Hebraica Stuttgartensia* (Stuttgart: German Bible Society, 1985).

4. Lexicons

The two most comprehensive lexicons for biblical Hebrew were described on p. 75. Although Holladay is useful for beginners in exegesis, the larger lexicons should be consulted for their more extensive entries.

> Brown, Francis; Driver, S. R.; and Briggs, Charles A. *A Hebrew and English Lexicon of the Old Testament with an Appendix Containing the Biblical Aramaic*. Oxford: Clarendon, 1907. This has recently been reprinted with an alphabetical index as *The New Brown-Driver-Briggs-Gesenius Hebrew and English Lexicon* (Peabody, MA: Hendrickson, 1979).

Koehler, Ludwig, and Baumgartner, Walter. *Lexicon in Veteris Testamenti Libros: A Dictionary of the Hebrew Old Testament in English and German.* II vols. Leiden: E. J. Brill; Grand Rapids: Wm. B. Eerdmans, 1951-53. *Supplementum*, 1958.

A helpful tool to be used only as a last resort is the following analytical lexicon that lists alphabetically every form as it appears in the Hebrew Bible and gives the full parsing. This is a reprint of an old work, so that some of the grammatical terminology is no longer in use (future = imperfect; preterite = perfect).

Davidson, Benjamin. *The Analytical Hebrew and Chaldee Lexicon.* London: Samuel Bagster & Sons, 1848; reprint, Grand Rapids: Zondervan, 1970.

5. Concordances

There are several concordances to English versions of the Bible that are indexed with the transliterated Hebrew words. But those who have studied Hebrew are equipped to use the two complete Hebrew concordances.

Lisowsky, Gerhard. *Konkordanz zum hebräischen Alten Testament.* 2nd ed. Stuttgart: Württembergische Bibelanstalt, 1958.

Mandelkern, Solomon. *Veteris Testamenti concordantiae hebraicae atque chaldaicae.* 9th ed. Jerusalem: Schocken Books, 1971. (Originally published in 1896).

6. Textual Criticism

Because of the centuries of both oral and written transmission of the Hebrew Bible, textual criticism is necessary to deal with problems in the text as it has come down to us. The following works introduce the field of textual criticism.

McCarter, P. Kyle, Jr. *Textual Criticism: Recovering the Text of the Hebrew Bible.* Guides to Biblical Scholarship, Old Testament Series. Ed. Gene M. Tucker. Philadelphia: Fortress, 1986.

Roberts, Bleddyn J. *The Old Testament Text and Versions: The Hebrew Text in Transmission and the History of the Ancient Versions.* Cardiff: University of Wales, 1951.

Würthwein, Ernst. *The Text of the Old Testament: An Introduction to the Biblia Hebraica.* Trans. Erroll F. Rhodes. 4th ed. Grand Rapids: Wm. B. Eerdmans, 1979.

APPENDIX II

VOCABULARY LISTING

The following alphabetical listing of 444 Hebrew words includes all words that occur 100 times or more in the Hebrew Bible. Also a few other important words of less frequency that were included among the vocabulary words are listed.

Some words did not appear in any of the readings in the *Workbook* but were listed in the additional vocabulary lessons on pp. 204-206.

This listing can serve as a glossary for the vocabulary words in the *Workbook*. Students may write in translations of the vocabulary words as they are encountered in the readings.

The lexicon form of the word is given at the outer margin of the page. In brackets is the number of times the word occurs in the Hebrew Bible. The count depends mainly on that of Larry A. Mitchel, *A Student's Vocabulary for Biblical Hebrew and Aramaic* (Grand Rapids: Zondervan, 1984). Then the passage where the word was first encountered in the *Workbook* is given with the *Workbook's* word number in parentheses. Finally, a brief quotation of the context of the word in that passage is provided, so that the student will not only learn the lexicon form but remember the word in a biblical context.

אֶל־אַבְרָהָם אָבִיו :(53) Gn 22:7	[1568]	אָב
וּלְהַאֲבִיד וְלַהֲרוֹס :(308) Jr 1:10	[183]	אבד
עַל־שְׁנֵי לֻחֹת אֲבָנִים :(187) Dt 5:22	[268]	אֶבֶן
וְהָאֱלֹהִים נִסָּה אֶת־אַבְרָהָם :(9) Gn 22:1	[172]	אַבְרָהָם
וַיֹּאמֶר יהוה אֶל־אַבְרָם :Gn 12:1	[60]	אַבְרָם
(407)	[107]	אַבְשָׁלוֹם
(408)	[112]	אֱדוֹם
כָּל־עַבְדֵי אֲדֹנָיו :(251) II Sm 11:9	[770]	אָדוֹן
נַעֲשֶׂה אָדָם בְּצַלְמֵנוּ :(295) Gn 1:26	[553]	אָדָם
כֹּל מִשְׁפְּחֹת הָאֲדָמָה :(96) Gn 12:3	[225]	אֲדָמָה

8

אהב	[205]	אֲשֶׁר־אָהַ֫בְתָּ (17): Gn 22:2
אֹ֫הֶל	[342]	וַיֵּט אָהֳלֹה (113): Gn 12:8
אַהֲרוֹן	[347]	וָאֶשְׁלַח אֶת־מֹשֶׁה וְאֶת־אַהֲרֹן (198): Js 24:5
אוֹ	[311]	(334)
אוֹר	[125]	יְהִי אוֹר וַיְהִי־אוֹר (288): Gn 1:3
אוֹת I	[79]	אֶת־הָאֹתוֹת הַגְּדֹלוֹת הָאֵלֶּה (222): Js 24:17
אָז	[141]	וְהַכְּנַעֲנִי אָז בָּאָ֫רֶץ (108): Gn 12:6
אֹ֫זֶן	[187]	אָנֹכִי דֹּבֵר בְּאָזְנֵיכֶם (147): Dt 5:1
אָח II	[626]	וְאֶת־לוֹט בֶּן־אָחִיו (104): Gn 12:5
אֶחָד	[959]	עַל אַחַד הֶהָרִים (26): Gn 22:2
אָחוֹת	[114]	אִמְרִי־נָא אֲחֹ֫תִי אָ֑תְּ (125): Gn 12:13
אַחֵר	[166]	לֹא יִהְיֶה־לְךָ אֱלֹהִים אֲחֵרִים (159): Dt 5:7
אַחַר, אַחֲרֵי	[713]	וַיְהִי אַחַר הַדְּבָרִים הָאֵלֶּה (2): Gn 22:1
אֹיֵב	[281]	אֵת שַׁ֫עַר אֹיְבָיו (87): Gn 22:17
אַ֫יִל I	[161]	וַיַּרְא וְהִנֵּה־אַ֫יִל אַחַר (71): Gn 22:13
אַ֫יִן I	[773]	וְלָרָשׁ אֵין־כֹּל (266): II Sm 12:3
אִישׁ I	[2149]	וַיְצַוּוּ עָלָיו פַּרְעֹה אֲנָשִׁים (141): Gn 12:20
אַךְ	[160]	(365)
אכל	[795]	אַתֶּם אֹכְלִים (214): Js 24:13
אַל I	[738]	אַל־תִּשְׁלַח יָדְךָ (63): Gn 22:12
אֵל V	[236]	אָנֹכִי יהוה אֱלֹהֶיךָ אֵל קַנָּא (162): Dt 5:9
אֶל	[5000+]	וַיֹּ֫אמֶר אֵלָיו (11): Gn 22:1
אֵ֫לֶּה	[738]	אַחַר הַדְּבָרִים הָאֵלֶּה (5): Gn 22:1
אֱלֹהִים	[2706] (see אֱלוֹהַּ)	וְהָאֱלֹהִים נִסָּה אַבְרָהָם (7): Gn 22:1
אֶ֫לֶף II	[494]	וְעֹ֫שֶׂה חֶ֫סֶד לַאֲלָפִים (167): Dt 5:10
אֵם	[219]	כַּבֵּד אָבִיךָ וְאֶת־אִמֶּ֫ךָ (180): Dt 5:16
אִם	[1046]	וְאִם רַע בְּעֵינֵיכֶם (217): Js 24:15

8

(335)	[226]	I אַמָּה
(409)	[100]	I אמן
וַיֹּאמֶר אֵלָיו (10) Gn 22:1	[5000+]	I אמר
וַעֲבְדוּ אֹתוֹ בְּתָמִים וּבֶאֱמֶת (215) Js 24:14	[127]	אֶמֶת
כִּי אִתָּנוּ אֲנַחְנוּ אֵלֶּה פֹה הַיּוֹם (152) Dt 5:3	[156]	אֲנַחְנוּ
וַאֲנִי וְהַנַּעַר נֵלְכָה עַד־כֹּה (45) Gn 22:5	[1316]	אֲנִי
אָנֹכִי דֹּבֵר בְּאָזְנֵיכֶם (146) Dt 5:1		אָנֹכִי
וַיֶּאֱסֹף יְהוֹשֻׁעַ אֶת־כָּל־...יִשְׂרָאֵל (188) Js 24:1	[203]	אסף
(366)	[130]	I אַף
וַיִּחַר־אַף דָּוִד בָּאִישׁ מְאֹד (268) II Sm 12:5	[279]	II אַף
(336)	[182]	אֶפְרַיִם
(337)	[315]	I אַרְבַּע
(367)	[129]	אַרְבָּעִים
הָאָרוֹן וְיִשְׂרָאֵל וִיהוּדָה יֹשְׁבִים בַּסֻּכּוֹת (252) II Sm 11:11	[202]	אֲרוֹן
(368)	[155]	אֲרָם
אֶל־אֶרֶץ הַמֹּרִיָּה (21) Gn 22:2	[2498]	אֶרֶץ
וַיִּקַּח בְּיָדוֹ אֶת־הָאֵשׁ (52) Gn 22:6	[375]	I אֵשׁ
וַיִּקַּח אַבְרָם אֶת־שָׂרַי אִשְׁתּוֹ (103) Gn 12:5	[779]	אִשָּׁה
(369)	[152]	אַשּׁוּר
קַח־נָא אֶת־בִּנְךָ...אֲשֶׁר־אָהַבְתָּ (16) Gn 22:2	[5000+]	אֲשֶׁר
כִּי אִשָּׁה יְפַת־מַרְאֶה אָתְּ (122) Gn 12:11	[53]	אַתְּ
וְהָאֱלֹהִים נִסָּה אֶת־אַבְרָהָם (8) Gn 22:1	[5000+]	I אֶת־, אֵת
וַיִּקַּח אֶת־שְׁנֵי נְעָרָיו אִתּוֹ (33) Gn 22:3	[5000+]	II אֶת־, אֵת
כִּי־יְרֵא אֱלֹהִים אַתָּה (69) Gn 22:12	[740]	אַתָּה
אַתֶּם אֹכְלִים (213) Js 24:13	[278]	אַתֶּם
וַיַּשְׁכֵּם אַבְרָהָם בַּבֹּקֶר (28) Gn 22:3	[5000+]	בְּ־---
(338)	[288]	בָּבֶל

8

Hebrew	[No.]	Example
בֶּ֫גֶד II	[214]	(339)
בְּהֵמָה	[192]	וְכָל־בְּהֶמְתֶּ֫ךָ (174): Dt 5:14
בּוֹא	[2530]	וַיָּבֹ֫אוּ אֶל־הַמָּקוֹם (54): Gn 22:9
בּוֹשׁ I	[126]	(370)
בחר I	[173]	בַּחֲרוּ לָכֶם הַיּוֹם (219): Js 24:15
בטח I	[119]	(410)
בִּין	[171]	וַיָּ֫בֶן דָּוִד כִּי מֵת הַיֶּ֫לֶד (280): II Sm 12:19
בֵּין	[396]	אָנֹכִי עֹמֵד בֵּין־יהוה וּבֵינֵיכֶם (157): Dt 5:5
בַּ֫יִת I	[2039]	וּמִבֵּית אָבִ֫יךָ (92): Gn 12:1
בֵּית־אֵל	[70]	מִקֶּ֫דֶם בֵּית־אֵל (111): Gn 12:8
בכה	[114]	בַּעֲבוּר הַיֶּ֫לֶד חַי צַ֫מְתָּ וַתֵּבְךְּ (281): II Sm 12:21
בְּכוֹר	[122]	(411)
בִּלְתִּי	[111]	(412)
בָּמָה	[103]	(413)
בֵּן I	[4887]	קַח־נָא אֶת־בִּנְךָ (15): Gn 22:2
בנה	[373]	וַיִּ֫בֶן שָׁם אַבְרָהָם אֶת־הַמִּזְבֵּ֫חַ (55): Gn 22:9
בִּנְיָמִין	[180]	בְּאֶ֫רֶץ בִּנְיָמִן (300): Jr 1:1
בַּ֫עַד I	[101]	בְּעַד הַנָּ֫עַר (278): II Sm 12:16
בַּ֫עַל I	[198]	וַיִּלָּחֲמוּ בָכֶם בַּעֲלֵי־יְרִיחוֹ (210): Js 24:11
בָּקָר	[183]	וַיְהִי־לוֹ צֹאן־וּבָקָר (134): Gn 12:16
בֹּ֫קֶר II	[200]	וַיַּשְׁכֵּם אַבְרָהָם בַּבֹּ֫קֶר (29): Gn 22:3
בקשׁ	[225]	וַיְבַקֵּשׁ דָּוִד אֶת־הָאֱלֹהִים (277): II Sm 12:16
ברא I	[48]	בְּרֵאשִׁית בָּרָא אֱלֹהִים (286): Gn 1:1
בְּרִית	[287]	יהוה אֱלֹהֵ֫ינוּ כָּרַת עִמָּ֫נוּ בְּרִית (151): Dt 5:2
ברך II	[328]	כִּי־בָרֵךְ אֲבָרֶכְךָ (79): Gn 22:17
בָּשָׂר	[270]	(340)
בַּת I	[582]	אַתָּה וּבִנְךָ־וּבִתֶּ֫ךָ (173): Dt 5:13

8

(414)	[104]	גָּאַל I
(341)	[241]	גְּבוּל
(371)	[161]	גִּבּוֹר
וְאֶעֶשְׂךָ לְגוֹי גָּדוֹל (93) Gn 12:2:	[525]	גָּדוֹל
וַאֲגַדְּלָה שְׁמֶךָ (94) Gn 12:2:	[122]	גדל
כֹּל גּוֹיֵי הָאָרֶץ (89) Gn 22:18:	[545]	גּוֹי
וַיֵּרֶד אַבְרָם מִצְרַיְמָה לָגוּר שָׁם (119) Gn 12:10:	[81]	גּוּר I
עַד־גְּלוֹת יְרוּשָׁלִַם (304) Jr 1:3:	[187]	גלה
(415)	[108]	גִּלְעָד
גַּם־אֲנַחְנוּ נַעֲבֹד אֶת־יהוה (224) Js 24:18:	[812]	גַּם
כַּאֲשֶׁר דִּבֶּר אֵלָיו יהוה (98) Gn 12:4:	[1130]	דבר II
אַחַר הַדְּבָרִים הָאֵלֶּה (4) Gn 22:1:	[1426]	דָּבָר
וְדָוִד יוֹשֵׁב בִּירוּשָׁלִָם (236) II Sm 11:1:	[1031]	דָּוִד
(372)	[169]	דּוֹר II
הַצִּילֵנִי מִדָּמִים (326) Ps 51:16:	[356]	דָּם
וַיִּשְׁמְרֵנוּ בְּכָל־הַדֶּרֶךְ (223) Js 24:17:	[698]	דֶּרֶךְ
וַיִּשְׁלַח דָּוִד וַיִּדְרֹשׁ לָאִשָּׁה (243) II Sm 11:3:	[163]	דרשׁ
אַחַר הַדְּבָרִים הָאֵלֶּה (3) Gn 22:1:	[5000+]	הַ‑ֶ‑‑
וַיֹּאמֶר הֲלוֹא־זֹאת בַּת־שֶׁבַע (244) II Sm 11:3:	[5000+]	הֲ‑‑‑
וַיִּקְרָא אַבְרָהָם שֵׁם־הַמָּקוֹם הַהוּא (74) Gn 22:14:	[1533]	הוּא
כִּי־יָפָה הִוא מְאֹד (128) Gn 12:14:	[541]	הִיא
וַיְהִי (1) Gn 22:1:	[3514]	היה
(416)	[80]	הֵיכָל
וְלֶךְ־לְךָ אֶל־אֶרֶץ הַמֹּרִיָּה (19) Gn 22:2:	[1504]	הלך
וַיְהַלְלוּ אֹתָהּ אֶל־פַּרְעֹה (132) Gn 12:15:	[145]	הלל I
(342)	[1553]	הֵם, הֵמָּה
הֵן־בְּעָווֹן חוֹלָלְתִּי (320) Ps 51:7:	[100]	הֵן I

8

Word	Freq.	Note	Example
הִנֵּה	[1037]		וַיֹּאמֶר הִנֵּנִי (12) :Gn 22:1
הַר	[554]		עַל אַחַד הֶהָרִים (27) :Gn 22:2
הרג	[168]		וְהָרְגוּ אֹתִי וְאֹתָךְ יְחַיּוּ (123) :Gn 12:12
וְ ---	[5000+]		וְהָאֱלֹהִים נִסָּה אֶת־אַבְרָהָם (6) :Gn 22:1
זֹאת	[598]		לְזַרְעֲךָ אֶתֵּן אֶת־הָאָרֶץ הַזֹּאת (110) :Gn 12:7
זבח	[136]		(373)
זֶבַח I	[162]		כִּי לֹא־תַחְפֹּץ זֶבַח (329) :Ps 51:18
זֶה	[1154]		כִּי יַעַן אֲשֶׁר עָשִׂיתָ אֶת־הַדָּבָר הַזֶּה (78) :Gn 22:16
זָהָב	[383]		(343)
זכר	[230]		וְזָכַרְתָּ כִּי־עֶבֶד הָיִיתָ (177) :Dt 5:15
זָקֵן	[178]		וַיִּקְרָא לְזִקְנֵי יִשְׂרָאֵל (191) :Js 24:1
זֶרַע	[228]		וְהִרְבָּה אַרְבֶּה אֶת־זַרְעֶךָ (81) :Gn 22:17
חֹדֶשׁ I	[278]		עַד־גְּלוֹת יְרוּשָׁלַםִ בַּחֹדֶשׁ הַחֲמִישִׁי (305) :Jr 1:3
חוה II	[174]	(cf. שחה)	נֵלְכָה עַד־כֹּה וְנִשְׁתַּחֲוֶה (48) :Gn 22:5
חוֹמָה	[133]		יֹרוּ מֵעַל הַחוֹמָה (262) :II Sm 11:20
חוּץ	[165]		(374)
חזק	[288]		הַחֲזֵק מִלְחַמְתְּךָ אֶל־הָעִיר (264) :II Sm 11:25
חִזְקִיָּ(הוּ)	[131]		(375)
חטא	[237]		חָטָאתִי לַיהוה (276) :II Sm 12:13
חַטָּאת	[296]		לֹא־יִשָּׂא לְפִשְׁעֲכֶם וּלְחַטֹּאותֵיכֶם (228) :Js 24:19
חַי II	[233]		כֻּלָּנוּ חַיִּים (153) :Dt 5:3
חיה	[281]		וְהָרְגוּ אֹתִי וְאֹתָךְ יְחַיּוּ (124) :Gn 12:12
חַיָּה I	[97]		וְאֵת כָּל־נֶפֶשׁ הַחַיָּה (292) :Gn 1:21
חַיִּים	[153]	(see I חַי)	(376)
חַיִל	[246]		אֲשֶׁר יָדַע כִּי אַנְשֵׁי־חַיִל שָׁם (258) :II Sm 11:16
חָכָם	[138]		(377)
חָכְמָה	[152]		וּבְסָתֻם חָכְמָה תוֹדִיעֵנִי (321) :Ps 51:8

8

(378)	[134]	חלל I
אִם־תַּעֲלֶה חֲמַת הַמֶּלֶךְ (260) II Sm 11:20	[126]	חֵמָה
וַיַּחֲבֹשׁ אֶת־חֲמֹרוֹ (30) Gn 22:3	[97]	חֲמוֹר I
וְאַבְרָם בֶּן־חָמֵשׁ שָׁנִים וְשִׁבְעִים שָׁנָה (99) Gn 12:4	[324]	חָמֵשׁ
(379)	[154]	חֲמִשִּׁים
וַעֲבְדֵי אֲדֹנִי עַל־פְּנֵי הַשָּׂדֶה חֹנִים (254) II Sm 11:11	[143]	חנה I
וְעֹשֶׂה חֶסֶד לַאֲלָפִים (166) Dt 5:10	[250]	חֶסֶד II
(417)	[123]	חֲצִי
(344)	[193]	חָצֵר
שְׁמַע יִשְׂרָאֵל אֶת־הַחֻקִּים (144) Dt 5:1	[128]	חֹק
(418)	[104]	חֻקָּה
לֹא בְחַרְבְּךָ וְלֹא בְקַשְׁתֶּךָ (210) Js 24:12	[407]	חֶרֶב
(419)	[124]	חשׁב
וְהָאִשָּׁה טוֹבַת מַרְאֶה מְאֹד (242) II Sm 11:2	[612]	טוֹב I
(380)	[161]	טמא
וַיִּקַּח בְּיָדוֹ אֶת־הָאֵשׁ (51) Gn 22:6	[1580]	יָד
(420)	[115]	ידה II
כִּי עַתָּה יָדַעְתִּי (67) Gn 22:12	[924]	ידע
הָאָרוֹן וְיִשְׂרָאֵל וִיהוּדָה (253) II Sm 11:11	[889]	יְהוּדָה
וַיִּקְרָא אֵלָיו מַלְאַךְ יהוה (61) Gn 22:11	[5000+]	יהוה
(421)	[124]	יְהוֹנָתָן
וַיֶּאֱסֹף יְהוֹשֻׁעַ אֶת־כָּל־...יִשְׂרָאֵל (189) Js 24:1	[247]	יְהוֹשֻׁעַ
וַיִּשְׁלַח דָּוִד אֶת־יוֹאָב (237) II Sm 11:1	[146]	יוֹאָב
בַּיּוֹם הַשְּׁלִישִׁי (37) Gn 22:4	[2241]	יוֹם I
(345)	[214]	יוֹסֵף
לְמַעַן יִיטַב־לִי (127) Gn 12:13	[120]	יטב
(381)	[141]	יַיִן

8

יכל	[194]	לֹא תוּכְלוּ לַעֲבֹד אֶת־יהוה (225): Js 24:19
ילד	[488]	וַתֵּלֶד לוֹ בֵּן (265): II Sm 11:27
יָם	[392]	וְכַחוֹל אֲשֶׁר עַל־שְׂפַת הַיָּם (84): Gn 22:17
יָמִין I	[139]	(382)
יסף	[212]	וְלֹא יָסָף (185): Dt 5:22
יַעֲקֹב	[348]	וָאֶתֵּן לְיִצְחָק אֶת־יַעֲקֹב (197): Js 24:4
יצא	[1055]	בְּצֵאתוֹ מֵחָרָן (102): Gn 12:4
יִצְחָק	[112]	קַח־נָא אֶת־בִּנְךָ...אֶת־יִצְחָק (18): Gn 22:2
ירא I	[377]	כִּי־יְרֵא אֱלֹהִים אַתָּה (68): Gn 22:12
יָרָבְעָם	[104]	(422)
ירד	[380]	וַיֵּרֶד אַבְרָם מִצְרַיְמָה (117): Gn 12:10
יַרְדֵּן	[181]	הַיּוֹשֵׁב בְּעֵבֶר הַיַּרְדֵּן (205): Js 24:8
יְרוּשָׁלַם	[667]	וְדָוִד יוֹשֵׁב בִּירוּשָׁלָם (240): II Sm 11:1
יִרְמְיָהוּ	[147]	דִּבְרֵי יִרְמְיָהוּ בֶּן־חִלְקִיָּהוּ (298): Jr 1:1
ירשׁ I	[231]	וְיִרַשׁ זַרְעֲךָ אֵת שַׁעַר אֹיְבָיו (85): Gn 22:17
יִשְׂרָאֵל	[2513]	שְׁמַע יִשְׂרָאֵל (143): Dt 5:1
יֵשׁ	[139]	(383)
ישׁב	[1078]	שְׁבוּ־לָכֶם פֹּה עִם־הַחֲמוֹר (43): Gn 22:5
יְשׁוּעָה	[78]	(423)
ישׁע	[205]	(346)
יָשָׁר	[119]	(424)
יתר	[106]	(425)
כְּ---	[5000+]	כְּכוֹכְבֵי הַשָּׁמַיִם (82): Gn 22:17
כַּאֲשֶׁר	[504]	כַּאֲשֶׁר דִּבֶּר אֵלָיו יהוה (97): Gn 12:4
כבד	[114]	כַּבֵּד אֶת־אָבִיךָ וְאֶת־אִמֶּךָ (179): Dt 5:16
כָּבוֹד	[200]	(347)
כֶּבֶשׂ	[129]	כִּי אִם־כִּבְשָׂה אַחַת (167): II Sm 12:3

8

Reference	[No.]	Word
Gn 22:5 (47): נֵלְכָה עַד־כֹּה	[554]	כֹּה
Jr 1:1 (299): מִן־הַכֹּהֲנִים אֲשֶׁר בַּעֲנָתוֹת	[749]	כֹּהֵן
Ps 51:12 (324): וְרוּחַ נָכוֹן חַדֵּשׁ בְּקִרְבִּי	[219]	כּוּן
(384)	[125]	כֹּחַ I
Gn 22:12 (65): כִּי עַתָּה יָדַעְתִּי כִּי־יְרֵא אֱלֹהִים אַתָּה	[4395]	כִּי II
Gn 22:18 (88): כֹּל גּוֹיֵי הָאָרֶץ	[5000+]	כֹּל
Js 24:20 (230): וְכִלָּה אֶתְכֶם	[204]	כלה I
(348)	[324]	כְּלִי
Dt 5:14 (176): לְמַעַן יָנוּחַ עַבְדְּךָ וַאֲמָתְךָ כָּמוֹךָ	[139]	כְּמוֹ
Dt 5:15 (178): עַל־כֵּן צִוְּךָ יהוה אֱלֹהֶיךָ	[707]	כֵּן II
Gn 12:5 (106): וַיֵּצְאוּ לָלֶכֶת אַרְצָה כְּנַעַן	[92]	כְּנַעַן
Gn 12:6: וְהַכְּנַעֲנִי אָז בָּאָרֶץ	[71]	כְּנַעֲנִי
Gn 1:21 (293): וְאֵת כָּל־עוֹף כָּנָף לְמִינֵהוּ	[110]	כָּנָף
Jr 1:15 (310): וְנָתְנוּ אִישׁ כִּסְאוֹ	[136]	כִּסֵּא
Js 24:7 (202): וַיָּבֵא עָלָיו אֶת־הַיָּם וַיְכַסֵּהוּ	[157]	כסה
(349)	[399]	כֶּסֶף
(350)	[192]	כַּף
(426)	[102]	כפר
Dt 5:2 (150): יהוה אֱלֹהֵינוּ כָּרַת עִמָּנוּ בְּרִית	[287]	כרת
Dt 5:22 (186): וַיִּכְתְּבֵם עַל־שְׁנֵי לֻחֹת אֲבָנִים	[222]	כתב
Gn 22:2 (20): וְלֶךְ־לְךָ	[5000+]	לְ___ I
Gn 22:12 (70): וְלֹא חָשַׂכְתָּ אֶת־בִּנְךָ	[4973]	לֹא
Ps 51:12 (323): לֵב טָהוֹר בְּרָא־לִי אֱלֹהִים	[579]	לֵב
Js 24:23 (231): וְהַטּוּ אֶת־לְבַבְכֶם אֶל־יהוה	[265]	לֵבָב
Ps 51:6 (319): לְךָ לְבַדְּךָ חָטָאתִי	[155]	לְבַד
(427)	[113]	לבש
351)	[353]	לֵוִי

8

לָחַם I	[171]		וַיִּלָּחֲמוּ אִתְּכֶם (206): Js 24:8
לֶחֶם	[296]		וְלֹא־בָרָא אִתָּם לָחֶם (279): II Sm 12:17
לַיְלָה	[231]		וְלַחֹשֶׁךְ קָרָא לָיְלָה (289): Gn 1:5
לָכַד	[121]		(428)
לָכֵן	[196]		(352)
לָמַד	[85]		וְלִמַּדְתֶּם אֹתָם (148): Dt 5:1
לָמָה, לָמָה	[173] (see מָה)		לָמָה לֹא־הִגַּדְתָּ לִי (138): Gn 12:18
לְמַעַן	[269] (see מַעַן)		לְמַעַן יִיטַב־לִי (126): Gn 12:13
לָקַח	[964]		קַח־נָא אֶת־בִּנְךָ (13): Gn 22:2
לָשׁוֹן	[117]		תְּרַנֵּן לְשׁוֹנִי צִדְקָתֶךָ (329): Ps 51:16
מְאֹד	[287]		כִּי־יָפָה הוּא מְאֹד (129): Gn 12:14
מֵאָה I	[577]		(353)
מִגְרָשׁ	[115]		(429)
מִדְבָּר	[271]		וַתֵּשְׁבוּ בַמִּדְבָּר (203): Js 24:7
מָה	[760]		מַה־זֹּאת עָשִׂיתָ לִּי (137): Gn 12:18
מוֹאָב	[199]		בָּלָק...מֶלֶךְ מוֹאָב (208): Js 24:9
מוֹעֵד	[223]		וְהָיוּ לְאֹתֹת וּלְמוֹעֲדִים (291): Gn 1:14
מוּת	[737]		וְנִכָּה וָמֵת (256): II Sm 11:15
מָוֶת	[159]		כִּי בֶן־מָוֶת הָאִישׁ (269): II Sm 12:5
מִזְבֵּחַ	[401]		וַיִּבֶן שָׁם אַבְרָהָם אֶת־הַמִּזְבֵּחַ (56): Gn 22:9
מַחֲנֶה	[219]		(354)
מַטֶּה	[252]		(355)
מִי	[406]		בַּחֲרוּ לָכֶם הַיּוֹם אֶת־מִי תַעֲבֹדוּן (220): Js 24:15
מַיִם	[574]		וַאֲשֶׁר בַּמַּיִם מִתַּחַת לָאָרֶץ (160): Dt 5:8
מָלֵא	[250]		וּמִלְאוּ אֶת־הַמַּיִם בַּיַּמִּים (294): Gn 1:22
מַלְאָךְ	[214]		וַיִּקְרָא אֵלָיו מַלְאַךְ יהוה (60): Gn 22:11
מְלָאכָה	[167]		וְעָשִׂיתָ כָּל־מְלַאכְתֶּךָ (172): Dt 5:13

8

וְלִשְׁלוֹם הַמִּלְחָמָה (248) II Sm 11:7	[319]	מִלְחָמָה
בִּשְׁלֹשׁ־עֶשְׂרֵה שָׁנָה לְמָלְכוֹ (303) Jr 1:2	[347]	מָלַךְ I
בָּלָק...מֶלֶךְ מוֹאָב (207) Js 24:9	[2522]	מֶלֶךְ I
וְעַל־הַמַּמְלָכוֹת (307) Jr 1:10	[117]	מַמְלָכָה
וַיַּרְא אֶת־הַמָּקוֹם מֵרָחֹק (42) Gn 22:4	[1279]	מִן
(356)	[211]	מִנְחָה
(385)	[150]	מְנַשֶּׁה
(386)	[134]	מִסְפָּר I
וְאִם־מְעָט (273) II Sm 12:8	[96]	מְעַט
עַל־הַמִּזְבֵּחַ מִמַּעַל לָעֵצִים (57) Gn 22:9	[138]	מַעַל II
וַיִּשְׁתַּחֲווּ לְמַעֲשֵׂי יְדֵיהֶם (314) Jr 1:16	[235]	מַעֲשֶׂה
(357)	[451]	מצא
וּלְשֹׁמְרֵי מִצְוֹתָו (168) Dt 5:10	[181]	מִצְוָה
וַיֵּרֶד אַבְרָם מִצְרַיְמָה (118) Gn 12:10	[708]	מִצְרַיִם
וַיֵּלֶךְ אֶל־הַמָּקוֹם (36) Gn 22:3	[399]	מָקוֹם
כִּי אִשָּׁה יְפַת־מַרְאֶה אָתְּ (121) Gn 12:11	[103]	מַרְאֶה
וַיִּקְרָא מֹשֶׁה אֶל־כָּל־יִשְׂרָאֵל (142) Dt 5:1	[763]	מֹשֶׁה
אָנֹכִי מְשַׁחְתִּיךָ לְמֶלֶךְ עַל־יִשְׂרָאֵל (271) II Sm 12:7	[70]	משח
(387)	[139]	מִשְׁכָּן
כֹּל מִשְׁפְּחֹת הָאֲדָמָה (95) Gn 12:3	[300]	מִשְׁפָּחָה
שְׁמַע יִשְׂרָאֵל...אֶת־הַמִּשְׁפָּטִים (145) Dt 5:1	[425]	מִשְׁפָּט
קַח־נָא אֶת־בִּנְךָ (14) Gn 22:2	[401]	נָא I
נְאֻם־יהוה (77) Gn 22:16	[378]	נְאֻם
(430)	[115]	נבא
וַיִּשְׁלַח בְּיַד נָתָן הַנָּבִיא (285) II Sm 12:25	[313]	נָבִיא
וַיִּסַּע אַבְרָם...הַנֶּגְבָּה (115) Gn 12:9	[110]	נֶגֶב
לָמָּה לֹא־הִגַּדְתָּ לִּי (139) Gn 12:18	[369]	נגד

8

נֶגֶד	[151]	וְנֶגֶד הַשֶּׁמֶשׁ (275): II Sm 12:12
נגע	[150]	וַיְנַגַּע יהוה אֶת־פַּרְעֹה (136): Gn 12:17
נגשׁ	[125]	מַדּוּעַ נִגַּשְׁתֶּם אֶל־הָעִיר (261): II Sm 11:20
נָהָר	[117]	בְּעֵבֶר הַנָּהָר (195): Js 24:2
נוּחַ I	[143]	לְמַעַן יָנוּחַ עַבְדְּךָ (175): Dt 5:14
נוּס	[160]	(388)
נָחַל I	[138]	(389)
נַחֲלָה I	[223]	אִישׁ לְנַחֲלָתוֹ (235): Js 24:28
נחם	[108]	וַיְנַחֵם דָּוִד אֵת בַּת־שֶׁבַע אִשְׁתּוֹ (283): II Sm 12:24
נְחֹשֶׁת I	[139]	וּלְחֹמוֹת נְחֹשֶׁת (316): Jr 1:18
נטה	[215]	וַיֵּט אָהֳלֹה (112): Gn 12:8
נכה	[504]	וְנִכָּה וָמֵת (256): II Sm 11:15
נסע	[146]	וַיִּסַּע אַבְרָם הָלוֹךְ וְנָסוֹעַ (114): Gn 12:9
נַעַר	[240]	וַיִּקַּח אֶת־שְׁנֵי נְעָרָיו (32): Gn 22:3
נפל	[433]	וַיִּפֹּל מִן־הָעָם מֵעַבְדֵי דָוִד (259): II Sm 11:17
נֶפֶשׁ	[753]	וְאֶת־הַנֶּפֶשׁ אֲשֶׁר־עָשׂוּ בְחָרָן (105): Gn 12:5
נצל	[208]	וָאַצִּל אֶתְכֶם מִיָּדוֹ (209): Js 24:10
נשׂא	[651]	וַיִּשָּׂא אַבְרָהָם אֶת־עֵינָיו (39): Gn 22:4
נָשִׂיא I	[133]	(390)
נתן	[1994]	לְזַרְעֲךָ אֶתֵּן אֶת־הָאָרֶץ הַזֹּאת (109): Gn 12:7
סבב	[162]	(391)
סָבִיב	[309]	וְעַל כָּל־חוֹמֹתֶיהָ סָבִיב (312): Jr 1:15
סוּס I	[139]	(392)
סוּר	[298]	וְהָסִירוּ אֶת־אֱלֹהִים אֲשֶׁר עָבְדוּ אֲבוֹתֵיכֶם (216): Js 24:14
ספר	[162]	(393)
סֵפֶר I	[185]	בְּסֵפֶר תּוֹרַת אֱלֹהִים (232): Js 24:26
עבד	[289]	וְלֹא תָעָבְדֵם (161): Dt 5:9

וַיְהִי־לוֹ...וַעֲבָדִים וּשְׁפָחֹת :(135) Gn 12:16	[800]	עֶבֶד I
(394)	[143]	עֲבֹדָה
וַיַּעֲבֹר אַבְרָם בָּאָרֶץ :(107) Gn 12:6	[539]	עבר I
נֵלְכָה עַד־כֹּה :(46) Gn 22:5	[1246]	עַד II
(395)	[149]	עֵדָה I
בְּעוֹד הַיֶּלֶד חַי צַמְתִּי :(282) II Sm 12:22	[481]	עוֹד
יָשְׁבוּ אֲבוֹתֵיכֶם מֵעוֹלָם :(196) Js 24:2	[434]	עוֹלָם
פֹּקֵד עֲוֹן אָבוֹת עַל־בָּנִים :(164) Dt 5:9	[231]	עָוֹן
חָלִילָה לָּנוּ מֵעֲזֹב אֶת־יהוה :(221) Js 24:16	[212]	עזב I
וַיִּשָּׂא אַבְרָהָם אֶת־עֵינָיו :(40) Gn 22:4	[867]	עַיִן
וְעָרִים אֲשֶׁר לֹא־בְנִיתֶם :(212) Js 24:13	[1080]	עִיר I
עַל אַחַד הֶהָרִים :(25) Gn 22:2	[4898]	עַל II
וְהַעֲלֵהוּ שָׁם לְעֹלָה :(22) Gn 22:2	[879]	עלה
וְהַעֲלֵנוּ שָׁם לְעֹלָה :(24) Gn 22:2	[288]	עֹלָה I
וַיֹּאמֶר יְהוֹשֻׁעַ אֶל־כָּל־הָעָם :(194) Js 24:2	[1827]	עַם II
שְׁבוּ־לָכֶם פֹּה עִם־הַחֲמוֹר :(44) Gn 22:5	[1076]	עִם
אָנֹכִי עֹמֵד בֵּין־יהוה וּבֵינֵיכֶם :(156) Dt 5:5	[519]	עמד
וּלְעַמּוּד בַּרְזֶל :(315) Jr 1:18	[111]	עַמּוּד
וַיִּשְׁתַּחוּ אֶת־בְּנֵי עַמּוֹן :(239) II Sm 11:1	[122]	עַמּוֹן
וְלֹא־תַעֲנֶה בְרֵעֲךָ עֵד שָׁוְא :(181) Dt 5:20	[314]	ענה I
(431)	[110]	עָפָר
וַיְבַקַּע עֲצֵי עֹלָה :(34) Gn 22:3	[330]	עֵץ
תָּגֵלְנָה עַצְמוֹת דִּכִּיתָ :(322) Ps 51:10	[123]	עֶצֶם I
וַיְהִי לְעֵת הָעֶרֶב :(241) II Sm 11:2	[134]	עֶרֶב II
וְאַל־תַּעַשׂ לוֹ מְאוּמָה :(64) Gn 22:12	[2573]	עשׂה
בִּשְׁלֹשׁ־עֶשְׂרֵה שָׁנָה :(302) Jr 1:2	[350]	עָשָׂר ,עֶשְׂרֵה
(358)	[315]	עֶשְׂרִים

8

8

קָדוֹשׁ	[115]	כִּי־אֱלֹהִים קְדֹשִׁים הוּא (226) Js 24:19
קֹדֶשׁ	[172]	שָׁמוֹר אֶת־יוֹם הַשַּׁבָּת לְקַדְּשׁוֹ (170) Dt 5:12
קֹדֶשׁ	[430]	וְרוּחַ קָדְשְׁךָ (325) Ps 51:13
קָהָל	[123]	דִּבֶּר יהוה אֶל־כָּל־קְהַלְכֶם (184) Dt 5:22
קוֹל	[499]	עֵקֶב אֲשֶׁר שָׁמַעְתָּ בְּקֹלִי (91) Gn 22:18
קוּם	[624]	וַיָּקָם וַיֵּלֶךְ אֶל־הַמָּקוֹם (35) Gn 22:3
קטר	[116]	וַיְקַטְּרוּ לֵאלֹהִים אֲחֵרִים (313) Jr 1:16
קרא I	[730]	וַיִּקְרָא אֵלָיו מַלְאַךְ יהוה (59) Gn 22:11
קרא II	[139]	(399)
קרב	[291]	כַּאֲשֶׁר הִקְרִיב לָבוֹא מִצְרָיְמָה (120) Gn 12:11
קֶרֶב	[227]	כַּאֲשֶׁר עָשִׂיתִי בְּקִרְבּוֹ (199) Js 24:5
ראה	[1294]	וַיַּרְא אֶת־הַמָּקוֹם מֵרָחֹק (41) Gn 22:4
רֹאשׁ I	[593]	וַיִּקְרָא לְזִקְנֵי יִשְׂרָאֵל וּלְרָאשָׁיו (192) Js 24:1
רִאשׁוֹן	[182]	(361)
רַב	[475]	יָמִים רַבִּים (204) Js 24:7
רֹב	[153]	כְּרֹב רַחֲמֶיךָ (317) Ps 51:3
רבה I	[226]	וְהַרְבָּה אַרְבֶּה אֶת־זַרְעֲךָ (80) Gn 22:17
רֶגֶל	[252]	וּרְחַץ רַגְלֶיךָ (249) II Sm 11:8
רדף	[143]	וַיִּרְדְּפוּ מִצְרַיִם אַחֲרֵי אֲבוֹתֵיכֶם (200) Js 24:6
רוּחַ	[376]	וְרוּחַ אֱלֹהִים (287) Gn 1:2
רוּם	[195]	(362)
רוּץ	[103]	(434)
רֹחַב I	[101]	(435)
רֶכֶב	[120]	וַיִּרְדְּפוּ...בְּרֶכֶב וּבְפָרָשִׁים (201) Js 24:6
רָע ,רַע	[661]	וְאִם רַע בְּעֵינֵיכֶם (218) Js 24:15
רֵעַ II	[195]	לֹא־תַעֲנֶה בְרֵעֲךָ עֵד שָׁוְא (182) Dt 5:20
רָעָב	[103]	וַיְהִי רָעָב בָּאָרֶץ (116) Gn 12:10

8

רעה I	[171]			(400)
רעע I	[99]		וְשָׁב וְהֵרַע לָכֶם	Js 24:20 (229):
רַק II	[108]			(436)
רָשָׁע	[264]			(363)
שָׂדֶה	[332]		וְלֹא תִתְאַוֶּה בֵּית רֵעֶךָ שָׂדֵהוּ	Dt 5:21 (183):
שִׂים I	[584]		וַיָּשֶׂם עַל־יִצְחָק בְּנוֹ	Gn 22:6 (50):
שׂמח	[156]			(401)
שׂנא	[148]		לְשֹׂנְאָי	Dt 5:9 (165):
שָׂפָה	[178]		וְכַחוֹל אֲשֶׁר עַל־שְׂפַת הַיָּם	Gn 22:17 (83):
שַׂר	[412]		וַיִּרְאוּ אֹתָהּ שָׂרֵי פַרְעֹה	Gn 12:15 (130):
שׂרף	[117]			(437)
שֶׁ---	[139]	(see שֵׁ)		(402)
שָׁאוּל	[406]		וְאָנֹכִי הִצַּלְתִּיךָ מִיַּד שָׁאוּל	II Sm 12:7 (272):
שׁאל	[173]		וַיִּשְׁאַל דָּוִד לִשְׁלוֹם יוֹאָב	II Sm 11:7 (246):
שׁאר	[133]			(403)
שֵׁבֶט	[190]		אֶת־כָּל־שִׁבְטֵי יִשְׂרָאֵל	Js 24:1 (190):
שׁבע	[186]		כִּי נִשְׁבַּעְתִּי	Gn 22:16 (76):
שֶׁבַע, שִׁבְעִים I	[492]		בֶּן־חָמֵשׁ שָׁנִים וְשִׁבְעִים שָׁנָה	Gn 12:4 (101):
שׁבר I	[149]		רוּחַ נִשְׁבָּרָה לֵב־נִשְׁבָּר	Ps 51:19 (330):
שׁבת	[71]		וַיִּשְׁבֹּת בַּיּוֹם הַשְּׁבִיעִי	Gn 2:2 (297):
שַׁבָּת	[106]		שָׁמוֹר אֶת־יוֹם הַשַּׁבָּת	Dt 5:12 (169):
שׁוּב I	[1055]		שְׁבוּ־לָכֶם פֹּה	Gn 22:5 (49):
שׁחה	(see II חוה)			
שׁחת	[161]		וַיַּשְׁחִתוּ אֶת־בְּנֵי עַמּוֹן	II Sm 11:1 (238):
שׁכב	[221]		וַיִּשְׁכַּב עִמָּהּ	II Sm 11:4 (245):
שׁכח	[102]			(438)
שׁכן	[130]			(404)

8

שָׁלוֹם	[242]	II Sm 11:7 (247): וַיִּשְׁאַל דָּוִד לְשָׁלוֹם יוֹאָב
שׁלח	[839]	Gn 22:10 (58): וַיִּשְׁלַח אַבְרָהָם אֶת־יָדוֹ
שְׁלִישִׁי	[107]	Gn 22:4 (38): בַּיּוֹם הַשְּׁלִישִׁי
שׁלך	[125]	II Sm 11:21 (263): הֲלוֹא־אִשָּׁה הִשְׁלִיכָה עָלָיו
שׁלם	[117]	II Sm 12:6 (270): וְאֶת־הַכִּבְשָׂה יְשַׁלֵּם אַרְבַּעְתָּיִם
שְׁלֹמֹה	[293]	II Sm 12:24 (284): וַיִּקְרָא אֶת־שְׁמוֹ שְׁלֹמֹה
שָׁלֹשׁ	[412]	Jr 1:2 (301): בִּשְׁלֹשׁ־עֶשְׂרֵה שָׁנָה
שְׁלֹשִׁים	[174]	(405)
שָׁם	[817]	Gn 22:2 (23): וְהַעֲלֵהוּ שָׁם לְעֹלָה
שֵׁם I	[862]	Gn 22:14 (73): וַיִּקְרָא אַבְרָהָם שֵׁם־הַמָּקוֹם הַהוּא
שְׁמוּאֵל	[139]	(406)
שָׁמַיִם	[419]	Gn 22:11 (62): וַיִּקְרָא אֵלָיו מַלְאַךְ יהוה מִן־הַשָּׁמַיִם
שֶׁמֶן	[192]	(364)
שְׁמֹנֶה	[109]	(439)
שׁמע	[1136]	Gn 22:18 (90): עֵקֶב אֲשֶׁר שָׁמַעְתָּ בְּקֹלִי
שׁמר	[465]	Dt 5:1 (149): וּשְׁמַרְתֶּם לַעֲשֹׂתָם
שֹׁמְרוֹן	[112]	(440)
שֶׁמֶשׁ	[134]	II Sm 12:11 (274): וְנֶגֶד הַשָּׁמֶשׁ
שָׁנָה	[871]	Gn 12:4 (100): בֶּן־חָמֵשׁ שָׁנִים וְשִׁבְעִים שָׁנָה
שֵׁנִי	[156]	Gn 22:15 (75): וַיִּקְרָא...שֵׁנִית מִן־הַשָּׁמָיִם
שְׁנַיִם	[739]	Gn 22:3 (31): וַיִּקַּח אֶת־שְׁנֵי נְעָרָיו אִתּוֹ
שַׁעַר I	[368]	Gn 22:17 (86): וְיִרַשׁ זַרְעֲךָ אֵת שַׁעַר אֹיְבָיו
שׁפט	[203]	Js 24:1 (193): וַיִּקְרָא לְזִקְנֵי יִשְׂרָאֵל...וּלְשֹׁפְטָיו
שׁפך	[116]	(441)
שֶׁקֶר	[113]	(442)
שֵׁשׁ I	[216]	Dt 5:13 (171): שֵׁשֶׁת יָמִים תַּעֲבֹד
שׁתה II	[217]	II Sm 11:11 (255): לֶאֱכֹל וְלִשְׁתּוֹת

8

תָּוֶךְ	[416]	מִתּוֹךְ הָאֵשׁ (155): Dt 5:4
תּוֹעֵבָה	[118]	(443)
תּוֹרָה	[220]	בְּסֵפֶר תּוֹרַת אֱלֹהִים (233): Js 24:26
תַּחַת I	[490]	וַיַּעֲלֵהוּ לְעֹלָה תַּחַת בְּנוֹ (72): Gn 22:13
תָּמִיד	[104]	וְחַטָּאתִי נֶגְדִּי תָמִיד (318): Ps 51:5
תְּפִלָּה	[78]	(444)

8

INDEX OF SPECIAL NOTES, CHARTS,
AND COMMENTS ON HEBREW WORDS

italic number = page number
c + number = Chart
n + number = Note
w + number = Word
bold = Summary Note
[The note and chart numbers correspond to page numbers, but the word numbers do not.]

GENERAL INDEX

italic number = page number
n + number   = Note
c + number   = Chart
bold   = Summary Note
numbers in parentheses = Academic pronunciation
[The note and chart numbers correspond to page numbers.]

234